THE CAMPER'S GUIDE TO OUTDOOR PURSUITS:

FINDING SAFE, NATURE-FRIENDLY, AND COMFORTABLE PASSAGE THROUGH WILD PLACES

Second Edition

Jack Drury and Eric Holmlund

Illustrations by John A. Drury

SAGAMORE PUBLISHING L.L.C.

Champaign, IL

©2006 Sagamore Publishing L.L.C.
All rights reserved.

Interior Design: Janet Wahlfeldt
Cover Design: Michael Morgan
Editor: Cindy McNew

Cover Photo: Brad Mitchell Photography at bradmitchellphoto.com

Illustrations: John A. Drury

ISBN: 1-57167-559-0
Library of Congress Catalog Card Number: 2006921448

Sagamore Publishing L.L.C.
804 N. Neil St. Suite 100
Champaign, IL 61824
www.sagamorepub.com

10 9 8 7 6 5 4 3 2 1

In memory of my parents, Kitty and Maynard,
for introducing me to the outdoors and instilling a love for it.

In memory of Paul K. Petzoldt for teaching me how to use and care for the outdoors
and share ways to teach others.

JKD

To all the people who have inspired me to spend so many days and nights in untamed landscapes:
- *My parents, Elaine and Richard, who opened the door to the National Parks,*
- *My students at Paul Smith's College and the Wilderness Education Association, who provided energy and enthusiasm in remote wilderness areas,*
- *My wife Kim and children, Dana, John, and Will, who are my dear companions now and on future adventures into nature.*

ERH

CONTENTS

ACKNOWLEDGMENTS

As with any project of this magnitude, there are many people other than the authors who make the final product possible. We would like to thank Eric Bennett, Christy Blanchard, Bruce Bonney, Dave Cockrell, Doug Fitzgerald, Jim Glover, Dick and Elaine Holmlund, Kim Massari, Mitch Sakofs, Greg Smith, Buck Tilton, Ben Woodard, and many others for their help in providing important and valued feedback on this undertaking. Joe Bannon, Doug Sanders, and Janet Wahlfeldt of Sagamore Publishing provided the vision and turned our work into a reality. We appreciate Doc Forgey's support in taking on the project . . . The Wilderness Education Association for granting permission to use the book *The Backcountry Classroom: Lessons, Tools and Activities for Teaching Outdoor Leaders* as the foundation for this book. Finally, we would like to thank all our students for their feedback and friendship both in the classroom and in the backcountry.

INTRODUCTION

WHO SHOULD READ *THE CAMPER'S GUIDE*?

The Camper's Guide contains technical guidance, trip planning, and leadership information appropriate for all outdoor skill levels. If you are a three-trip-a-year camper who has learned about the outdoors from your Uncle Buck, your fishing friends, or the friendly neighbor down the street who always tells you about the great trips her family takes to the national parks, this book is for you. If you have been camping for years but just want to be sure that you've got all the facts straight, this book is for you.

This book is also for you if you've been going on adventures for many years to exotic and rugged wilderness areas where the challenges are as big as the mountains. For some of you, trips often end in frustration as you find you forgot some important piece of information, one critical piece of gear suddenly fails, or your knowledge of map and compass begins to show as many holes as your socks. You manage to limp home overtired and overextended and then sit on the couch afterward and wonder why the trip was so much work when it was supposed to be a fantastic renewal of body and spirit.

Finally, this book is for you if you are contemplating joining the millions of tanned, healthy, and well-adjusted outdoor people who are camping, hiking, canoeing, and biking in undeveloped and beautiful natural areas. You may hesitate because of the intimidating expense of high-performance outdoor gear on the market and the seemingly immense amount of information and skills that successful outdoor hikers, campers, and recreational explorers must possess. Don't worry; most of those hikers on the magazine covers are really sunburned and bug-bitten, and they aren't all that well-adjusted!

WHAT MAKES *THE CAMPER'S GUIDE* SPECIAL?
(OR, NOT ANOTHER BOOK ABOUT CAMPING!)

In *The Camper's Guide* we try to cover the entire array of outdoor living skills and topics in more depth and with more fun than any book we've seen. *The Camper's Guide* covers all the minimal-impact camping skills that are becoming required in many public and private backcountry settings, along with information about current clothing and equipment ranging from underwear to backpacks. We attempt to cover a more complete and detailed list of outdoor clothing than we could find anywhere.

Beyond the basics, we address the sometimes challenging and confusing topics of map and compass and their places in backcountry navigation. We look at hiking and methods to conserve energy while on the trail. We cover food selection, nutrition, and food planning for long and short expeditions. We address risk management and safety practices that apply to both recreational campers and outdoor professionals.

Perhaps most unique to *The Camper's Guide* is the chapter on outdoor leadership and group dynamics. Most current books don't even address these topics. *The Camper's Guide* offers a detailed and perceptive treatment of leadership issues in the outdoors. You will find that each person on an outdoor venture can be a leader and that casual trips as well as guided trips require some form of leadership. After reading this book, you will have greater awareness, appreciation, and skill in facilitating groups and leading yourself and others in the outdoors.

We think *The Camper's Guide* is the most user-friendly and fun outdoor skills book available. You'll enjoy reading it! Don't expect a dry, academic book that sounds like it was written from an armchair in the Explorer's Club. We strongly believe that outdoor activities should be fun, challenging, and invigorating. We have made every effort to create a book that makes this philosophy come to life. Our off-the-wall characters and bad jokes will make reading *The Camper's Guide* a lighthearted, sometimes wacky experience that will hone your outdoor skills and inspire you to reach new heights of outdoor fun!

HELPING YOU "LEAVE NO TRACE"

The Camper's Guide also contains information and guidelines that are consistent with Leave No Trace Outdoor Skills and Ethics. Leave No Trace is an organization created in 1991 to promote responsible and ecologically sound camping practices. Leave No Trace, a partnership of the National Outdoor Leadership School, the National Park Service, the United States Forest Service, the Bureau of Land Management, the United States Fish and Wildlife Service, and the outdoor industry, provides camping guidelines upheld by these federal land management agencies.[1] Millions of federal land users need to know and abide by these important guidelines if we are to safeguard the quality of water, soils, and wildlife habitat, as well as the human experience in wild lands. The Camper's Guide helps in this important educational mission.

HOW TO USE THIS BOOK

This introduction is also designed to get you ready to use the book. We want to acquaint you with the features and devices we use to tell the story of wilderness camping and the other skills you need to travel in the backcountry.

The Camper's Guide is designed to be as easy to use as possible. We have tried to create a format that is an enjoyable alternative to the sometimes tedious textbooks that have been written about the outdoors. The Camper's Guide uses icons, tips, characters, and real-life anecdotes to illustrate outdoor travel and camping principles.

Icons and Tips

The Camper's Guide is chock-full of information, and we want to be sure that you take the most important points with you. In order to help you through the information, we have highlighted sections of the book and set them aside for your special attention. We call these sections our "Tips," and each tip is indicated by a graphic or icon. Some of the seven different kinds of tips are essential, and others are meant to be read by those of you with particular interests. It may sound complex, but you'll get the hang of it soon! The following list describes each type of tip.

 ### BOTTOM-LINE TIP

The Bottom-Line Tip is probably our most important tip. It repeats, condenses, and highlights the essential information from a passage of text. Have you ever had a conversation with someone who rambled on and on and you just wanted to say, "Stop talking for a second! Could you just tell me the bottom line?" We know how you feel.

 ### ENVIRONMENTAL TIP

The Environmental Tip also condenses and highlights essential information from the book. These tips underscore certain ethical points that help protect natural ecosystems.

PHILOSOPHY TIP

The Philosophy Tip is for the thinker in you. Most people go to wild places for deeply personal, intellectual, or spiritual reasons. The Philosophy Tip investigates the "why" in everything we do. Don't worry—the Philosophy Tip isn't as "deep" as it sounds!

QUALITY CAMPER TIP

The Quality Camper Tip is for the camper who wants to "go the extra mile" in practicing camping and travel techniques. Generally, the Quality Camper Tip gives techniques that appeal to the perfectionist in us, or simply that part of us that wants to look extra sharp in the backcountry. We urge you to go for it!

SAFETY TIP

The Safety Tip underscores and condenses essential safety information that will help you avoid injury and accidents while traveling and camping.

TECHWEENIE TIP

The Techweenie Tip is for the "gear head" in all of us. When they have the time and inclination, most campers have an interest in the science behind many of the high-technology products that are available for backcountry users today. How many times have you wondered, "Now, just how does that work?" We've chosen to answer some of those questions in the Techweenie Tip. And by the way, "Techweenie" is a term of endearment!

TRICKS OF THE TRADE

Tricks of the Trade are the little secrets that experienced campers all seem to know. On the other hand, you'll always find that somebody has a simpler or more creative way to do simple camping tasks. We learn new Tricks of the Trade all the time from both new and veteran campers. We've chosen a few that we use and passed them on to you!

Characters and Scenarios

The Stumps

We have created two distinct scenarios that appear throughout the book in order to bring important concepts to life. The first scenario involves an American family, the Stumps, who are typical in that they are not a "model" family. Things go wrong with the Stumps. Sometimes they don't treat each other as well as they should. Sometimes they don't plan their camping trips very well. We hope you learn from their successes and challenges and enjoy reading about their adventures.

Forrest Stump, the father, also has a distinguished extended family. He frequently recalls famous relatives from different eras in history to illustrate points about camping. You'll come to understand that nothing is too far out for Forrest and his seemingly endless supply of nutty ancestors!

The Muskrat Pack

Our second scenario involves a small group of adult canoeists who call themselves the Muskrat Pack. These longtime friends occasionally take time from their careers to plan daylong canoe trips together. We'll join them as they plan their first multiday canoe trip in a large wilderness canoe area. They have many dynamics and concerns that are different from a family group.

Authors' Anecdotes

In addition to our fictional scenarios, we'll draw on our own experiences as outdoor educators and recreators. Because there are two of us writing the book, we have chosen to refer to ourselves in the "third person" when we want to share a story that we feel is particularly relevant. In other words, you will read that "Jack remembers when . . ." or "Eric once had a student who . . ." and so forth. Please realize that Jack and Eric are real people and not fictional relatives of Forrest Stump or members of the Muskrat Pack!

A FINAL THOUGHT: WHERE ARE YOU GOING?

Both literally and figuratively, this book can help you get where you want to go. By providing the information to hone your backcountry living and traveling skills, this book can help you reach the beautiful wild places you've dreamed about visiting. By sharing lessons from our years of experience, this book can also help you become the resourceful, thoughtful, and successful backcountry outdoor person that you want to be.

Combined with hours, days, and years of field experience, the information in this book will help you choose equipment for quality and value, plan and prepare healthy and delicious backcountry meals, use state-of-the-art minimal impact camping techniques, be able to interpret topographic maps and use navigational compasses, and plan and lead safe, enjoyable trips.

If this is where you want to go, you're reading the right book to help you begin your journey into the backcountry and onward to greater success as a wilderness trip leader!

Notes

[1]National Outdoor Leadership School. (1994). *Leave No Trace: Outdoor Skills and Ethics: Rocky Mountains*. [Manual]. Lander, WY: National Outdoor Leadership School.

CHAPTER 1

Before You Take the First Step

"The journey of a thousand miles begins with one step."
—Lao Tzu

While Lao Tzu, the influential thinker and proponent of the Chinese mystic tradition Taoism, hits the proverbial bull's-eye with most of his perceptive writings, we wouldn't recommend that you hire him as your guide for a backcountry trip. Oh, sure, he'd be great around the campfire for talks about philosophy and the meaning of life, but we're not sure he would have brought the right map or thought much about how many calories each person should have in his or her provisions. So instead, we might say, "A journey of a thousand miles begins *a couple of months before* the first step."

The Camper's Guide is all about what happens *before*

Figure 1.1
An interesting conversationalist?
Certainly—but we don't recommend hiring
Lao Tzu as a backcountry guide!

and *after* your trip, as well as what happens while you're in beautiful wild country.

WHY ARE PEOPLE GOING TO WILD PLACES LIKE NEVER BEFORE?

It seems like everyone's doing it. Now as never before, people stream to National Parks, forests, wilderness areas, and almost any undeveloped expanse of public land to travel, explore, and recreate. The Outdoor Industry Association reports especially large increases in participation in kayaking, canoeing, trail running, cross-country skiing, and snowshoeing. Further, nearly two-thirds of Americans over age 16 participate in human-powered outdoor recreation, representing more than 140 million people.[1] What brings recreation participants into wild places from the towns, suburbs, and urban centers? Why have so many people caught the wilderness bug?

We've found that people go "wild" for a number of reasons. Many simply want to escape from the humdrum routines and hassles of complex civilized life. Cynics say that campers merely exchange them for the humdrum routines and hassles of wet socks, mosquitoes, and camp-cooked macaroni and cheese. Go figure!

Others look to the wilderness for physical challenge and immersion in a natural setting. Some look to study nature, reach stunning vistas in remote locations, explore the lesser-known corners of the country, and test sporting skills against the challenges of the wilderness. Some people look for solitude, others for quality social experiences with family and friends. The list goes on and on.

People have a wide spectrum of goals and activities. Not all people can get the "wilderness experience" that they want from a given outdoor setting. We find that this range of goals and preferences is best met in a variety of areas with vastly different characteristics. As mountaineer and wilderness educator Paul Petzoldt might say, wilderness is like love; it means different things to different people.

WHAT DOES WILDERNESS MEAN TO YOU?

Ask a dozen people to define wilderness and you will probably get two dozen answers. What people look for in a wilderness experience is extremely personal. That's what makes wilderness so special. To some people, wilderness is Central Park or the state campground in the mountains. To others, true wilderness is the Brooks Range in Alaska.

When we think of wilderness, we think of a description of certain conditions. People often use terms like "naturalness," "minimum signs of human presence," "solitude," "undeveloped," "beautiful," "allowing for escape," "self-powered travel," and "primitive conditions." Wilderness historian Roderick Nash suggests that wilderness lies along "a spectrum of conditions or environments ranging from the purely wild on one end to the purely civilized on the other."[2]

The idea of a spectrum (Figure 1.2) makes sense to us. It allows for people to have a range of outdoor experiences in a variety of environments. "Wilderness" becomes a relative term, depending on the available land resource and the mindset of the outdoor person. In the range of wilderness conditions, some are more "pure" than others. Throughout this book we use the term "wilderness" generally to describe the range of outdoor experiences at the "purely wild" end of the outdoor spectrum. We use the term "backcountry" synonymously.

Figure 1.2
The Wilderness Spectrum

Sometimes it is easier to define what wilderness is not, rather than what it is. Wilderness is not about large numbers of people. By and large, it is not about those activities that can be done in non-wilderness settings. For example, dirt-bike travel, large-group picnics, and rowdy parties can all occur in non-wilderness settings. You don't need to be 7 miles back in the Bob Marshall Wilderness in Montana to throw a graduation party. These activities can and should take place closer to civilization, in less wild, yet still substantially natural areas.

Even though wilderness is not about large numbers of people, we think people naturally belong in wilderness settings, as long as their presence does not adversely alter natural conditions. We will see, however, that people often do have a negative impact on natural conditions in wild areas. Our challenge is to learn to minimize this often unintentional environmental impact.

Figure 1.3
As the number of human visitors to the backcountry increases, so too do their effects on the wilderness.

WHAT'S HAPPENING TO OUR WILDERNESS AREAS?

A cursory tour through many of our national and state parks reveals a "natural" landscape severely affected by the presence of humans and their play. Parking lots, eroded trails, flattened campsites that spread from year to year, braided trails that run everywhere and nowhere, garbage, dependent wildlife, cut trees, filthy fireplaces, human waste, overflowing outhouses, and scores of other effects mar the beauty and scar the ecosystems in our wild places.

Some people are sickened by the carnage, while others scarcely observe that it exists. Of this last group of outdoor people, many have never known an alternative and simply don't realize that their actions cause the aesthetic and ecological consequences that they do. However, most people at some level recognize the increasing shabbiness of overused areas.

In addition to scars on the land, outdoor people affect each other and themselves through unsafe practices. Misinterpreted maps and compasses lead many people into danger and exposure in rugged country. Lack of appropriate clothing leads to great discomfort or dangerous hypothermia for campers in weather both foul and fair. Stove flare-ups cause a great many burns in backcountry campsites. The underlying source of all of these unfortunate mishaps is a lack of outdoor judgment in backcountry travelers. People just seem to make the wrong decisions at the wrong time or make good decisions far too late.

How can you avoid these hazards of life in the wild? Reading this book is one small, but important step in developing solid outdoor skills and judgment. It contains the distillation of over 50 years of the authors' combined backcountry expedition leadership experience in areas ranging from the Adirondack Mountains of New York to the desert southwest to Denali in Alaska. This book offers information essential for safe, environmentally sound, and enjoyable backcountry travel for people pursuing everything from overnight trips to monthlong expeditions.

WHO, ME, AN OUTDOOR LEADER?

Many of the people who pick up this book have absolutely no aspirations to lead anybody anywhere, especially into the wild outdoors. They may think, "What is the one thing I can do to ruin both my experience and that of people around me? Answer: Try to be the leader." Most people go to the outdoors for relaxation, challenge, fun, and natural beauty. They may think leadership is for the military, the Boy and Girl Scouts, or for marching bands.

In the following pages, you'll find that leadership doesn't have to be "Leadership" and that you don't have to deliver "Win One for the Gipper" speeches or bark orders like Napoleon on your next camping trip. You'll also find that safe, enjoyable outdoor experiences require leadership in the form of skills, knowledge, and working with your own as well as other campers' emotions and preferences.

SAFETY, THE ENVIRONMENT, COMFORT: THE BIG THREE

The Camper's Guide's subtitle, "Finding safe, nature-friendly, and comfortable passage through wild places," states the three major themes that run through each chapter of this book. We call these our three priorities when it comes to making decisions, both in the backcountry and when planning the trip. For that matter, the "Big Three" priorities come into play when you are standing in the sporting goods store or supermarket trying to make decisions about what to buy for your trip.

Safety

Our first priority, safety, makes everything else possible in the backcountry. We're not suggesting that you strive to eliminate risk and challenge from your outings; in fact, risk and challenge are two of the most attractive qualities that the backcountry offers for many people. We do suggest that you plan for risk and challenge within a framework of safety and risk management. You may find that planning your trip well allows you to have more challenge *and* more safety.

Planning a safe trip, using safe equipment, and making safe leadership decisions along the trail or stream allow you and the people around you to experience the beauty and rigor of the outdoors as you planned and wished to. Preventing emergencies by reducing or eliminating risk minimizes the chances that your trip will be shortened or altered by illness, injury, or poor decisions. You'll find out how safety plays into every aspect of trip planning and activities once you're in the woods.

The Environment

As members of the increasingly large wave of recreators in beautiful undeveloped places, it has become critically important for each one of us to consider the effect our actions and choices have on the natural systems around us, especially in delicate and highly used backcountry destinations. You will learn how to shape your practices to minimize the impact your presence has on ecosystems and how to become as unobtrusive as possible during your stay in the wild outdoors. Most people find that learning these simple techniques actually adds to the pleasure of their experience in the outdoors, since they have a feeling of responsibility and service that comes with ethical camping practices.

Comfort

Only after the first two priorities are met can we focus on comfort. We want you to come back to the outdoors once you get home again. We don't want campers to be so exhausted and uncomfortable from their outdoor adventures that they (or their children) vow never to leave their recliners and home theater systems. We want people to say "No!" to virtual reality and "Yes!" to actual reality! One way we can make sure people and their families and friends return to the wild outdoors time and time again is to make outdoor living comfortable. You don't need to prove that you can survive for a week by sucking on pebbles, unless you're trying to live out a Jack London fantasy. (In that case, more power to you, and give this book to your neighbor!) Camping and outdoor travel don't need to be ordeals. With modern fabrics, packs, boots, and other products, we can live in the sun, rain, wind, and cold with relative comfort. Why not use your information and resources to help you have a good time?

INSIDE *THE CAMPER'S GUIDE*

As we mentioned in the introduction, *The Camper's Guide* is different. Instead of page after page of facts and testimonials from the dusty corridors of the authors' memories, we present important camping concepts in ways that the reader may find fun, challenging, and vivid. We use stories and characters. Our characters are meant to be symbolic or representative of many outdoor campers and adventurers and the struggles and challenges they go through in planning and participating in outdoor camping trips. We hope you find these people interesting, frustrating, and most of all, stimulating to the imagination! The bottom line is that we want you to think about the concepts in this book in an active and realistic way.

Who Are the Stumps?

We'd like to introduce our literary family, the Stumps, who will pop up from time to time in *The Camper's Guide*. The Stumps are a "normal" American family with standard family traits. Forrest is the father, who thinks of himself as benevolent dictator, exasperated coach, overworked referee, and family doormat. He is profoundly excited about camping and often tells stories about the wide-ranging Stump family and its famous (and not-so-famous) relatives. Holly, the mother, offers a realistic and gentle counterpoint to the sometimes hectic family scene. Woody, the oldest child at 18, loves the "high adrenaline" side of outdoor pursuits and is hard at work stockpiling a full array of high-technology gear. Willow, 16, and Moss, 12, are the sometimes loving daughter and son who have an ambivalent attitude toward family camping. Together, the Stump family and the menagerie of Stump relatives illustrate many of the camping concepts throughout *The Camper's Guide*.

Figure 1.4
Introducing the Stumps: Holly, Forrest, Moss, Willow, Woody, and Friend.

Introducing the Muskrat Pack

We will also describe a group of adults who have loosely organized a social paddling club they call the "Muskrat Pack," after the funny little rodents that they encounter on certain slow-moving rivers. As a group of adult peers, the Muskrat Pack has different needs and issues from the Stumps. They interact differently, plan trips differently, and have had many experiences outside of their group.

The extraordinary thing about the Muskrat Pack is that *you* are a member! We decided to write you, the reader, into the action. We have given you a part, along with a job and certain abilities and limitations. We did this to connect both with adult outdoor people and people new to camping. Any questions? Well, read on. . .

You and three friends from Wynotgota College, Juan, Anne, and Stella, created an informal paddling club, the Muskrat Pack, several years after graduation. Most of the Muskrat Pack's activity in *The Camper's Guide* revolves around planning for a late spring canoe trip in the Drifting Paddle National Canoe Area. Anne is your best paddler. In the winter she's a ski instructor at Killington, Vermont, and during the rest of the year she is a rafting guide in West Virginia. She's also a certified American Canoe Association white-water canoe instructor. Juan, a Pittsburgh marketing executive for Heinz, Inc., is looking for the 58th variety. He is the only person in the group who has been to the Drifting Paddle Canoe Area, having canoed there a few years ago. Stella is a seventh-grade biology teacher from Mystic, Connecticut. Stella has great camping skills, and last summer she took a National Outdoor Leadership School course in which she backpacked for a month and learned camping and adventure skills in Wyoming.

Figure 1.5
The Muskrat Pack—you're about to embark on a wilderness adventure!

You, however, have never gone camping in your life. You're the victim of peer pressure—Juan called you up and recruited you to go on your first overnight trip. Maybe that's why you're reading this book! You do, however, have the most experience working with groups of people from your job as assistant director of the Butternut Substance Abuse Center in Big Boulder, Arkansas. You're anticipating the trip, perhaps with a bit of trepidation, but you trust that your friends know what they're doing and expect to learn a great deal about camping and outdoor travel.

LET'S GO! TAKING THE FIRST STEP

At this point, we've presented our wilderness philosophy and our priorities for planning and participating in great outdoor trips and have introduced some of the characters who will accompany you through *The Camper's Guide*. You will also encounter various tips that underscore and highlight important bits of information. In other words, we've laid the groundwork for your "journey" through this book. You're now ready to take the first step in your thousand-mile journey. Have fun!

Notes
[1] Outdoor Industry Association. (2004). *Outdoor Recreation Participation Study for the United States* (6th ed.). Boulder, CO: Outdoor Industry Association.
[2] Nash, R. (1982). *Wilderness and the American Mind* (3rd ed.). New Haven, CT: Yale University Press, p. 6.

CHAPTER 2
High-Country Fashion

"The important rule governing dress for any hike in wilderness regions is that a party be able to survive one night in case of injury, becoming lost or other emergency."

—Paul K. Petzoldt

Topics:
- Heat Loss and Gain
- Fabrics
- Clothing Selection
- The Clothing List
- Using Backcountry Clothing

ZAK STUMP'S CLOTHING DILEMMA: 1 MILLION YEARS BC

The sun rose over the mountains on the first morning of the Stump family camping trip to the Cascades. "I know it's early, kids, but have I ever told you about your great-great-great, well, prehistoric Uncle Zak?" said Forrest Stump to Willow, Moss, and Woody, who were in the back seat of the family van. Holly Stump groaned as she prepared for another of her husband's half-baked stories about famous family forebears.

"He had it rough, you know. He didn't have Lycra and Gore-Tex when he wanted to stagger across the frozen tundra. No way. But that was *really* living."

"Please, not again, dad," said Willow. "You keep telling us about these ancestors of ours that nobody's ever heard of. Do we have a Stump relative everywhere, at every point in recorded history?"

"And even before, Willow," said Forrest. "Your ancestor Zak couldn't even write! These stories were passed around orally."

"Sounds like strep throat," said Moss.

"Well, anyway," said Forrest, "whenever our Neanderthal predecessor Zak Stump crawled out of his cave to clobber a saber-toothed rabbit for dinner, he slipped on his loincloth, fur shirt, and buffalo-head cloak. Before he could worry about food, equipment, or self-actualization, Zak had to decide whether to wear the fur mukluks or the sandals and which tie matched his elkskin. His first thought was to protect himself from the elements with adequate clothing. Think about that when you climb out of your tent in the morning."

The point of Forrest's musings is that shelter is the oldest and most basic human concern, and it should be the camper's as well. Clothing is the most basic and essential shelter. Before we launch into specialized fabrics and clothing items like Polartec and mitten shells, we'll investigate the whys of clothing: the physics of heat loss and the principles behind dressing warmly.

 BOTTOM-LINE TIP: Heat Loss and Gain
An understanding of heat loss and heat gain equips the camper with the ability to keep optimally warm in all situations.

The following section explores the technical aspects of heat loss and provides suggestions for keeping warm in the outdoors.

Some of us think complete comfort means reclining on an overstuffed couch while dressed in a robe and slippers with the thermostat set at 80° F. Anything less and we start to whimper. Unfortunately, we can maintain such complete comfort only deep inside layers of vinyl siding, plywood, and pink fiberglass insulation. The moment we step outside our cozy houses, we're suddenly cold, alone, and naked. And then it's okay to whimper.

Our bodies can't adjust beyond a narrow range of temperatures, so we have trouble maintaining the couch-bound total comfort state without help. We must shield ourselves with specialized layers, much like the house described above, each performing a different function, from the outside to the skin. Outdoor travelers must work hard to keep their bodies in thermal homeostasis—that is, not too hot, and not too cold. We recommend 98.6° F.

Figure 2.1
Zak Stump, 1 million years BC

Figure 2.2
One version of complete comfort for Forrest.

HEAT LOSS AND GAIN

A great way to think about our specialized layers of clothing is in terms of preventing unwanted heat loss and heat gain. Practical knowledge of this sort enables us to make informed choices based on how clothing functions.

Conduction is our first major concept. Heat-energy moves from warm to cool surfaces and objects, so when our bodies directly touch an external surface that is cooler than we are, we lose heat to it and feel colder. When our bodies touch an external surface warmer than we are, we gain heat from it and feel warmer. For example, if we sit on a cold rock, we cool rapidly, just as we will when standing on snow while wearing thin-soled sneakers. Clothing must provide a barrier between our skin and external, cooling objects. When the surface is hotter than we are, it transmits heat to us, sometimes rapidly. That's why we use gloves when handling hot pots around the fire.

Radiation is the loss of infrared heat from exposed skin to the air. Our bodies emit infrared radiation continuously, like lightbulbs or radiators. Unless properly covered, exposed skin radiates large amounts of heat. Our circulatory system functions like a hot water radiator heating system. Instead of water, our bodies use blood to carry heat throughout the body. Areas with high blood flow and great surface area, such as the head and neck, radiate heat rapidly. If we cover areas prone to high radiative heat loss, like our heads, our bodies can warm other areas, like our feet. So, just like mom told us, if your feet are cold, put on a hat!

Figure 2.3
Understanding heat loss can help Willow stay warm.

Similarly, we can also gain heat from radiation. If we are outdoors in the hot sun, we may suffer heat-related injury or sunburn from direct exposure to the largest source of radiative energy in our immediate galactic neighborhood: the sun. The solution, again, is to cover up your skin, putting some form of barrier between yourself and the source of radiative heat. Hats, long-sleeved shirts, pants, and sunscreen work just fine!

Convection is heat loss through the action of moving air. Most of us have little difficulty imagining the "wind chill" concept when we hear *Today Show* weather forecaster Al Roker grimly chuckle about the 70-below-zero wind chill in North Dakota. Wind cuts through our clothing and blows away the thin layer of warm air that our bodies generate next to the skin. We can stop heat loss from convection by wearing windproof fabrics such as nylon taffeta and polyester microfiber.

The last major concept is heat loss through *Evaporation*. Most people are thankful that we have a different heat-shedding system than the Stump's dog, Chip, who can only lose heat through evaporation from his feet and panting tongue, since he lacks the widespread sweat glands of his owners. People shed excess heat by perspiring, and in order for perspiration to change to vapor, our bodies must generate a great deal of heat energy. We want to avoid sweat, since our bodies must expend unnecessary energy to produce and evaporate perspiration. In addition to the energy loss, the moisture often winds up soaking our layers of clothing, which increases conductive heat loss.

FABRICS

Now that we've discussed the importance of heat loss, what should clothes be made of? Do we set out for the woods in our golf shirt and slacks? How about blue jeans and a sweatshirt? Although these outfits work well in suburban settings, they should be scrutinized for their merits in the outdoors.

Unfortunately, you often see campers wearing casual "street" clothing in the backcountry while enjoying nature in the summer. If these people are lucky, they will have a fine day, with little discomfort or hazard to life. But when a sudden rainstorm or chill wind blows in, or if someone needs to spend an emergency night out away from the motor home, these poorly-dressed campers will be uncomfortable or even in grave danger because of the limitations of their street clothing. Most street clothing functions better in town than on the trail and is often made of comfortable and inexpensive cotton fabric. However, we will see that cotton is a cool killer when wet and should be practically eliminated from the camper's clothing list.

SAFETY TIP: Dressing for Safety
Every user of wild lands has the responsibility to dress properly, both for their own safety and that of family members, friends, and clients who are traveling with them. Campers should also bear in mind the efforts of the rescuers who may have to venture into the backcountry, risking their own lives to find and help them.

Let's take a look at the three most common fabrics used, for good or ill, in camping today: cotton, wool, and various forms of synthetics. We'll evaluate each fabric's characteristics and look at its relative advantages and disadvantages.

Cotton

Although cotton field shirts, khakis, and hats are the garments of choice for master outdoor people like Indiana Jones and the Crocodile Hunter, bear in mind that this fabric performs best in the arid outback for driving topless Land Rovers. Indisputably the most comfortable of the major fibers, cotton should be chosen only in situations suited to its characteristics.

Cotton fibers breathe well, allowing perspiration vapor to escape to the environment. However, because it also absorbs a high volume of water compared to its weight (7% of its weight in moisture[1]), cotton is a cool fabric to wear when wet because of evaporative heat loss. Cotton clothing lasts for years, is relatively inexpensive, and can be easily laundered. Just remember to bring your iron to take care of those unsightly wrinkles!

Figure 2.4
Never underestimate the dangers of cotton clothing.

Cotton's disadvantages are consequences of some of its advantages. Have you ever gone swimming with a cotton T-shirt on? When you get out of the water, sometimes the wind feels so cold on the wet T-shirt that it seems warmer to remain in the water. We generally want to eliminate this rapid cooling characteristic in our outdoor clothing, unless we travel in extremely hot and arid regions. Cotton is a good thermal conductor and thus is a poor insulator. In fact, many outdoor professionals strongly discourage the use of cotton in most temperate regions. Some of them have a clear and somewhat grim fabric philosophy: "Cotton kills."

BOTTOM-LINE TIP: Cotton Garments

Simply put, cotton garments such as jeans and sweatshirts have no place in the backcountry and should be used by campers only in mild temperatures and when staying close to vehicles or shelters. Pete Fish, a legendary retired forest ranger in New York's highly used Adirondack Mountains, warns the public, "All of our best-dressed corpses wear cotton."

Wool

When was the last time you saw a cold sheep? They must be doing something right. Wool is an effective outdoor fabric that has been used for many centuries by cultures around the world. The reasons for wool's effectiveness lie in the fiber's structure. The coarse, heavy fibers trap a great deal of air and form an effective thermal barrier. The fibers themselves conduct little heat (one third as much as cotton[2]), so the heat remains next to the skin.

The greatest advantage of wool is that it retains much of its power to insulate even when wet. This feature is very important to campers, who should understand that sooner or later everyone will spend a day or a night soaked to the skin due to sweat, rain, or an unplanned swim. The warm-when-wet phenomenon occurs because of the residual oils left in the unprocessed or "virgin" fibers. These oils are "hydrophobic" and shed water. This property means that some wool garments dry relatively quickly when worn. Relying on this principle, the camper can dry out a soaked wool sweater in the morning by wringing it out and wearing it all day. Don't try this with your New England Patriots cotton sweatshirt!

Figure 2.5
Wool: the natural outdoor fabric.

Of course wool can't perform miracles or satisfy every outdoor person. In fact, many people can't stand wearing wool because of its scratchiness, and some develop rashes from the irritating fibers. Some fastidious campers wrinkle their noses at the wet-dog smell that wool gives off when damp. Wool is also relatively heavy and bulky, compared to new synthetic fabrics. Watch out that you don't wash wool in hot water or leave it in the dryer unless you want to outfit the Munchkin Bobsled Team with tiny woollies!

Overall, wool has been the traditional choice for outdoor clothes in many cultures for centuries, because it performs remarkably well year after year in all sorts of nasty weather. Wool is also plentiful, easy to obtain, and relatively inexpensive.

Synthetics

Many people turn to the outdoors to sample an alternative to our techno-crazed culture, longing for simplicity, tradition, and natural things for the fleeting duration of their vacation. The last thing they want to wear is a new gizmo. However, we would be well served to consider the newcomers of the clothing family—synthetics-that outperform wool without wool's disadvantages. Once the uniform of used car dealers and lounge lizards, synthetic fabrics no longer shimmer beneath disco lights or have the texture of pantyhose.

Figure 2.6
Some synthetic polyester garments are better left in the closet.

Synthetic fabrics have three general uses in outdoor clothing: undergarments, middle-layer fabrics, and outer-shell fabrics. Synthetic insulating fills are discussed in Chapter 3. Synthetic undergarments like Thermax, Capilene, Quik-Dri, and Lifa and fleece products including Polartec, Polarplus, and Synchilla are derivatives of the original fiber-polyester. Polypropylene, a common synthetic, is in most simple terms a strand of plastic woven into thread. It absorbs almost no water, conducts little heat (less even than wool), and transports ("wicks") water away from the skin, keeping the wearer warm and dry. Polypropylene and its spinoffs are extremely lightweight, fairly durable, mildew resistant, and easy to wash. Many outdoor professionals choose these "space-age" fabrics because of their performance, comfort, simple care, and durability.

ENVIRONMENTAL TIP: Recycled Fleece Garments

Synthetics objectors, people who choose not to buy synthetics because they are processed from petroleum products, now have a reasonable excuse to try the high-functioning outdoor fabrics. Several national outdoor clothing and equipment retailers offer recycled fleece garments made from used soft drink bottles. The recycled fleece performs just as well as newly processed fleece, costs about the same, and is much easier on the environmental conscience! Look for products using ECO Fleece (up to 89% recycled materials) and Polartec, which states that it tries to use as much recycled material as possible in all its fabrics. Try Patagonia's post-consumer recycled (PCR) fleeces and shells and The North Face and other suppliers for recycled fleece garments.

Synthetic garments have their share of disadvantages. Some people recoil philosophically, politically, and aesthetically at the thought of wearing petroleum products. Synthetics melt at low temperatures, and we advise users to stand clear of fires, stoves, candles, and matches. Don't use your sleeve as a pot holder! Synthetic fleece garments allow wind to blow through with little resistance. Bring a wind shell to wear over synthetic fleece to address this problem or buy "wind-blocking" fleece products that sandwich a layer of windproof material within the garment. Finally, synthetics tend to hold on to odors, and after a sweaty expedition, garments retain unwelcome aromatic memories of places and bodies.

TECHWEENIE TIP: Synthetic Fleece

One of the most common brand names for synthetic fleece you will find is the Polartec series by Malden Mills. The fabric comes in three weights: Polartec 100, 200, and 300, also called "Polarplus." The higher the number, the thicker and warmer the fabric. Choose a fabric weight according to your activity needs.

TECHWEENIE TIP: Fabric Terms, from Warp to Denier

To understand the materials used to make both clothing and equipment, it might help to understand a few textile terms. *Warp* refers to the strands of thread on the weaving loom. The *fill* is the threads woven at a right angle to the warp. Fabrics such as nylon ripstops and taffetas are described by the thread count of the warp and fill. For example a 100 × 75 thread count means that there are 100 strands of thread per inch in the warp and 75 strands per inch in the fill. The higher the thread count, the tighter the weave and the more windproof the fabric will be.

Heavier fabrics in particular are often described in terms of thread weight. Cordura, the heavy canvas-like nylon, is often advertised in either 500 or 1,000 denier weights. The denier is the unit of measurement for thread weight. What does that mean to the average consumer? The higher the denier, the heavier duty the material. Nylon ripstops and taffetas are usually made with 70 denier thread while pack material is typically made from 400 to 1,000 denier thread.

GENERAL PRINCIPLES FOR CLOTHING SELECTION

We shortened our list of 10 general principles to 8, eliminating two of the more advanced ones. If you're curious, Clothing Selection Principle Number 9 was "Clothing must have Head, Leg, and Armholes," and Number 10 was "Clothing must be Wearable at Two or More Social Functions." Ahem. Well, on with the show.

We offer eight concepts or principles that can help you choose clothing that is safe and comfortable for rugged outdoor use. We also discuss quality construction, durability and value.

1. Clothing Should Be Roomy and Comfortable

Large, loose-fitting clothes have become quite fashionable. You've probably seen (or worn!) pants with knee-level crotches and sweatshirts big enough for professional wrestlers.

Figure 2.7
Clothing should allow freedom of movement as well as provide insulation.

Although such unusual tailoring may seem extreme, we have a few notes on the function provided by this style.

In addition to being chic, *reasonably* roomy clothing is comfortable and non-constricting, allowing campers to hike, paddle, or climb with ease. Such clothing allows blood to circulate freely, especially around ankles and cuffs, and allows for wearing layers of clothes.

On the other side of the fence, some of the new stretch synthetics, like Spiderman's long johns, conform to the body and provide the same warmth and freedom of movement as the loose clothes we describe above.

2. Clothing Must Insulate the Wearer

If we think of clothing as the layers of a house, some articles of clothing must serve the same purpose as the pink fiberglass insulation in the walls. Clothing layers, like home insulation, must trap air in pockets between the garment fibers. This "dead air space" acts to prevent conductive and radiative heat loss by creating a thermal barrier between you and the outside. Sweaters, thermal underwear, pants and shirts can create good insulating dead air spaces.

 ### BOTTOM-LINE TIP: Layers for Warmth

Wear clothing in separate multiple layers. Like the construction of a house, the spaces between layers trap air to keep you warm. Two lighter layers are almost always a better clothing choice than one heavy layer, since multiple layers are more adjustable in terms of regulating body heat. A final tip: keep your Superman costume closest to your skin in case someone needs to be rescued.

Clothing must be made of materials that keep you warm even when the clothing has been dampened by rain or perspiration. That is why wool and synthetic clothing are so valuable.

3. Clothing Must Keep You Dry

The equivalent of vinyl siding in the camper's wardrobe is rain- and wind-gear. You can buy a set of rain pants and jacket and a set of wind pants and jacket, or you can try one of the products that claim to be both wind- and rain-proof, such as Gore-Tex, Helly-Tech, Schoeller-WB and Omni-Tech. In the rest of the book, we will refer generically to clothing using these fabrics as "waterproof/breathable garments."

 ### TECHWEENIE TIP: Waterproof and Breathable Fabrics

Waterproof/breathable fabrics are extremely thin films of plastic laminated to more durable fabrics. The film has millions of microscopic pores that allow the passage of very small molecules. Thus, perspiration vapor is small enough to escape through the membrane, while water droplets are too big to soak through from the outside. Wow! Does it work? Well . . . ask two people and you'll get two different answers. Jeanne-Claude Stump, Forrest Stump's Olympic skiing sister, says that when she really gets moving, her "miracle fabric" jacket feels like a Swedish sauna. And when it rains, breathability decreases even more. The casual day or overnight camper may have great success with a waterproof/breathable garment, especially when it is new. Virtually all waterproof/breathable garments have a lifetime warranty, which comes in handy if you camp near a dealer. If you have the money and patience to try one of these high-tech fabrics, you may be pleasantly rewarded. But be forewarned!

Coated nylon and PVC are less-expensive options for rain gear. Campers often confuse ordinary untreated wind-gear for waterproof rain gear and are mystified (and irritated!) when they wear wind-gear in the rain and get wet. Read the labels. Urethane or polyurethane-coated nylon fibers are waterproof. Some treatments such as sprays or special weaves are only water repellent and may soak through in heavy rains.

Make sure your clothes don't soak you from the inside via perspiration. Look for clothes made with many zippers and vents, which allow perspiration to escape. Inner layers of clothing should be made of fabrics that do not absorb moisture. Synthetics and wool are the best choices. Layers that absorb little moisture will also dry rapidly.

4. Clothing Must Be Sturdy

Choose outdoor clothing built for poor weather, rugged terrain, scrapes, falls, and many years of vigorous use. Often, cheap clothing is just that: cheap. When purchasing new clothing, recognize that quality does come with a price. But don't despair, because you don't always have to pay top dollar for high-tech functional clothing. Comparison shopping among outdoor suppliers often yields significant savings. Look for rugged fabrics; double-stitched seams; heavy-duty zippers; and reinforced elbows, knees, seats, and crotches.

5. Clothing Should Have Multiple Uses

Try to find multiple purposes for clothing. Thermal underwear becomes pajamas. A sweater becomes a pillow. Nylon shorts double as swim trunks. A thermal underwear top becomes an outer layer by itself in temperate weather. Carry only one hat for both sun and rain.

PHILOSOPHY TIP: Less Is More

Ideally, you should have a limited number of clothing items. Think of traveling light, like Wyatt Earp riding the range, not like Queen Victoria touring Europe. Paring everything down when camping becomes a sort of philosophical challenge. Simplicity in everything reduces complexity, headaches, impact on resources, and cost. Remember Thoreau? "Simplicity, simplicity, simplicity! I say let your affairs be as two or three and not a hundred or a thousand." Or, as Moss Stump says, "If you've got too much stuff, you lose it."

6. Clothing Should Be Lightweight and Stuffable

Don't bring the 9-pound varsity letter sweater or the wool trenchcoat. All items should be absolutely necessary and as light as possible.

Figure 2.8
**As H.D. Thoreau would say, remember—
keep it simple!**

TRICKS OF THE TRADE: Stuffing Versus Folding

Forget about folding your shirts carefully and placing them in matching luggage. Most campers stuff clothing vigorously into ditty bags, stuff sacks, and backpacks. Stuffed clothing usually takes less space than when carefully folded and fills gaps in your backpack.

7. Clothing Should Be Well-designed and Functional

Campers need to find a balance between clothing best suited for country-club weddings and the neon zipper-festooned NASA rejects that claim to be the latest in high-tech outdoor gear. Look for a reasonable number of large, expandable pockets with durable fasteners, comfortable and roomy hoods, half- or full-zipped legs on rain and wind pants, and workable closures on wrists and ankles. Healthy skepticism, common sense, and Thoreau's simplicity should guide you through the consumer jungle. Clothing selection and purchase provides the camper with the first opportunity to practice quality decision making. Use a decision-making process based on experience and knowledge, and don't fall prey to the latest outdoor clothing fad.

8. Clothing Should Be Easy to Maintain and Repair

Sturdily constructed clothing should be able to withstand many washings and weeks of abuse in the field. It should feature non-clogging zippers and a minimum of fancy, easily destroyed decorations.

TRICKS OF THE TRADE: Secondhand Clothes

Although apparel companies make millions on fantastic outdoor clothes, outfitting your group or family doesn't have to cost a fortune. Before you mortgage the house for outdoor gear, pull down the stairs to the attic and poke around. You might find mothballed relics of yesteryear that would make ideal clothing for camping. Grandpa's WWII woollies, your older sister's prized cashmere sweater, or Uncle Walt's suspenders would all add style and sturdy function to your gear list. Also, Salvation Army, Goodwill, and other secondhand stores are great places to spend rainy days before heading into the woods. For some outdoor people, finding a perfectly fitting used wool shirt is as rewarding as finding a trout-filled mountain pond.

THE CLOTHING LIST

Clothing Items, from Underwear to Outerwear

As a reference, we suggest using the outdoor clothing list developed by the Wilderness Education Association (WEA) for outfitting students on their month-long outdoor leadership field courses. The list is intended for three-season (spring, summer, and fall) backpacking for an average person. You may have to modify the list for your personal needs. For instance, if you tend to feel chilly, add the optional items for additional layers. Even though the list was made for month-long trips, we find that we usually need all the items even for a shorter trip.

The list illustrates the eight clothing principles described above. The camper should look for lightness, simplicity, and flexibility of layers. The concept of layering for greater warmth, humidity control, and comfort guides all of our choices. The list actually provides a vast number of combinations for optimizing comfort and warmth. We divided the list into sections: under-wear, middlewear, outerwear, head and hands, and footwear. We'll present the list and then comment on each item.

Underwear
    1. Boxer shorts (2 pairs)
    2. Synthetic or synthetic/wool blend underwear top (1 or 2)
    3. Long underwear bottom (optional—1 or 2 pairs)

Middlewear
    4. Long-sleeved cotton/polyester, light-weave dress shirt (1)
    5. Wool or pile trousers with belt/suspenders (1 pair)
    6. Shorts (1 or 2 pairs)
    7. Heavy C.P.O. type wool or pile shirt (1)
    8. Sweaters (1 or 2); wool, pile, or fleece; thin and layerable

Outerwear
    9. Rain parka (1); coated nylon or waterproof/breathable type
   10. Rain pants (1 pair)
   11. Wind parka (1); breathable (uncoated) nylon
   12. Wind pants (1 pair)

Head and Hands
   13. Ski cap made of wool, synthetic, or blend (1); covers ears and back of neck
   14. Brimmed cap (1); wide brimmed wool felt or wool baseball-style
   15. Gloves made of wool, synthetic, or blend (1 pair); may be glove liners
   16. Mittens made of wool, synthetic, or blend (1 pair)
   17. Cotton work gloves (1 pair)
   18. Bandannas (2 or more)
   19. Sunglasses (1 pair)

Footwear
   20. Socks, lightweight wool or synthetic liners (2 pairs); mid- or heavyweight wool or synthetic (2–4 pairs)
   21. Boots (1 pair)
   22. Sneakers or shoes (1 pair); lightweight nylon or canvas
   23. Sandals (optional; 1 pair); nylon/rubber

Backcountry Clothing List Notes
So there you have it. Simple, right? But now you want to know, "Why?" Why boxer shorts? Why a polyester dress shirt? Why both a rain suit and a wind suit? We'll explain each item from #1 to #23.

Underwear
1. Two pairs of boxer shorts. We have found that most men and women prefer some loose-fitting garment for their crotch region. The looseness aids in ventilation and the length of the boxer short prevents the chafing that often occurs when hikers walk many miles. If you're skeptical, bring one pair along on your next trip and try them. We think you'll find that you have less chafing and a smile at the end of a long day. Take two pairs so that you can wash one and wear the other.

2/3. Synthetic or wool-blend long underwear set. Long underwear functions primarily as an insulating layer, worn against the skin and under other layers, in order to provide warmth. The fabric should be synthetic (polypropylene, Thermax, Capilene, Quik-Dri, etc.) or wool in order to "wick" away moisture to the outside and insulate when wet. Your underwear top often becomes your main daily garment when camping, so many campers bring two that can be worn in layers or washed when necessary.

**Figure 2.9
The King of the Trail wears a
poly/cotton dress shirt.**

Middlewear

4. Long-sleeved cotton/polyester dress shirt. This item usually causes the most confusion. How is an Abercrombie and Fitch button-down shirt suited for use in the backcountry? Do we think we'll be invited to a backwoods board meeting? Are we selling insurance to our tent partners? Surprisingly, this common item performs with high function and versatility in the outdoors. Intended for warm days, the long sleeves provide protection from the sun and wind, bug bites, scrapes, and poison ivy. Roll up the sleeves if you get warm. For that matter, unbutton it to the navel for the Elvis look. The light weave and polyester fibers dry quickly, leaving you comfortable even when you sweat out a rendition of "Jail House Rock." These shirts are also inexpensive and readily available, especially if acquired in your father's trunk of retired clothing.

Many outdoor clothing suppliers, including L.L. Bean, R.E.I., E.M.S., Patagonia, and The North Face have jumped on the band wagon in providing stylish polyester shirts for outdoor wear. Try one, and we think you'll appreciate the simplicity and high function.

5. Synthetic fleece (pile) or wool trousers with belt or suspenders. We strongly recommend synthetic fleece or wool rather than jeans or cotton khakis because of the dangerous water-retaining characteristic of cotton. We forbid cotton clothing (except for the listed items) on our expeditions.

Synthetic fleece pants (Polartec, Polarplus, microfleece, etc.) have become the choice for campers with healthy clothing budgets. They perform like wool yet absorb less water, weigh less, and dry much more quickly. Many people find synthetic fleece pants more comfortable against the skin. Their disadvantages are that they wear out more quickly, generally cost more than wool, and are harder to find secondhand.

Wool trousers have long been a favorite of outdoor people, mail carriers, and the military for temperate, rainy, and cold-weather situations. Light or mid-weight wool trousers get high marks for comfort in cool and warm weather. In hot weather, wool pants are comfortable because they "breathe" well and don't hold as much moisture as cotton. If they do get too hot, simply take them off and wear shorts. Remember to obtain trousers that are roomy enough to wear with all your clothing on and still allow you to tuck in shirttails and sweaters. Do you know why campers wear red suspenders or belts? To keep their pants up! Don't forget yours!

6. Shorts. To be brief, our concerns are fabric and function. Choose nylon or polyester material to provide durability, warmth when wet, and quick-drying ability. For optimal function, consider bringing shorts that double as swim trunks or underwear. Women may want to bring nylon, polyester, or synthetic swimming apparel as well as shorts. Some synthetics, like Supplex, have a comfortable cotton-like feel together with the quick-drying capability of nylon.

7. Synthetic fleece or heavy wool shirt. Use the synthetic fleece zip-front jacket as an all-purpose insulating layer. Look for the heaviest fleece for your activity level and purpose. The traditional heavyweight wool shirt remains a strong seller among hunters and other outdoor enthusiasts. Also called a "C.P.O." shirt, this garment still provides the high function that won it a place in every outdoor person's wardrobe before the advent of synthetics.

8. Synthetic fleece and wool sweaters. Synthetic fleece pullovers and light jackets serve as additional insulating layers. We've found that inexpensive fleece tops available at discount retailers are very functional, but "pill" sooner than higher-grade garments. Alternatively, find two mid- or lightweight wool sweaters that can fit over one another for layering.

TRICKS OF THE TRADE: Double-length Sweaters
Some resourceful campers cut the body off one sweater below the sleeves and sew it to the bottom of another to form a super long-trunked sweater that cannot come untucked during vigorous activity. These long-trunked sweaters are great in the winter for playing in the snow.

**Figure 2.10
Make sure to tuck in your double-length
sweater.**

Outerwear

9/10. Rain gear. We recommend both a rain jacket and pants, or some form of covering for your legs in the event of a two- or three-day soaker. Some people say that ponchos and cagoules (rain jackets that extend to the knees or lower) work well. Make sure your jacket has a roomy and comfortable hood, or that you are prepared to cover your head with a waterproof hat.

BOTTOM-LINE TIP: Waterproof Versus Water-resistant Garments

Many people get very confused when it comes to fabrics for rain gear. Do not assume that any garment that is shiny and made from nylon will be waterproof and suitable as rain gear. Your gear must say "Waterproof" on the tag and be made of urethane-coated nylon, PVC-coated nylon, or have a waterproof/breathable-type laminate. "Water repellent" and "water resistant" are not good enough for an extended or rugged camping trip. You will get wet with these treatments! Some people say you will get wet no matter what type of rain gear you bring. Don't be surprised if you find yourself agreeing after your first couple of trips.

Stay away from vinyl or disposable ponchos, jackets, or pants. These fall apart in the backcountry and should be left for fans at football stadiums who can run into their warm SUVs at the end of the day. Do yourself a favor and spend a little money on quality waterproof rain gear.

SAFETY TIP: The Importance of Quality Rain Gear

Choosing good rain gear involves more than comfort. Considering the dangers of hypothermia, choosing good rain gear involves safety and can save lives.

11/12. Wind gear. Do you need both wind gear and rain gear? Doesn't your rain gear stop the wind? Why spend all that money? Rain gear does stop the wind and can perform the same function, if you plan to stand around without perspiring. Coated rain gear does not breathe, meaning it does not let perspiration escape. When you start perspiring, the water vapor remains trapped inside the rain gear, turning your slicker into a steam-bath. If the wind blows while you are walking, paddling, or mountain climbing, wear an uncoated, breathable nylon wind layer on your torso and legs to keep warm and dry. Nylon windbreakers are relatively inexpensive and light. We recommend purchasing wind pants as well for a versatile, easily packed layer. Wind gear also protects undergarments from excessive wear and tear.

What about waterproof/breathable fabric? Is it the exception to the rule? It's supposed to be good for rain and wind, right? Well, yes, sort of. Refer to the discussion of waterproof/breathable laminates under Clothing Principle #3 for the fabric's strengths and weaknesses. Jack's guide-series (heavy-duty) Gore-Tex shell from L.L. Bean is actually too hot during periods of heavy exertion. He complains about overheating and sweating, thus dampening his inner garments and defeating the purpose of wearing a "breathable" garment. Lighter-weight waterproof breathable shells are on the market, however. The bottom line is, unless you have waterproof/breathable garments, you should bring both wind and rain gear.

Head and Hands

13. Wool, synthetic or wool/synthetic blend hat. These hats should provide warmth during extreme daytime weather, cold nights, or periods of inactivity. They should be thick, snug, and functional, covering the ears, the entire head, and the back of the neck. Ideally, they should fit inside the hoods of your rain and wind jackets.

Many people consider skipping head gear, especially in the summer, but we teach our outdoor leaders at the WEA to carry a warm hat at all times to provide quick warmth. The dangers of hypothermia exist in all seasons and in all temperatures wherever wind and water are present. For its use in preventing hypothermia, a hat becomes an important tool for administering backcountry first aid.

14. Brimmed hat. The brim keeps sun and rain out of the eyes and offers some protection against branches when off trail. As reported in a scientific journal, in order to combat the steadily rising incidence of facial skin cancers, donning a brimmed hat keeps 70% of damaging solar rays from hitting the face[3]. Look for wool or synthetic fabric and ear flaps for additional protection. A wool felt "Crusher" hat with a round, wide brim also works well, but beware of considerable shrinkage when it gets soaked.

15/16. Wool or synthetic gloves and mittens. Gloves or mittens are necessary to keep the hands warm and healthy. Avoid leather, as it provides marginal insulation and performs poorly when wet.

Gloves function especially well for high-dexterity tasks such as refueling a stove or tying knots. We find thin polypropylene glove liners work best for fine handwork. Mittens make great partners to the gloves since they can be worn over them. Mittens provide greater warmth than gloves by reducing exposed surface area and allowing fingers to warm each other. A coated nylon or waterproof/breathable mitten overshell can be added for extreme weather conditions.

17. Cotton work gloves. Now wait a second. Cotton? Rogue of fabrics? You bet! We recommend bringing one pair of cotton garden or work gloves for use around the fire or stove. Gloves are an extremely helpful, not to mention safe, cooking aid to handle hot pans, fuel wood, or shovels. Cotton works well because it won't melt like synthetics and lasts longer than wool. For this situation, we're not concerned with its inability to insulate when wet.

18. Bandannas. We always bring two or three bandannas for a wide variety of uses. The colorful cotton cloths can serve as handkerchiefs, pot holders, washcloths, or towels. People wear them on their heads, sprinkle them with insect repellent and wear them as neckties, and use them in emergencies to bandage wounds and for lashing stretchers. It's hard to beat bandannas for all-around versatility.

19. Sunglasses. We recommend sunglasses for overall eye protection from the sun and potentially hazardous objects, such as pointed twigs, dust, or food fights. A good pair of sunglasses is a great investment, as they can avert eyestrain, headaches, and in extreme cases, glare-related injury such as snow blindness.

Footwear

Footwear and foot care are two of the camper's greatest concerns and challenges. Healthy feet bring heightened enjoyment of the outdoors with safe access. Painful or blistered feet can cut a trip short, keep a team off a long-awaited mountain summit, or cause an expensive and risky evacuation from the backcountry.

 **BOTTOM-LINE TIP: Foot Power**
We say to hikers on WEA expeditions that the feet are your "diesel" power in the backcountry. "Diesel get you into the woods and diesel get you out." You get the idea. Maintaining healthy feet is of critical importance.

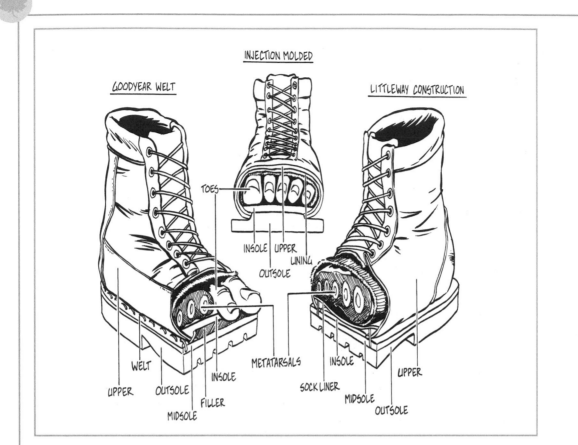

INJECTION MOLDED

GOODYEAR WELT

LITTLEWAY CONSTRUCTION

TOES

INSOLE | UPPER

LINING

OUTSOLE

WELT

UPPER

OUTSOLE

INSOLE

FILLER

MIDSOLE

METATARSALS

INSOLE

SOCK LINER

MIDSOLE

OUTSOLE

UPPER

Figure 2.11
Common methods of boot construction.

20. Mid-weight wool or wool/synthetic socks. For fabrics, we again look to wool and synthetics or blends of the two. The purpose of the inner sock is to rub against the outer sock, which transfers friction away from the feet. Athletes almost always wear two layers of socks in order to minimize chafing, hot spots, and blisters. We recommend the same. Cushioned hiking socks such as Thor-lo work well. Jack swears by the Thor-lo Trekker, while Eric sings the praises of Smart-Wool and other merino wool socks. Thin polypropylene or silk liner socks wick perspiration to the outer sock, keeping the foot dry and comfortable. Bring a minimum of four pairs of socks so that you always have one dry pair in reserve. For lengthy trips, we recommend that campers bring six pairs of socks: two pairs of thin liners and four pairs of mid-weight wool socks.

PHILOSOPHY TIP: The Outdoor Athlete
Backpackers and trekkers can think of themselves as athletes and should prepare themselves accordingly. Outdoor athletes should train as conscientiously as the level of planned activity dictates, paying heed to gear, training, and discipline. But only if you want to. If the outdoors ceases to be fun, take another look at how you approach it.

21. Boots. The single most critical item for the success and enjoyment of a backcountry trip is a good pair of boots. Well-fitting boots appropriate for the chosen terrain make life much easier. Fortunately or unfortunately, the hiking boot market has mushroomed into a bewildering emporium of options, styles, technology, and prices. How can you make a good choice? Be skeptical, patient, and persistent, armed with good information.

Boot Weight. The first foot-gear decision, which will greatly narrow the field of options, is to determine the appropriate boot weight for the type of hiking you will be doing. The market has three broad boot classifications: lightweight, midweight, and heavyweight.

Lightweight hiking boots are modifications of tennis shoes designed for unencumbered or lightly encumbered day walks in easy to moderate terrain. They usually have fabric and suede uppers, which offer flexibility and breathability. If you plan to dayhike from a central location or walk around town, these boots are very comfortable and light on your feet. Do not try to carry heavy loads, though, unless you have ankles of steel.

Midweight boots generally have uppers similar to the lightweights, but have heavier soles and more rugged construction overall. These boots are good for transporting moderate loads (20–45 pounds) over moderate terrain for relatively short trips. Jack finds that his Nike ACG Gore-Tex Air Wallowa Mid II boots are a great compromise between ruggedness and comfort. He says he wouldn't wear them when carrying a heavy pack, but has used them for extended day hikes when carrying a day pack. Boots such as these offer a great combination of fit, support, and breathability with no break-in period (Figure 2.11).

Heavyweight boots generally have full-grain leather uppers (not split leather with a suede nap) for strength, support, durability, and weatherproofing. The soles are thick and rugged, attached to the uppers with cement or a stitched welt. Look for stitches between the upper and the sole. The sole often has a "shank," a stiff piece of metal, fiberglass, or plastic, deep inside under the footbed. The shank greatly stiffens the sole, allowing the hiker to walk over pointed rocks or uneven terrain with security and greater comfort. Notice we say "greater" comfort. We mean greater comfort than walking barefoot. Your feet still can hurt after 7 miles with a full pack.

Heavyweight boots are your choice for carrying moderate to heavy loads (45 pounds and greater) over rugged terrain for extended backcountry trips. The trick in choosing a boot weight is to honestly appraise your level of activity. Lightweight boots just don't cut it under heavy loads when you need the support of full-grain leather.

Boots should protect the sole of your foot and support the ankles. Many boots cover the ankles and allow free movement for the Achilles tendon at the back of the foot. This is an important feature, as many hikers experience an irritation of this tendon. Look for quality laces, grommets, eyelets, and lace hooks (speed lacing).

❖❖❖❖❖❖❖❖❖❖

TECHWEENIE TIP: Boot Construction

Full-grain leather uses the entire thickness of the animal hide, lending durability, stiffness, and some degree of water repellency to the boot. Less sturdy boots use split-grain leather, which is a veneer or layer of leather. Split-grain leather often has a suede-like nap and is much thinner than full-grain leather. It is also a good idea to count the seams on a boot. Generally, the fewer seams the better. Single-piece leather construction is usually the hallmark of a good-quality boot. Several pieces of leather stitched together to form the upper leave a great number of seams, which weaken the boot and allow more entrances for water.

❖❖❖❖❖❖❖❖❖❖

Like ideal rainwear, boots should shed rain and water and allow perspiration vapor to escape. In practice, we've found no leather boot to be completely waterproof, but in general we regard leather as superior to synthetic composite boots for overall performance. Waterproof/breathable fabric-lined boots have improved in their ability to keep your feet dry, but remain relatively expensive and short-lived in their effectiveness.

Fitting boots. Once you have chosen the weight and style of boots you want, you should try on several styles and sizes to arrive at the "perfect" fit. Choose boots large enough for two pairs of socks and to allow for good circulation, yet small enough to avoid excessive slippage, which may cause blisters. Put on two pairs of hiking socks and slip on the boots. With the boots unlaced, you should be able to insert one finger between your heel and the back of the boot. When you lace up, the boots should feel comfortable. Your feet should just touch the insides, and your toes should wiggle comfortably.

The arches of the boots should meet the arch of your feet. Kick your toe against a step or a solid object. Your toes should not touch the front of the boot with each kick. This action simulates descending steep slopes. Finally, does the boot "feel" right? Often your instincts about fit, comfort, and quality are correct.

TRICKS OF THE TRADE: Boot Quality

A note about quality and durability in boots: ask the experts. However, the experts you should ask don't always work in the boot department of gear stores. Ask friends or teachers who are backcountry veterans. Which boots do they choose? How did they use the boots? What types of terrain did they hike on, for how many miles, and how much weight were they carrying? Do the "hot" hiking boots really hold up? We've seen many boots from supposedly top-of-the-line boot companies self-destruct after rugged field use.

22. Sneakers or shoes. In addition to pickup ultimate matches and bear races, soft-soled sneakers or shoes function well around the backcountry campsite. After a long day on the trail, there are few greater pleasures than peeling off the sweaty boots you've trekked in all day, powdering your feet, and donning your comfy old running shoes.

Aside from comfort, camp shoes should have relatively smooth soles for preserving campsite vegetation and soil. The hungry lugs of hiking boots rapidly chew up heavily-trafficked passages near campsites, killing vegetation and increasing erosion. Campsite impact takes years to recover. An extra pair of sneakers also helps during river crossings if footing is relatively easy and the sup-

Figure 2.12
Woody changes into camp shoes after a long hike.

port of hiking boots can be traded for dryness. Choose old sneakers or shoes made from nylon, Cordura, or other synthetics. Avoid footwear constructed with foam padding or leather, as these shoes take ages to dry and often become moldy.

Many retailers are now offering aquatic sport shoes, which look like a sneaker sole with a porous synthetic top. Some models lace up, while others use Velcro closures or simply slip on. These products offer good foot protection as well as the ability to dry relatively quickly when worn in the open air after immersion. You might want to try reinforced neoprene booties, some of which come with rugged rubber soles for walking down to the river's edge and wading. In addition, some outdoor suppliers market a simple canvas "canoe shoe," which is nothing more than a simplified version of the old Converse "Chuck Taylor" basketball sneaker still popular with skateboarders and Beaver Cleaver fans. These canvas canoe shoes work well in warm weather when their lengthy drying time is not a significant disadvantage.

While these specialized aquatic shoes are quite functional, remember that when backpacking, you'll have to carry them on your back. Try to keep the number of changes of footwear to a minimum. Your boots plus one other alternative should be sufficient.

23. Sandals. Nylon and rubber sandals have swept the country as a recent craze in outdoor clothing, shodding the feet of legions of campers in a sort of Ben-Hur revival. These would-be Roman Centurions wear Velcro or buckle-fastened sandals originally designed by river guides. Now, campers wear sandals on day hikes, while lounging around camp, swimming, and even carrying heavy backpacks. We suggest caution in using sandals for activities other than those they were designed for.

The simple design of sandals offers great coolness, air circulation, and freedom, but also exposes the feet to injury, abrasion, cuts, stings, poison ivy, and sunburn. We've found that Velcro straps don't hold for very long and that the sandals actually fall off when you swim. So much for river running. Don't river guides ever fall off their rafts and have to swim to shore?

Overall, nylon/rubber sandals are comfortable and fun, but generally we don't bring them on serious backcountry trips. Many people disagree, and you will find armies of sandal wearers in outdoor settings from Rome to Reno. However, since they expose your all-important feet to injury, we judge that sandals pose more trouble than they are worth.

USING BACKCOUNTRY CLOTHING

In this final section about clothing we address how you actually use clothing in the backcountry by reviewing some critical concepts. When selecting items for your backcountry wardrobe, style and appearance should be your lowest priorities.

BOTTOM-LINE TIP: Clothing Selection
Choose the perfect wardrobe based on function, lightness, durability, fabrics, versatility, and value.

SAFETY TIP: Bring It All!
Bring all of the items on the list. Just because the weather is 70° F and cheerful, you shouldn't leave your sweaters or rain gear behind. Our list of 23 items is as short as our judgment, based on years of outdoor experience, can allow. Trust us, at least until you have logged several months in the field! As crusty (but still living!) outdoor travelers say, "Better to have it and not need it than need it and not have it."

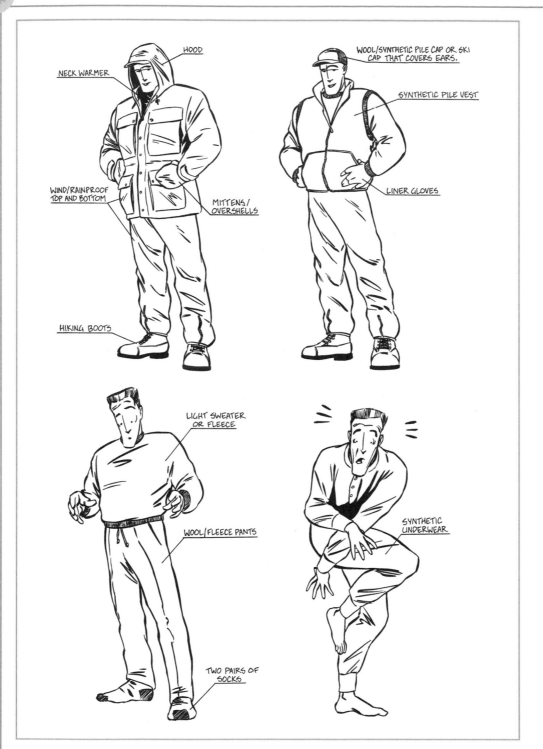

NECK WARMER

HOOD

WOOL/SYNTHETIC PILE CAP OR SKI CAP THAT COVERS EARS.

SYNTHETIC PILE VEST

WIND/RAINPROOF TOP AND BOTTOM

MITTENS/OVERSHELLS

LINER GLOVES

HIKING BOOTS

LIGHT SWEATER OR FLEECE

WOOL/FLEECE PANTS

SYNTHETIC UNDERWEAR

TWO PAIRS OF SOCKS

Figure 2.13
The many layers of the wilderness adventure.

In short, you can think about three concepts to help guide your decisions: climate control, layering, and accessibility.

Climate control means regulating your body's temperature to maintain relative comfort. Choose clothing items from your backpack to fit weather and temperature conditions appropriate for the warmth of your body. It is wise to remember the controllable means of heat loss: conduction, convection, radiation, and evaporation through perspiration. Heat creation and retention are caused by exercise and effective use of insulation from clothing. Think about how you can minimize or maximize heat loss from each process, depending on your body's needs, by using clothing wisely and moderating the rate of exercise (e.g., how fast you're hiking, pedaling, or paddling).

Our primary tool for maximizing comfort and warmth in the backcountry is layering (Figure 2.13). *Layering* involves wearing specialized clothing items over one another to create a weatherproof, warm, and comfortable environment. Think in three layers: the skin layer, the insulating layer, and the wind/rain layer. Simple!

The final concept, *accessibility* of clothing, allows the camper to control his or her climate by changing clothing layers. Basically, in order to take layers off before soaking them or to put layers on before a chill sets in, clothes must be easily accessible to the backcountry traveler. The wise and comfortable backcountry traveler plans to change layers by packing items such as rain gear, hats, and an extra sweater near the top of the pack and does not hesitate to stop and adjust clothing.

To cool off while you are walking, try adjusting your clothing by taking off your hat, opening your shirt, taking off gloves, and rolling up sleeves. To warm up, try the reverse. Think of climate control, ventilation, and layering as a challenge of your skills. Try to proactively modify your layers and physical activity so that you never soak a layer, never get out of breath, and always remain comfortable.

 **BOTTOM-LINE TIP: Climate Control Through Layering**

Campers must wear enough clothing to keep warm, but not enough to cause discomfort and heat loss through perspiration. You maintain climate control through effective layering. Simply put, if you are cold, put on another thin layer or increase physical activity or both. If you are too warm, take a layer off, increase ventilation, or decrease physical activity.

Wilderness travel and backcountry camping are wonderful activities, but to engage in them without appropriate clothing is like driving a car without a seat belt. Are the consequences worth the gamble?

Notes

[1]Drury, J., Ed. (2005). *The backcountry classroom: Lessons, tools and activities for teaching outdoor leaders*. Guilford, CT: Falcon Guide.
[2]Ibid.
[3]*Science News*. (1994, January 22). *145*, 55.

References

Denner, J.C. (1990). *A Primer on Clothing Systems for Cold-Weather Field Work*. (Open-File Report 89-415). U.S. Department of the Interior. Bow, NH: U.S. Geological Survey.

Drury, J., Ed. (2005). *The backcountry classroom: Lessons, tools and activities for teaching outdoor leaders*. Guilford, CT: Falcon Guide.

Forgey, W.W. (1985). *Hypothermia: Death by Exposure*. Merrilville, IN: ICS Books, Inc.

Hart, J. (1977). *Walking Softly in the Wilderness*. San Francisco: Sierra Club Books.

Petzoldt, P. (1984). *The New Wilderness Handbook* (2nd ed.). New York: W.W. Norton & Company. (Original work published in 1974).

Simer, P., & Sullivan, J. (1983). *The National Outdoor Leadership School's Wilderness Guide*. New York: Simon and Schuster.

CHAPTER 3

Outdoor Tools and Toys

"Some swear by it and some swear at it . . ."
—Granny Stump

"Better to have it and not need it than to need it and not have it."
—Jack Drury

> **Topics:**
> • Packs
> • Sleeping Bags and Pads
> • Shelter
> • Single-Burner Cookstoves
> • Miscellaneous Equipment
> • Personal Care Items

When you ask some veteran outdoor travelers about their equipment, you'd better be prepared for a good long talk. This is true especially of "techweenies," or those people smitten by the design, materials, and engineering of the outdoor gadgetry cornucopia. Discussing equipment sends techweenies into nirvana. They can spend hours discussing the pros and cons of every piece and style of equipment.

Equipment can become a very personal and emotional issue. We have friends who have had such strong arguments over the merit of one type of backpack versus another that they now agree to disagree and choose not to speak about gear. The left-brained, rational side of us might say, "That's crazy," but the right-brained, playful side says, "Why not? After all, half the fun of camping is the chance to play with our new outdoor toys."

PHILOSOPHY TIP: There's More Fun to It than Just Doing It

Recreation theorists talk about five stages of a recreational experience: planning the activity, traveling to the recreation site, having the experience, returning from the experience, and reflecting on the experience. Researching, analyzing, purchasing, and maintaining equipment are all valid and necessary aspects of the recreational experience.

PRIORITIES FOR SELECTING EQUIPMENT

To help us through the maze of marketing and advertising, we have some guidelines that make equipment purchases easier. To start, the equipment we select should help provide for our safety and then help us protect the environment. After those two needs are met, equipment can be selected to increase our enjoyment and comfort in the outdoors.

GETTING COMFORTABLE WITH COMFORT

The question of comfort always arises in wilderness travel. What exactly does a particular person mean by comfort? We have found that there is no easy answer. What is comfortable for one person is torture for another. We feel wilderness travel is like many of life's adventures: without effort there is no benefit.

People often ask, "How can you enjoy carrying a heavy pack in the rain and cold?" First, we think that comfort is relative, and we can honestly say that we are rarely uncomfortable in the outdoors. Second, people do many things in life that are uncomfortable in hopes of a greater reward. For example, look at the social drinker who wakes up with a hangover. We would rather be sore from carrying a heavy pack. What about the college athlete who works for years in the hope he or she may make first string, be elected captain, be selected All-American, and succeed as a professional athlete? How about the medical student who slaves away for six or more years? Pain and pleasure are extremely personal.

Most people engaged in activities they find personally rewarding find that discomfort soon disappears. In fact, their definition of comfort often expands to include what they once thought was uncomfortable. Wilderness travel is somewhat like that. To us, the rewards associated with wilderness travel far outweigh what we consider to be a few mild discomforts.

The first time Jack met wilderness educator Paul Petzoldt was in 1969 when Paul was promoting the National Outdoor Leadership School (NOLS). An audience member asked, "Why is it that every time I go outdoors I get wet, cold, and hungry; develop blisters; and have a miserable time?" Paul's response stayed with Jack. Paul said, "We have a saying at NOLS. 'If you're uncomfortable, you're not doing it right.'" That comment struck home. Even now, if we find ourselves uncomfortable, we try to figure out what we're doing wrong.

CHOOSING IDEAL OUTDOOR EQUIPMENT

A good piece of equipment should be like a good knot: it should serve very well the purpose for which it was designed. Unfortunately, our experience tells us that there is a lot of equipment that doesn't always meet this standard. After safety and environmental needs are met, selecting equipment can also be like selecting your underwear: It's very personal! One person may like silk boxers, while the other prefers lycra bikini briefs. In matters of preference, there is no right or wrong.

Our equipment choices work for our type of wilderness travel. We don't necessarily endorse the brand names we mention, but when we like something, we'll tell you. After some field experience of your own, you may find our choices unacceptable for your wilderness adventures. Develop and use your own judgment and learn what works best for you. We encourage you to be open-minded and willing to try new things. Most importantly, we encourage you to make your critical gear purchases based on the priorities we talk about. If all wilderness users accept responsibility for their own safety and make a great effort to take care of the signs of their passing, we all might be able to use the wilderness with less governmental regulation.

Keep in mind that technology is changing so fast that whatever we write will quickly become outdated. We are confident, however, that what we talk about works and has worked for hundreds of college students on monthlong expeditions. Be aware that this doesn't mean that there isn't a newer and better option out there.

Finally, it is important to remember that your goal is to get into the outdoors and safely enjoy the natural surroundings. High-tech gadgetry should make this easier, not more complex. If you spend more time caring for your equipment than enjoying the outdoors, then perhaps your passion lies in the equipment and not the outdoors. That is okay, but just understand and appreciate your priorities.

THE "BIG TICKET" ITEMS

We'll look at equipment in three categories. "Big Ticket" items are expensive but necessary and include backpacks, sleeping bags and pads, shelters, and stoves. We also discuss miscellaneous items from altimeters to water bottles, and personal care items which include sunscreen, sunglasses, toilet paper, and others.

PACKS

Backpacks

Since the backpack carries your gear to your destination, it is a crucial piece of equipment. Your backpack determines what you bring, how comfortable you will be, and—if it can't hold your stuff—what you might lose along the way. You will find dozens of choices in today's backpack market. Let's look at what kind of packs the Stump family owns. Forrest Stump has an older Kelty aluminum external frame pack that he purchased in the mid-1970s. (Those were the BC years, Before Children, when he and Holly were doing a lot of backpacking.) The Kelty has held up well and is relatively simple by today's standards. The frame comes in sizes ranging from extra-large to small and has padded shoulder straps with minimum adjustment and a padded waist belt with stabilizer straps. The packbag has one compartment with four side pockets and space below to tie on the sleeping bag. It isn't very sophisticated, but it is simple to adjust and has better overall design than the pack Dick Kelty originated in the '60s. Twenty years later, Forrest still finds it fairly comfortable and in good condition. It was obviously built to last.

Holly had an old external frame Camp Trails pack that she traded in for a Lowe internal frame pack during the mid-1980s when she and Forrest did a lot of canoe camping with the children. They found camping by canoe made it easier to take the kids while not having to worry as much about carrying heavy equipment. She likes the Lowe. It has two parallel aluminum stays, which provide rigidity and support sewn into the sleeves. The stays can be bent to fit the contours of her back. With the stays and the sophisticated harness system, she can carry loads of up to 45 pounds in relative comfort. The harness system of shoulder straps, shoulder stabilizers, sternum strap, waist belt and waist belt, stabilizers, although not as sophisticated as some newer backpacks, still seems more complex than she would like.

Willow has an external frame pack marketed for "women of the 21st century." It looks very similar to her Dad's old Kelty with a few high-tech "doodads" and contemporary colors. The packbag has been lowered with the idea of putting the sleeping bag on top instead of on the bottom. Willow finds the pack functional, given the little backpacking she does. She loves the color and thinks it "looks cool." When the manufacturer was asked about what research this "women's" pack was based on, they admitted they had used none; the women-oriented approach was basically a marketing strategy.

Moss has his mother's old Camp Trails frame pack, which is much like his dad's old Kelty pack: simple, functional, and relatively indestructible.

Woody is the "expert" backpacker of the family. He went on an NOLS adventure course two summers ago and is hoping to go to a Wilderness Education Association (WEA) affiliated college next year. He has a Dana Designs Astralplane OK (the OK stands for "overkill," meaning the pack is extra-heavy-duty to withstand years of abuse). It will hold enough gear for a month-long expedition, and it cost him a fortune ($425), but he hopes it will last him as long as his dad's Kelty. It has state-of-the-art everything, with well-designed shoulder pads, stabilizers, internal plastic reinforcement, and a super-comfortable waist belt. The Dana is a techweenie's dream, but at least all the features are based on function.

Pack Analysis

Let's evaluate the Stumps' backpacks in terms of our wilderness priorities: safety, protection of the environment, comfort, and enjoyment.

Safety

A backpack should allow you to carry relatively heavy weights without straining or otherwise injuring your back. In addition, it should allow you to maintain your balance and minimize the chance of falling down. By and large, external frame packs allow you to carry heavier weights due to their higher center of gravity and efficiency in distributing the weight throughout the frame. Internal frame packs provide better balance as they hug the wearer's back and provide a lower center of gravity. The type of activities you participate in help determine which pack would be best for you. Forrest's old Kelty, Willow's "women of the 21st century pack," and Moss's hand-me-down Camp Trails are all frame packs that, in theory, carry heavy weights but provide less balance. Holly's Lowe and Woody's Dana are internal frame packs and so provide better balance but might not carry heavier weights as comfortably. However, today's best internal frame packs are designed to carry heavy loads comfortably.

Volume is another factor in pack safety. Can your pack carry what you need? If you can't fit into the pack what you need for survival, then your pack is too small. Pack volumes vary considerably. One old adage advises campers to purchase the smallest pack they can so they don't bring anything more than what is absolutely necessary. Although this minimizes pack weight, we find that people with too-small packs tie gear and clothes to the outside of their pack. These dangling items either get damaged or fall off and get lost. We suggest that you purchase a pack slightly larger than you will need and then use good judgment in adding weight to your load.

A frame pack's volume is affected by the placement of the sleeping bag. Forrest, Willow, and Moss have packs designed for the sleeping bag to be tied on outside the packbag, directly onto the frame. Most frame packs with this external-sleeping-bag design have volumes in the 3,500-cubic-inch range. If you want the sleeping bag and other gear to fit inside the pack, the pack should have a 5,500- to 6,500-cubic-inch capacity. Some people contend that a pack this big is larger than anyone needs, but we prefer to fit everything inside the pack, including the tent, sleeping pad, fry pan, and, of course, the kitchen sink. A streamlined, self-contained pack saves gear from falling off, getting caught in branches, clanging and banging, and giving you the look of an old-time snake-oil seller.

Figure 3.1
A backcountry enthusiast or a snake-oil seller?

Whether a pack has an external or internal frame has little to do with its volume. Holly's internal-frame Lowe has a capacity of 4,500 cubic inches, while Woody's internal-frame Dana Designs Astralplane has a monstrous capacity of 7,000 cubic inches.

Durability and quality also affect safety. If your pack has a poor design along with inferior materials and workmanship, it is going to fail when you need it most. Let's say you're backpacking with your niece and nephew over Mt. Washington and bad weather blows in. The kids come down with a 24-hour bug, and you decide to take a portion of their weight. If that's the time your pack blows out a major seam or the shoulder strap rips out, you could be in serious trouble. Fortunately, most brand-name packs are both durable and well made. Pack failure is uncommon with quality manufacturers.

 **BOTTOM-LINE TIP: Quality Outdoor Gear**
In general, you get what you pay for. Quality costs money.

Protecting the Environment

How does a pack help protect the environment? Let us count the ways. First, if it's big enough and you can fit everything inside, you will eliminate accidental litter through gear loss. If we had a dime for every piece of equipment we've found along the trail that had obviously fallen off packs—from fishing poles to frying pans and other trail flotsam—then we could buy a pack like Woody's Dana Designs Astralplane. A pack that holds everything does help minimize accidental litter.

Equipment and clothing color increases the aesthetic quality of wilderness for you and other campers. Using gear in shades of blue, brown, green, maroon, and gray can keep you from looking like the local camouflage-garbed militia unit but still keep you from clashing with the natural environment. Fluorescent colors are dead and we hope they stay that way. When bright colors were stylish, there was a saying: "Friends don't let friends wear neon." Research has shown that when people wear subtle colors, more campers can use an area without feeling crowded.

 PHILOSOPHY TIP: What Do We Really Need?
According to Maslow, people are motivated to satisfy five basic types of needs.[1] Unfortunately, taking care of the environment is fairly low on that list. Taking care of physiological needs—food, warmth, and shelter—comes first. Security needs, or keeping the lions and tigers at bay, comes second. Somewhere buried within the next three needs comes protecting the environment. What's the point? When you're tired, wet, and cold and your pack is digging into your back, unless you have incredible discipline, you start caring more about your comfort and physiological needs than you do about the environment. A backpack that helps keep you comfortable and well-rested will give you more energy to be a good low-impact camper.

One last environmental consideration concerns the eco-cost of manufacture. We should be low-impact consumers as well as low-impact campers. At this point, there isn't much evidence that one pack is made in a more environmentally friendly way than another, but it is something to think about. For an example of eco-friendly manufacturing, look for labels describing recycled materials or components. When it comes to other pieces of equipment, the choices are more difficult.

Comfort and Enjoyment

As we have already discussed, the definitions of comfort and enjoyment are elusive. When selecting a backpack, we recommend that you try on the pack with a little less than the maximum weight you are generally going to carry in it. Compare packs and find the one that is most comfortable. In general, comfort is a function of the harness system. Don't necessarily go for the most complex backpack or the one with the best salesperson. Buy the most comfortable pack!

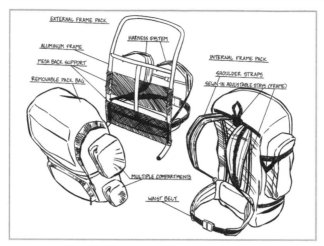

Figure 3.2
What type of frame will you need?
Choose your backpack based on what you plan to do.

 **BOTTOM-LINE TIP: Selecting a Backpack**

Select an internal- or external-frame pack (Figure 3.2) based upon the outdoor activities you normally do, and consider that external-frame backpacks are generally less expensive. Internal frames are better when you need balance or want to stow your pack in a boat, plane, or auto. External-frame packs generally carry heavier weights more comfortably and are easier to pack.

For trips longer than an overnight, select an external frame pack with at least 3,500 cubic inches and an internal frame pack with 5,500 cubic inches. In general, the more volume, the better. Try the pack on and buy the most comfortable one that you can afford. Look at this purchase as a once- (okay, maybe twice) in-a-lifetime purchase and try not to base the decision on price. Look for quality in every aspect of manufacture and try to select one in a relatively environmentally friendly color.

PACK COVERS

Even though packs are made of waterproof materials, water enters packs through seams and zippers. Unless you hike in rainless environments, consider a pack cover essential. Some argue that plastic bags make sufficient rain covers. We have two arguments against them. Firstly, they tear easily and litter the environment as you walk through the backcountry. Secondly, as environmentally conscious campers, we try to limit our use of disposable items. We would rather have a reusable pack cover than a disposable one. In our opinion, plastic bags have their place, but not as disposable pack covers.

DAY AND FANNY PACKS

In the backcountry, we prefer a sturdy day pack with side pockets and a functional waist belt to a fanny pack. A sternum strap is a nice extra because it provides greater stability and comfort. Choose a pack with a volume of at least 1,800 cubic inches. Anything less is too small to carry important gear for a safe day trip. Remember, you should carry enough items to survive the night. For that reason, we feel all but the largest fanny packs are too small for backcountry use.

SAFETY TIP: What to Take on a Day Trip
Paul Petzoldt, founder of the NOLS and the WEA and author of *The New Wilderness Handbook* says, "Clothing must enable a person to survive one night's bivouac in case of emergency."[2]

PACKING THE PACK

We like to use the initials C.B.S., Conveniently Balanced System, to help us remember the basic considerations in efficient packing.

Convenience

Convenience refers to having ready access to the most needed items, which maximizes the camper's use of time and energy and minimizes frustration. In other words, the day's plans might dictate where things are packed in the backpack. External pockets might carry the water bottle, snacks, foot care items, sunglasses, bug repellent, or camera. The water purification system, an extra layer, rain gear, and pack cover should also be readily available. Emergency gear, such as the first aid kit and repair kit should also be in a convenient location. All group members should know where the first aid kit is located in case of emergency.

Conversely, things like the tent, sleeping bag, cooking gear, and other items unlikely to be used on the trail can be stowed away in a relatively inaccessible location. Additionally, items requiring special protection from the elements might be packed inside waterproof stuff sacks. Extra clothing, cameras, books, binoculars, and sleeping bags might fit into this category.

Balance

Balance of the pack from left to right, top to bottom and front to back adds to the backpacker's safety and comfort. Heavy loads are most comfortably carried when the weight is placed directly in line with the largest and strongest bones and muscles: the pelvic girdle, upper thigh bones, and the muscles of the thighs and buttocks. The heaviest part of the pack should be centered as close to the body and as near to the top of the spinal column/base of the neck area as possible (Figure 3.3). The load should be centered between the shoulder blades. When packing the pack, the heaviest single item of equipment (e.g., food or tent) should be packed in or on the top half of the pack as close to the packer's back as possible.

When trying to balance the pack from left to right, items of similar weight should be packed on opposite sides of the pack so that neither side of the body is uncomfortably overburdened. For example, if a fuel bottle is packed in the upper left external pocket, a water bottle can be packed in the upper right external pocket.

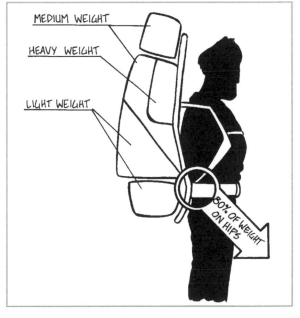

Figure 3.3
Distribute items in the pack for optimum load, comfort, and balance.

Generally speaking, it is easier to carry the heaviest components near the top of the back. However, heavy items should not be placed so high on the pack that they tip the backpacker forward. By the same token, items on the bottom should not be so heavy that they pull the backpacker backward.

You can usually tell which backpacker has the heaviest items packed away from the center of the back because they look so poorly balanced. Heavier items should be placed as close as possible to your back to minimize backward pull. For internal-frame packs or day packs that lack much protective cushioning, a sleeping pad, sweater, or jacket can be placed along the interior pack wall closest to the packer's back to protect it from rigid equipment like pots, stoves, and shovels.

Terrain also influences the way that weight is distributed in the pack. For flat, easily traveled terrain, pack the heaviest weight high and close to the shoulders. In rough terrain with steep inclines, the pack weight can be distributed slightly lower toward the middle of the back, which allows for greater balance and mobility. When boulder hopping, river crossing, traveling on scree and talus, or traversing slopes, you want to have the weight of the pack very low. This lowers the body's center of gravity and maximizes balance. With the weight in this position, the trade-off is a loss of comfort.

System

A pack that is organized with an efficient and consistent *system* speeds the process of daily packing and minimizes the chances that items are left behind or lost. A good system also minimizes tension between group members, since they don't have to hear, "Now, where did I put that? I know it's around here somewhere!" Some individual items can be grouped together and packed in separate stuff sacks.

Listed below are samples of grouped items.

- **Toilet kit:** toothbrush, toothpaste, comb, hand lotion, nail clippers, and so forth
- **Clothes bag:** socks, underwear, bandannas, and so forth
- **Food bag:** rations, bear rope, spice kit, eating utensils, cook pots, and so forth
- **Misc. bag:** flashlight, extra batteries, shoelaces, playing cards, whoopee cushion, and so forth
- **Repair kit:** pack parts, nylon cord, wire, small tools, and so forth

◆❖◆❖◆❖◆❖◆❖◆

QUALITY CAMPER TIP: A Neat Pack Is a Happy Pack!

One sign of a competent camper is how neat and organized he or she looks when hiking down the trail. Organization and neatness also allow the camper to maximize his or her enjoyment of the backcountry. When all equipment is placed inside the pack, in pockets, or securely lashed to the pack frame, nothing gets lost. If the camper eliminates protruding items from the pack, nothing catches on branches, wriggles free, or pokes other campers. Extra lengths of pack cord, webbing, and stuff sack drawstrings should be coiled up, tied off, and tucked in so they do not hang loosely from the pack and catch on branches, and so forth.

◆❖◆❖◆❖◆❖◆❖◆

Once a system has been developed that suits the packer's needs, it should be used consistently. Most items in the pack should be packed the same way and in the same place every time. All the same, don't be afraid to make allowance for small adjustments due to itinerary or terrain!

SLEEPING BAGS

The Stumps Go Shopping

The Stump family went shopping for sleeping bags. Papa Forrest Stump, being the meticulous researcher that he is, read all about sleeping bags and was surprised to find out that a sleeping bag is nothing more than a big bag of insulation designed to conserve the body's heat as it cools down during the inactivity of sleep. The more he read, the more it made sense to him. Anything that creates "dead air" space can be an insulator, including steel wool, ground-up newspaper (called cellulose when used in our homes), kapok, fiberglass batting, or Styrofoam.

Although these all make decent insulators, none of them make particularly good sleeping bag insulators because sleeping bags have other requirements. Weight, compressibility, ability to insulate when wet, and ease of laundering are the primary requirements. The type of camping a person plans to do determines the importance of these criteria.

Later that evening, Forrest shared his newfound knowledge with the family and asked each family member what they wanted a sleeping bag for—besides, of course, the upcoming family vacation. Woody said that, given his previous experience and his interest in making the outdoors a career, he wanted a sleeping bag that is light, durable, and will keep him warm during three seasons. "Oh yeah. It should dry out quickly, too. With all the rain we get, that's pretty important. Eventually I hope to get a winter bag once I have the opportunity to try winter camping."

Holly shared her concern about space, "I hate that claustrophobic feeling from tight-fitting mummy-shaped sleeping bags. Besides, I never camp in weather below 40°F. Oh yes!" she cooed bashfully, "I also want a bag that can zip together with yours, honey."

"Absolutely," said Forrest, "But I also want one that I can take with Woody when we go out together in colder weather. I wonder if we can get a matching pair if mine is warmer than yours?"

Moss stated that he didn't care, "as long as it's light and warm. When we go camping I always seem to be cold when everyone else is warm. Dad, you said the bag I have is rated to 20°F. If that's the case, I want one rated to 10°F because we've never camped in 20°F weather, but I always sleep cold."

"Good point," said Forrest, "You always seem to sleep cold—we need to get you a warmer bag."

Finally, Willow said, "I want my bag as light as possible. I don't need it extra warm 'cause I sleep great when camping, and I hate carrying the weight and trying to jam it in my pack. Keep my sleeping bag light and compact!"

 **BOTTOM-LINE TIP: Loft**
The warmth of a sleeping bag is primarily a function of sleeping bag thickness, or loft. The more loft, the warmer the bag. Compare sleeping bags of equal loft for equal warmth.

Let's look at the Stump family's sleeping bag needs. They wanted sleeping bags that were warm, lightweight, durable, roomy, and compact and that dry quickly when wet. Unfortunately, an exceptionally warm, lightweight, long-lasting, roomy, compact sleeping bag that will dry quickly when wet doesn't exist. To get some of those qualities, you have to give up others.

The warmth of a sleeping bag is a function of two things: the thickness of the insulation—or loft—and the amount of excess air space in the bag, or, in other words, the roominess. Just like the walls of your house, the thicker the insulation, the easier it is to heat the inside. With sleeping bags, the more loft they have, the more efficient they are in preserving your body heat. For this reason, the more loft, the warmer the bag. Of course, the trade-off is that more insulation makes for a heavier sleeping bag.

The shape of the sleeping bag determines how much excess air space there is in the bag, apart from that occupied by your body. The less air space your body has to heat up, the easier it is for you to stay warm. That is why a contoured, snug-fitting mummy bag with a hood is more efficient than a rectangular bag with no hood. Generally, the roomier the bag, the less warm it is. In addition, the roomier the bag, the more material is needed to make it, which increases the sleeping bag's overall weight.

BOTTOM-LINE TIP: Sleeping Warm

Your body is the heat source that keeps you warm when you sleep. You use a sleeping bag to try to keep your body heat inside the sleeping bag. As you get cooler, think about cutting down on heat loss (for more on heat loss, see Chapter 2). Add more insulation around and under you or encourage your body to produce more heat by eating or exercising. If you have to go to the bathroom in the middle of the night, definitely do so! Lying in the sleeping bag thinking about relieving yourself keeps you from sleeping. Besides, once you dispose of those body wastes, your body can more easily keep you warm rather than the waste in your bladder.

Fills

If weight and compressibility are requirements for our sleeping bags, then what insulators best meet those demands? The traditional insulating material is down, which is the wispy under-feathers of various types of fowl. Down-filled products such as parkas and sleeping bags "fluff up" to form immense, puffy gear that will turn you into an instant Pillsbury Doughboy, plump and warm as a toasted marshmallow. Down is remarkably light and compressible and retains its loft well after each compression. Amazing! The ideal outdoor insulator. Or so you'd think . . .

Besides its royal price tag, which ranges from 45 to 100% more per sleeping bag than alternative insulators, down has one absolutely damning attribute that eliminates it from many campers' backcountry wardrobes: Down is useless when wet. Once wet, down requires a calendar to measure the amount of time it takes to dry. When exposed to water, the feathers do just what you'd expect them to do: cling together in sodden, small, useless balls. Suddenly, your $300 down sleeping bag becomes a wet, skinny, lumpy nylon sack with no insulating value. What a letdown!

What is the alternative? Through the marvel of modern chemistry and multinational corporations, we have synthetic fibers. In the mid-1960s, the DuPont Corporation started using Dacron 88 for a rectangular car-camping type of sleeping bag. NOLS and WEA founder Paul Petzoldt pioneered the use of Dacron 88 at NOLS in the late '60s. In 1971, Dupont provided NOLS with its new insulation, called Fiberfill II, for an expedition up Denali, North America's highest peak at 20,320 feet.

Jack was fortunate to have been on that trip and attests to the value of this—at that time—new fiber. According to Jack's journal, "Yesterday, all the expedition members ferried supplies up to camp or up to a higher cache at nearly 15,000 feet. No one was left behind in camp, where we left our tents set up without rainflies [waterproof covers] on them. We had been assured by Tap and Ken [leaders] that above 10,000 feet the only precipitation we would get would be snow, which we could easily dust off of the tents when we returned later. A cloud layer came in yesterday afternoon and warmed things up. My rope team was climbing through wet snow at 14,000 feet, but it was raining back in camp.

"We got back to our campsite late yesterday afternoon only to find our tent filled with water. My sleeping bag was totally soaked. I must have wrung over a gallon of water out of it.

My tent partner and I splashed the water out of the tent, lay the wrung-out sleeping bags on our Ensolite pads and crawled in them. Within minutes we were toasty warm. With temperatures dipping down into the low teens we slept comfortably last night. This morning, as I lay here writing in my journal, the bag is completely dry except for some ice crystals covering the outside of the bag. If I had a down bag, I think I might be dead now. I'm sold on synthetic fibers. You'll never see me in a down sleeping bag!"

TECHWEENIE TIP: Types of Synthetic Fibers

Since 1971, the number of different synthetic fibers has increased considerably. Polarguard is unique because it is a continuous filament. The fibers are spun into a mass of fluffy batting, resembling a ball of incredibly fine, tangled fishing line or Albert Einstein's hair. Polarguard Delta is the latest version of Polarguard's synthetic insulation. Constructed of hollow-core continuous filaments, this insulation is lighter, more durable, and more thermally efficient than previous Polarguard products. Improvement is based on a higher-diameter fiber with more hollow space inside to create higher loft with less weight. Some argue that Polarguard is better for sleeping bags because its inherent stiffness isn't as critical as it is in clothing. PrimaLoft Sport, the latest version of PrimaLoft (outperforming PrimaLoft PL1 and PL2), supposedly has a softer feel and drapes more naturally. DuPont's Quallofil is a relatively high-loft, seven-channel polyester insulation with a softer feel than some of the other synthetics. Thinsulate is 3M's low-loft 35% polyester/65% olefin insulation. It claims to provide more warmth with minimal thickness. It is most often found in outerwear, footwear, and gloves. Its main criticism is its stiffness, preventing it from draping as naturally as down-filled products.

The biggest difference between synthetic insulators is the feel or draping characteristics of the sleeping bags made with these insulators. To a lesser extent, they differ in weight, compressibility, and durability.

BOTTOM-LINE TIP: Sleeping Bag Insulation

Although synthetic fills are somewhat heavier and less compressible than down, their abilities to insulate when wet and to dry rapidly provide an unsurpassed margin of safety and comfort. In our opinion, the only insulating material that has a place in most backcountry settings is some form of synthetic polyester. The reality of camping is that YOU WILL GET WET, and so will your gear. Sometime, someplace, probably in the least convenient or safe segment of the trip, you will get rain for 3 days, 6 inches of unexpected snow, your canoe will tip, or your 3-year-old will roll the sleeping bags into the lake.

What do sleeping bags look like through the lenses of our wilderness travel priorities of safety, environmental protection, comfort, and enjoyment?

Safety

A sleeping bag keeps you safe if it is warm enough for the conditions you expect to encounter and if the insulation works under virtually all weather conditions. Since down does not work when wet, our choice for safety is synthetic insulation.

Protecting the Environment

Sleeping bags have little environmental impact in the wilderness. Unfortunately, their eco-cost of manufacture is quite high. Synthetic-fill sleeping bags are made almost totally out of petroleum-derived products. Take care of your sleeping bag, make it last and perhaps we'll save a little oil.

Comfort and Enjoyment

A good, durable well-made sleeping bag will pay many dividends in terms of comfort and enjoyment. It will allow you to sleep soundly and be well rested for the physical demands of living in the outdoors. Fortunately, virtually all sleeping bags from brand name manufacturers found in quality backpacking stores meet those criteria. In fact, poorly designed backpacking sleeping bags are so rarely found in quality backpacking stores that we hesitate to include drawings of sleeping bag construction so typical of backpacking books. Quality sleeping bags all work. However, keep two points about sleeping bag construction and design in mind. Make sure there are no sewn-through seams. If the sleeping bag has stitching that penetrates all the way through, heat readily escapes, forming cold spots. Also, test the sleeping bag by getting inside it to make sure that it fits properly. Sleeping bags come in a variety of lengths, and some companies even make sleeping bags of various widths. Getting a proper fit allows you to carry as little sleeping bag as you need.

If you make wise compromises between sleeping bag weight and warmth you'll have a bag that isn't too heavy to schlep around. An average three-season synthetic-fill sleeping bag rated to 20° F will weigh about three pounds. A tightly fitting mummy bag might weigh a little less, while a roomier bag would weigh a little more.

Finally, care of your sleeping bag will maximize its useful life. Jack has a synthetic-fill North Face sleeping bag that has had steady use since 1974. Admittedly, it was rated for sleeping in 20° F temperatures when it was new and is now relegated to milder summer temperatures. Wash your sleeping bag as needed, but don't overdo it. After a certain point, the wear and tear of washing starts to shorten the bag's life. At home, store the sleeping bag unstuffed. If your living quarters don't allow that, then store it stuffed in a larger bag (like a laundry bag) rather than the stuff sack used for camping. Prolonged periods of compression greatly reduce sleeping bag loft. Keep sleeping bags out of direct sunlight when not in use, and of course, follow the manufacturer's directions for washing. A well maintained sleeping bag will serve you for many years.

TECHWEENIE TIP: Sleeping Bag Design Features

If you're the type who doesn't just grab the first sleeping bag you see in the color you like (and you must be or you wouldn't be reading this), then here are some things to look for in a good sleeping bag. We like a sleeping bag with the biggest zipper possible—preferably a #10 nylon coil. Look for a zipper draft flap (the insulation that prevents cold air from blowing through the zipper) that hangs down from the top of the sleeping bag when the bag is used. (If the zipper draft flap is attached to the ground side of the sleeping bag, gravity will pull it down and away from the zipper it is supposed to insulate.) The draft flap should be designed so the zipper doesn't catch on the shell material. Some people really like a full-length zipper. Unless you are looking for a sleeping bag to mate with another (an important safety and enjoyment consideration), we lean the other way. The shorter the zipper, the less area for heat to escape and cold to seep in. Unfortunately, not many manufacturers see it that way.

Continued

Look for even stitching with reinforced stress points. Sleeping bags should have a box foot or similar type of construction that maximizes insulation around your feet. Some feel that a good sleeping bag should have a differential cut—where the inner shell is cut considerably smaller than the outer shell. This minimizes the compression of insulation against the outer shell—except, of course, under your body.

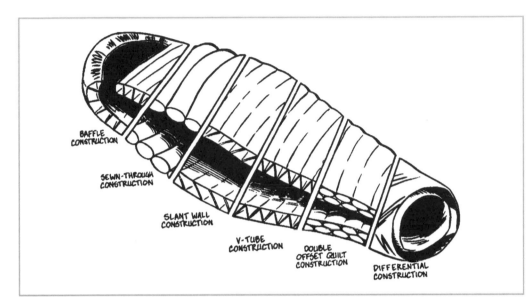

Figure 3.4
Several methods of sleeping bag construction.

SLEEPING PADS

When Jack camped with his family in the '50s, they used air mattresses. Air mattresses were great for comfort but were extremely heavy and not much help in keeping you warm. Fortunately, most of Jack's early family camping was from a motorboat in New York's Adirondacks. When he started backpacking in the late '60s and early '70s, a 1/4-in. closed-cell ensolite pad was considered more than adequate. The idea was not so much to provide comfort on the hard ground but to insulate from the cold ground. Insulation is still the most important purpose of a sleeping pad. The insulation of the sleeping bag is compressed under the user, which reduces its ability to retain heat. A good sleeping pad minimizes that heat loss and throws in comfort to boot.

As we already know, materials that trap dead air make good insulators. Although closed-cell foams do that best, they are fairly dense and not very comfortable. Open-cell foams insulate pretty well but absorb water and generally are too thick to pack easily. A good sleeping pad has to resist compression yet still fit into your pack—a tall order, for these are two contradicting needs. The closed-cell ensolite pad still does a decent job, and you can't beat the price of about $15 for a 3/8-in. thick 21 × 56-in. pad. When it comes to the second priority of providing comfort, however, the ensolite comes up woefully short.

Probably the finest sleeping pad to hit the market is Cascade Designs' Therm-a-Rest. Jack remembers the first time he slept on one in 1980. The owner of the pad proclaimed, "Once you sleep on it, you'll never want to go back to an ensolite pad." He was right. The joke at the time was that you have to be over 30 to appreciate a Therm-a-Rest. Now we tell people you have to be over 40 to appreciate them.

The Therm-a-Rest self-inflating sleeping pad consists of an open-cell pad encased in a coated nylon shell with an air valve in one corner. When the pad is rolled up, the air escapes through the valve. The valve can be closed once all the air is purged, leaving it quite compact. When the valve is opened and the pad is unrolled, the open-cell foam expands and sucks in air, thus making it self-inflating. There is no doubt in our minds that for a combination of comfort and insulation, you can't beat a self-inflating pad. Starting at $40, the price can be a little stiff for those on a limited budget. Any of the less expensive closed-cell pads will do a decent job of insulating you from the cold ground. Once you hit 40, though, you can purchase a Therm-a-Rest and really appreciate its wonders!

◇◇◇◇◇◇◇◇◇◇◇◇

TRICKS OF THE TRADE: Packing Your Sleeping Pad

Sleeping pads do not have to be rolled up. In fact, Therm-a-Rest pads can be folded. Jack has folded his Therm-a-Rest for nearly 15 years with no negative effect to the pad. We like to fold them because it allows us to put the sleeping pad inside the pack rather than on the outside where it can get punctured (even in a protective stuff sack). With an internal frame pack, the pad also provides a cushion against the wearer's back.

◇◇◇◇◇◇◇◇◇◇◇◇

SHELTER

Depending upon your location and season, your shelter must protect you from one or more of the following: precipitation, insects, wind, sun, and cold. Naturally, these criteria fit into our overall wilderness priorities.

Safety

A safe shelter is one that protects you adequately from precipitation and wind. With the exception of snow shelters (which are beyond the scope of this book), shelters should not be thought of as offering protection from the cold. Although in periods of extreme cold a tent with three or four people in it can be 10 to 20°F warmer inside than out, the temperature differential is not enough to protect you from the cold. In tropical environments, a tent can play an important role in protecting you from the sun. In general, however, we think a tent's primary safety role is to protect us from precipitation and wind.

Protecting the Environment

A good shelter protects the environment based upon the size of its "footprint" and how much manipulation of the environment is required to set it up.

For example, tarps or rainflies leave a small footprint, or area of disturbance, because they have no floor and so spare vegetation from most trampling. We have spent many nights with witch hobble or spruce saplings sprouting between our sleeping bags. If you have to move logs, remove branches, or flatten vegetation, however, then the tent has a larger footprint. Our rule of thumb: if you have to move rocks, logs, cut branches, dig trenches, or cause any major manipulation of the environment, you should look for another tent site.

Comfort and Enjoyment

In most areas, protection from insects is a comfort issue, although in regions where insects carry disease, bites can be a safety issue. If you've ever spent a sleepless night swatting mosquitoes or no-see-ums, you know what we mean. At least black flies go home when it gets dark! Although good campsite selection (choose a high, dry, windy site) can minimize insect encounters, a good insect-proof tent is essential in most parts of the world.

The Stumps Select a Tent

Given the criteria we look for in a shelter, let's see how the Stumps went about selecting tents and tarps for their family. One night, the Stumps employed the ritual of the family dinner to plan the next summer's big trip. They had bought their clothing, backpacks, and sleeping bags, but still needed to decide on types of shelters that would allow for flexibility and performance. Holly orchestrated a discussion and asked everyone to describe what they thought was most important in a tent or tarp for the family.

"Okay, everybody," said Holly. "What kind of tent do you want to sleep in for the big trip next summer?"

Woody said, "First off, we should get two shelters, not one. One shelter for all five of us might work for car camping but would be too heavy for backpacking. And anyway," he added, "We're close, but not that close. Who wants that much family togetherness?"

"Good point," added Forrest, his back aching just thinking about the prospect of carrying a shelter large enough for five people. "But we could split up the weight of a big tent to lighten the load."

"Anyway," said Holly, "two smaller tents are more versatile than one big one."

"All I know," whined Moss, "is that it better keep me dry. It always seems to rain when we go camping."

"I don't really care," chimed Willow, "'cause I don't really want to go camping with you guys anyway. If I *have* to go, I want to make sure the tent's bug-proof. I got eaten alive the last time we went camping."

Holly and Forrest looked at each other and thought to themselves, "Ah, the joys of raising adolescent children!" Holly reinforced Moss's point by saying, "Since it does seem to rain so much, I think we should have a tent with lots of room. That way, if we have to spend the day in the tent, at least we'll have room to stretch and maybe play some cards."

Forrest seemed to boil it all down. "It seems to me I've heard us talk about weight, keeping dry, and having enough room. I'd like to add that the shelters we choose should be durable. If we're going to spend a chunk of money on a good tent, let's be sure it's going to last. Are there any things we've missed?"

"Just one, Forrest," Holly stated emphatically. "It shouldn't take a rocket scientist to set the tents up."

Rainflies

Given the considerations the Stump family has listed: weight, protection from precipitation, protection from insects, roominess, durability, and a simple setup, what can they expect to find? First, a simple tarp or rainfly is worthy of close examination. A rectangular 10 × 10-foot rainfly is lightweight, compact, readily sheds rain, protects occupants from the wind if pitched properly, is roomy for two or three people, has a low-impact footprint, and has an economical price. However, rainflies (also called tarpaulins or "tarps") do not keep out insects, an issue all the more important with the increased concern regarding West Nile Virus; are tricky to set up; and have limited value in highly impacted campsites where the rain cannot be readily absorbed into the compacted soil.

TRICKS OF THE TRADE: Bring a Rainfly and Leave the Tent at Home!

If insects are not a major concern, camping is done in primitive campsites, and one is willing to learn the art of rainfly pitching, then consider taking a rainfly.

The key to working with a rainfly is knowing how to pitch it. A location with soils that absorb rain quickly is essential. If the weather forecast calls for fair weather with little or no

Figure 3.5
Pitch a rainfly for a lightweight and functional shelter.

wind and you like to take risks, pitch the fly high (4 1/2 to 6 feet off the ground). It will provide you with luxurious space and in a light rain will give you adequate protection. Be prepared, however, to lower the rainfly on the windward side to protect you from both the wind and rain. To take advantage of your campsite's characteristics and protect you from the elements, rainflies can be set up in a multitude of shapes. In stormy weather, we've sometimes set up our rainfly with barely enough headroom to sit up in. We kept dry, however, and were glad we had such an effective shelter that weighed only 2 pounds.

PHILOSOPHY TIP: Really Getting Back to Nature

Tom Brown, outdoor tracker, survival expert and author, talks about how modern people keep trying to put something between themselves and nature. Unlike the Native American, "the white man builds a shelter, and it becomes his prison. He shuts out the cleansing elements. He shuts out the sun, the wind, and the rain. He separates himself from the earth and refuses to budge."[3] Using a rainfly is a different type of camping that brings one a little closer to the earth. Don't be afraid to sit on the ground and lie in your sleeping bag with the openness of a rainfly around you. We recommend using a shelter with no floor to bring campers closer to nature.

Tents

If the idea of a rainfly doesn't float your boat—or perhaps "pup your tent" would be more appropriate—there are plenty of different tents to meet your needs. Since the early '70s, the evolution of tents has been nothing short of remarkable. Probably the single most important technological development in tent designs was the advent of flexible, strong, lightweight, small-diameter aluminum tent poles. Before this development, you could choose a tent that had either rigid aluminum or flexible fiberglass poles. The rigid aluminum poles limited tent designs, and the flexible fiberglass poles allowed for more creative tent designs but lacked the strength to hold up in high winds and heavy snows.

Tent Design Fundamentals

Most tents today are designed with a bathtub floor, breathable walls, and a waterproof rainfly. What does this mean? Quality tents use waterproof nylon for the floor and the bottom 6 to 16 in. of the tent walls. Manufacturers call this design the bathtub floor. The idea is to keep ground water and water that runs off the rainfly out of the tent. If any water gets trapped inside the tent, however, you'll really understand the "bathtub design." Don't forget your rubber ducky.

The reason that inner tent walls are breathable—which means air and moisture can pass through them—is because our breath gives off anywhere from a cup to a pint of moisture each night as we sleep. Multiply that times the number of people you have in a tent and you have a lot of hot, steamy air floating around. A tent with breathable walls allows most of that moisture to evaporate harmlessly through the walls of the tent. Outside the breathable inner wall, the waterproof rainfly generally sits 2 or 3 in. from the rest of the tent. This air space between the rainfly and the tent allows the humid air from inside to move away, while the rainfly is still able to protect the tent from rain, sleet, hail, snow, and squirt gun ambushes.

Figure 3.6
Forrest's "A-Frame" style tent from the seventies still does the trick. Note the waterproof rainfly.

TRICKS OF THE TRADE: Ventilation

Keep in mind that when it rains, the humidity inside a tent is very high, and the temperature on the outside of the tent is relatively cool. Moisture will condense on non-breathable surfaces very readily. We have had many students complain about a leaky tent, when in reality it was just a tremendous amount of moisture condensing on the interior walls of the tent. In rainy situations, even the relatively breathable fabric of the inner tent walls can't keep up with the humidity of the inside air without the help of an open tent door and window, which allow humid air to leave the tent. One way to minimize condensation is to ventilate the tent as much as possible. We suggest leaving the tent's vents, windows, and doors open as much as possible. If bugs are not a problem, open the netting as well. Anything that increases air circulation will decrease condensation.

Selecting the Tent

As we have seen, the primary factors in selecting a backpacking tent are roominess, weight, ease of set up, and cost. A roomier tent will probably be a heavier tent. A review of a recent outdoor catalog found two-person tents ranging in weight from 3 pounds to over 7 pounds. Floor area ranged from a little over 27 square feet to 45 square feet while prices ranged from $99 to $375. By and large, tents are like sleeping bags. If you buy a reputable brand from a reputable backpacking store or mail-order specialty store, you won't get burned. You will probably run into trouble if you try to buy a cheap tent from a discount department store or other store that doesn't specialize in outdoor gear. Finally, ease of setup is probably a function of learning style. Some people find some tents easier to set up than others, so it comes down to personal preference.

Also make sure there is adequate ventilation; the zippers are usable, snag-resistant, and big; the zippers are paired (two-way); there are inside pockets for organization (if desired); the tent has enough access for you (one or two entrances?); and the floor, wall, and rainfly fabric is durable and light enough for your purposes. Check that the windows and doors have no-see-um-bug proof netting. Most of today's tents do, but don't confuse no-see-um netting with mosquito netting. Mosquito netting keeps out mosquitoes and larger insects while no-see-um netting keeps out virtually all insects. The trade off is that no-see-um netting is so fine that it cuts down on air circulation.

TECHWEENIE TIP: Three-season or Four-season?

Some "higher end" manufacturers sell tents rated for four seasons. What's the difference between three- and four-season tents besides an extra $50–$200? Generally, a four-season tent is designed for winter camping and technical mountaineering, where wet, heavy snow (or simply tons of it) can fall on the tent overnight. You don't want your tent to play pancake in the middle of the night when it's -20° F. Four-season tents have extremely strong aircraft aluminum poles; thicker and tougher fabrics for the tent, rainfly and floor; and special rainflies that reach all the way to the ground to provide additional protection against snow and rain. They may also have more aerodynamic designs with extra lashing points for guy lines and vestibules (extra rooms outside the inner chamber but inside the rainfly) for cooking and gear storage in extreme conditions. Generally speaking, don't invest in a four-season tent unless

(left margin, vertical text) The Camper's Guide to Outdoor Pursuits

you're *sure* you'll use it in the winter. We advise campers to stick to three-season camping until they've mastered most of the basic outdoor living, navigation, and emergency skills.

Try a Tent on for Size

To find a tent that's right for you, we suggest you go to the store, pitch the tent, and get in it. Next, take a nap if the salesperson lets you. If you want a true test, after you have pitched it once, try pitching it again with your eyes closed. That will give you an idea of what it would be like trying to pitch the tent in the pouring rain or the dark of night. (Of course, the low-impact camper tries to avoid these situations as much as possible.) Keep in mind that only time will really tell if you got the right tent.

Tent Care

Taking care of your tent is not much different than taking care of other equipment—it's largely a function of good judgment. Pitch your tent correctly without branches sticking into it and avoid walking in it with your boots on, which will not only get the tent dirty but put extra wear on the fabric. Please, never ever walk in your tent with your ice crampons on! When you get home, machine-wash the tent if it's gotten particularly dirty. Otherwise, just hose it off or let it dry and wipe out the dirt. Most importantly, *let the tent dry thoroughly before storing it*. A damp tent will mildew, and although it doesn't really hurt the tent, not many people want to sleep in a tent that smells like a dank attic.

The Great Ground-Cloth Controversy

Although some say you should always use a ground cloth, we never do, even with tents that have served us for 20 years. A tent that costs top dollar should be sturdy enough to hold up to fair but rugged use. We carefully select good tentsites that are free of sharp objects, which not only affords a good night's sleep but also protects the tent floor. Further, if even a tiny corner of the ground cloth is left poking out from the tent floor, the ground cloth traps water between itself and the tent floor, preventing any water that does collect under the tent from draining into the soil. When this occurs, water inevitably seeps upward into the sleeping area. In this way, ground cloths cause the very problem that they are supposed to prevent: wetness inside the tent! In our opinion, if you want to save weight, leave the ground cloth at home.

Tentsite Selection and Pitching the Tent

Campsite selection is covered in Chapter 5, but some basic considerations for selecting your specific tentsite are appropriate here. Look for a well-drained site. Although we have never been flooded out of a campsite, we have had students who had to move in the middle of a rainy night. Find a relatively flat site. To ensure flatness, lie down on the prospective site and check it out. The low-impact camper resists the temptation to roll away rocks, pull out saplings, or take other measures to make the "perfect" tentsite. Be sure there are no obvious dead tree-tops or branches above your tent. Although we always check for these "widow makers," they are the things that worry us most when camping. We have seen relatively healthy trees come down in the middle of windy nights and just miss sleeping campers. You can't be too careful.

SAFETY TIP: Watch Out for Hanging Deadfall

Before you pitch your tent, look up. If you see a dead, leafless tree above, creaking in the wind, choose another site well out of range. Trees fall in the forest all the time, and you don't want to be the one who hears them up close.

We prefer to orient the tent with the door facing opposite the prevailing wind unless it's peak bug season, and then we'll face the door into the wind. The wind helps to keep bugs from loitering near the tent door. Sometimes we like to orient the door so it faces the morning sun for warmth and aesthetics. We always make sure to keep the tent well upwind and away from any places we might have a campfire. It's no fun to repair holes created by tiny embers.

Figure 3.6

Pitching the tent is a function of following the directions. There are, however, a couple of things we recommend. Learn a few knots. We find the slippery taut-line hitch in particular very useful for tying down tent guy lines. Bring the number of tent stakes you will need and don't count on carving them from the nearest branch. Placing them as shown in Figure 3.6 will minimize the chances of them pulling loose in high winds. More than once, we have returned from a day hike to see a tent blown downwind from camp.

QUALITY CAMPER TIP: A Well Pitched Tent Can Take You Far

Think of the tent, like your pack, as an extension of your personality and a reflection of who you are. Just as a neatly packed pack reflects a responsible hiker, so does a well-pitched tent. Be proud of your work, and let it show! A loose, unevenly taut tent not only looks sloppy but may become damaged from flapping in the wind.

The Envelope, Please: The Stump Family Shelters

After all their discussion, what kind of tents did the Stumps purchase, anyway? They ended up with one three-person tent for the kids, a two-person tent for mom and dad, and a rainfly. On longer trips, they bring the rainfly to cover the cooking area, and on shorter trips during the bug-free time of year, Forrest and Holly trade in their tent for the rainfly. Pretty smart!

SINGLE-BURNER COOKSTOVES

Because single-burner cookstoves are extremely handy when cooking quick meals after a hard day on the trail, we wouldn't think of traveling without one. In this section, we'll take a look at considerations in purchasing a stove. For a more in-depth discussion of stove operation and the pros and cons of campfires, refer to Chapter 5. Looking at our wilderness priorities, the advantages and disadvantages of stoves become quite clear.

Safety

Stoves provide us with a safe, reliable source of heat for cooking food and heating beverages. During inclement weather, a stove can provide a hot meal and so ward off hypothermia. On the other hand, after driving to the trailhead in automobiles, using stoves is the most statistically dangerous aspect of our outdoor recreational pursuits. Without proper care and operation, stoves can flare up, explode, spill boiling contents, and burn careless users. Stoves require constant attention and should be carefully used and maintained in order to minimize the chance of injury.

Protecting the Environment

Using a stove will help minimize the number of campfire scars, chopped-down trees, denuded forest floors, and forest fires. As advocates of low-impact camping, we see stoves as an important means of minimizing the negative effects of campfires. This isn't to say that campfires shouldn't be used, but that they just need to be used judiciously. When in doubt, however, we advocate the use of a stove over the use of a campfire.

In terms of the big picture, we must also look at whether the eco-cost of stoves and the fossil fuels they burn has a higher toll on our earth's resources than the use of campfires. Some people will say that downed firewood is a much more renewable resource than white gas or kerosene. Some aspects of this question depend on regional environmental conditions. Is there plenty of downed wood in a particular forest? In semi-arid regions, will it take 10 or more years to replenish downed wood supplies? In many of the heavily used forests of the west, fire danger and firewood depletion are causing park and forest agencies to require stoves in most instances. Finally, as the concept of commercial sustainability becomes more prevalent, the effect of equipment manufacture (stoves) needs to be computed into the impact equation.

Comfort and Enjoyment

For many, the idea of a crackling campfire is what outdoor travel is all about. For others, the idea of a smoky, sooty fire that always seems to get the food too hot or not hot enough does nothing for their idea of a relaxing leisure experience. To us, campfires have a special place in outdoor travel lore. We love them but realize that they take real skill to master and have a potential negative impact that has to be balanced against the benefits.

Stoves and their fuel entail extra weight, but their reliability and ease of use usually make them worth the effort.

Stove Design

Discussing stove design with a group of experienced campers is a bit like discussing automobiles with a bunch of car buffs. Everyone has his or her favorite make and model and thinks the other types don't compare. Stoves can be distinguished by the type of fuel they use. White gas (Coleman fuel), kerosene, unleaded gasoline, alcohol, solid/jellied fuels, butane, propane, and isobutane are the most common types of fuels you will find.

Liquid fuels (with the exception of alcohol) have to be vaporized and require a generator system to heat and vaporize the fuel. They often have a pump system to pressurize the fuel tank. The ability to regulate the amount of heat emanating from liquid-fuel stoves ranges from very good to poor. The ability to cook over low heat for long periods is an important feature for those of us who like to bake on top of a stove. Liquid-fuel stoves are generally the most complicated and require the most maintenance, although the level of complication and maintenance varies from one brand and model to another.

Alcohol stoves use a simple dish for burning the alcohol, which makes this option very simple and inexpensive. The temperature is regulated by sliding a cover over the top of the dish, allowing more or less alcohol to burn. The more the top is covered, the lower the heat. Solid fuel stoves (e.g., Sterno) work on the same principle.

Stoves that burn butane, propane, and isobutane are very simple, as the fuel is already in a gaseous state. The temperature is easy to regulate and simple to operate. These stoves are as simple to operate as a gas range at home.

Common Stove Fuels

White Gas

White gas is probably the most common fuel in the United States for backpacking stoves. It is very flammable, produces a large amount of heat and is relatively easy to use. Examples of white gas stoves include the Coleman Peak 1 Feather 400 and the Peak 1 APEX II, the MSR Whisperlite Shaker, MSR Dragonfly, and the Svea 123R. Because of this fuel's extreme flammability, use great caution when operating white gas stoves or filling fuel canisters.

Kerosene

Kerosene is not as flammable as white gas, so is safer to transport and store. It is probably the most common fuel found around the world. Because of its lower volatility it needs to be primed with another fuel (usually white gas, alcohol, or lighter fluid). Once ignited it is a very efficient fuel. The fuel has an oily texture that does not evaporate as readily as white gas. Multi-fuel stoves like the Coleman Exponent multi-fuel stove, the Peak 1 APEX multi-fuel stove, and the MSR Whisperlite Internationale burn kerosene as well as other fuels such as white gas, leaded, and unleaded gas.

Unleaded Gasoline

Unleaded gasoline is relatively inexpensive and widely available. Most multi-fuel stoves burn unleaded gasoline. In addition, the Coleman Exponent Feather 442 Dual-Fuel stove burns unleaded and white gas.

Alcohol and Solid Fuels

In our opinion, due to their relatively low heat output, these fuels are limited to emergency uses only. Jack recalls the time when a student brought a new alcohol stove on a winter overnight trip. The salesperson had convinced the student how great the fuel was, but when the student tried to heat water for a simple instant dinner, it took over an hour for the water to boil! That experience helped him decide that alcohol stoves have limited use.

Butane/Propane and Isobutane

The combination of 80% butane and 20% propane provides a fuel that works reasonably well in cold weather, although not as well as white gas. Butane/propane comes in cartridges and is convenient and easy to use. We don't like the non-recyclability of the cartridges. A variation of this fuel is isobutane, which is reputed to work well in extreme temperatures and at high elevations, although the reports of its effectiveness vary from very good to poor. Coleman, MSR, Snow Peak, and GAZ manufacture a variety of butane, propane, butane/propane, and isobutane stoves.

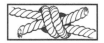 **BOTTOM-LINE TIP: Stove Selection**

The majority of our experience over the years has been with white gas stoves made by Coleman, MSR, and Optimus. All these stove manufacturers produce excellent products. Owning a stove is a little like having a pet animal, however. Each stove has its own personality and idiosyncrasies that must be understood before you can master its use. Jack leans toward the Coleman Peak 1 Feather 400 and the MSR Dragonfly because he desires a stove with a more adjustable flame. He actually prefers some of the older Coleman Peak 1 models because their flames were even more adjustable than today's versions. Eric leans toward the MSR Whisperlite for its effective operation and light weight. We have both become experts at maintaining these stoves, which is not difficult once you understand how they work and have the extra parts.

MISCELLANEOUS EQUIPMENT

The Muskrat Pack Packs Their Bags

You probably remember us introducing the Muskrat Pack in Chapter 1. They are the group of paddling buddies who have been canoeing together since their years at Wynotgota College and have kept in touch through their informal paddling club. You should remember the Muskrat Pack because we put *you* in it! The club is quite small; only Juan, Anne, Stella, and you remain from the glory days of yesteryear.

Figure 3.7
The Muskrat Pack's Anne, Juan, and Stella pack up.
You are left holding the trowel!

At this point, the Muskrat Pack is trying to decide which knickknacks, doodads and other miscellaneous equipment they are going to bring on the big trip to Drifting Paddle National Canoe Area. Everyone has their own opinion based on their personal camping experience. You, based on your personal camping experience (none), are completely lost. Who do you listen to?

Anne, the best paddler, has guided raft trips on the New River for three seasons and is a certified whitewater canoe instructor. Juan had a lot of experience hiking in New England and Colorado just after graduation but has been too involved with his big job at Heinz for the last several years to get out much. He's a bit rusty. Stella, your college study partner, takes her school kids out on overnights several times a year. She is also bursting with knowledge from the outdoor leadership expedition she took last summer.

You are struggling to decide what to bring and what to leave behind. Anne is organizing all the canoe gear, so you don't have to worry about that. Juan is taking care of the food, while you and Stella are responsible for group equipment. Of course, you also have to worry about your personal gear. Stella has helped you select the big-ticket items, and now you're down to the nitty-gritty. Stella tells of her instructor's suggestion that you create three piles of equipment. One pile is the essentials, those things you can't possibly do without. The second pile has those things you'd really like to bring but aren't necessary, and the third is of extravagant luxuries. The instructor suggested that campers take the entire essential pile and one item from the luxury pile, ignore the middle pile, and start hiking. Although we may suggest you bring a few additional items, you probably get the idea.

We encourage you to use our three priorities in selecting additional equipment. Look first for items that ensure safety and protection of the environment. If there is additional room or if you can carry the weight, then consider additional items for comfort and enjoyment.

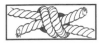

BOTTOM-LINE TIP: Weight
We use the phrase, "That don't weigh nuthin," to emphasize the point that everything weighs something. Four 4-oz items weigh a pound. Don't delude yourself into thinking that something "don't weigh nuthin." Make decisions based on the ability of the item to meet one or more of your camping priorities, rather than the fact that you don't think it weighs anything. Until we camp in a gravity-free environment, everything weighs something, and it adds up quickly!

In the following section we list alphabetically items you and Stella might consider bringing, depending on the objectives of your outdoor venture.

Altimeter

If you do much off-trail hiking, altimeters, which measure height above sea level, can be real assets. Jack and Eric have used a variety of different watches with built-in altimeters and have been very happy with them. With the advent of less expensive GPS receivers, you may want to consider using one of these units for providing elevation information. They even make a watch with an integrated GPS receiver unit. See Chapter 6 for more information on these instruments. However, if all your journeying is on the trail or in canoes, don't waste your money on an altimeter.

Axes and Saws

You might bring a saw, but leave the axe at home! If you need an axe to cut your wood, you are either cutting down trees—which is illegal on virtually all public lands—or burning wood too big for the fire. The largest wood you put on the fire should be about the size of your wrist, and you generally shouldn't need an axe or saw to break it. See Chapter 5 for more information on fires and firewood.

We used to carry a saw for building an emergency litter for carrying out an injured hiker, but the few times we have had to build a litter, we were able to construct one without a saw. Lightweight folding saws are handy if you must have a saw, but we recommend you leave both your saw and axe at home.

This is great—so far, we've listed three things you probably don't need!

Books

For us, a venture in the woods can also be an opportunity for some quality reading time. Bring a book or two, but keep them small and lightweight, and store them in waterproof bags. Be conservative, because it's better to run out of reading material than lug a bunch of books that you never open. Remember, wet books weigh about three times what dry books weigh. Keep them dry.

Camera

A lightweight camera is a great way to preserve precious memories. Depending on the trip, we either bring the whole Nikon system, a compact auto-everything, a recyclable point-and-shoot, or nothing. The decision is determined by what our trip goals are, the uniqueness of the country and people we're traveling with, and how heavy our pack is. Like your book, keep it in a waterproof container.

Candles, Candle Lantern

A couple of candles can be very handy to provide a low level of constant light. During the summer months, however, we find we rarely use them. During the rest of the year when days are shorter, a candle is almost indispensable. A candle lantern is by no means a necessity but does give you more flexibility in terms of protecting the candle flame from the wind and putting the light where you need it most.

Cell Phone or Two-way Radios

Should you or shouldn't you? While we think electronic communication certainly has its place and that each wilderness user must make up his or her own mind, in general we do not support electronic communication devices in wilderness areas, particularly phones.

Our concerns:

- They are not dependable. When you need them most they will probably not work. Most wilderness terrain does not lend itself to cell phone communication
- They create a sense of dependency. Traveling in the wilderness by its very nature requires skills, knowledge, and self-sufficiency. Cell phones negate that. There are verified stories of hikers getting to a trail intersection and calling the rescue dispatcher and asking which way they should go.
- They are counter to what wilderness is about. Wilderness is about getting away from civilization and being "on your own."

On the other hand:

- When traveling alone (something we don't recommend) they may be worthwhile "extra insurance." Jack sometimes hunts alone in the fall and will carry one, although he does not hunt in a wilderness area.

We put two-way radios in the same category. They can be very handy, but they should not replace sound judgment and are not an excuse for groups to split up—something we really discourage. Whatever you do, don't ever become dependent on electronic communication devices.

Chair

Ten years ago you would have never seen us include this item on the list. Although it definitely falls in the luxury category, if you spend a lot of time sitting down or canoeing where weight is not a factor, then you can't beat the comfort of folding fabric camping chairs. Crazy Creek and Therm-a-Rest as well as other manufacturers make back-saving chairs that may be worth bringing. We are not fans of the inexpensive collapsible metal-framed chairs that you can readily find in big-box stores. Our experience is that they break all too readily and then become garbage that you have to haul out.

Compass

Buy a quality compass immediately, learn how to use it, and don't ever venture into the woods without it. A compass can be a real lifesaver, but only if you know how to use it. We recommend the orienteering style of compass. There are three major manufacturers of orienteering compasses: Brunton, Silva, and Suunto. They all make reliable products, but the Silva Polaris Type 7 compass costs about $10 and is our favorite for teaching and learning beginning and intermediate navigation skills. See Chapter 6 for more information on compasses.

Cooking Gear and Eating Utensils

See Chapter 4 for a complete discussion of cooking gear.

First Aid Kit

We each have at least two first aid kits that we customize for the different types of trips we go on. A first aid kit and knowledge of how to use it are essential. Chapter 7 has additional information on first aid kits.

Food Bag

A medium size (approximately 9 × 20-in.) medium weight (8-oz pack cloth) zippered nylon duffel makes an excellent food bag (Figure 3.8). It provides easy access via the zipper compared to digging through the opening of a conventional stuff sack. Keep in mind, however, that most duffels are not completely rainproof, so an effort should be made to make sure the contents are.

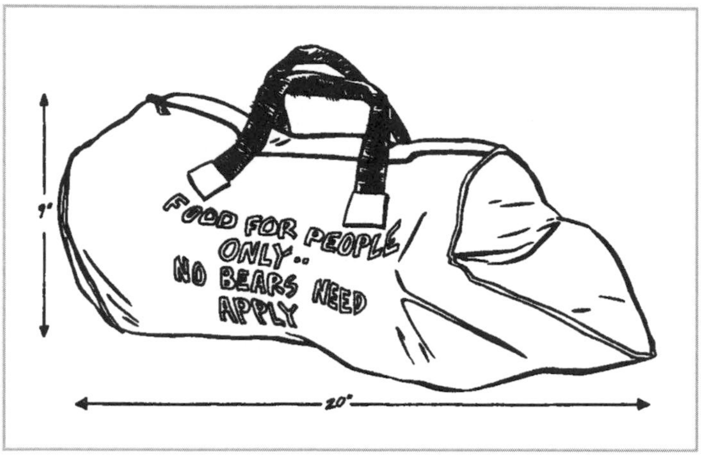

Figure 3.8
Food bag.

Flashlight

There has been nothing short of a revolution in flashlights in the last few years. LED flashlights have taken over the camping flashlight market because of their many advantages (see techweenie tip below). About the only disadvantage of LED flashlights is their lack of a focused long-distance beam. This is generally not an issue for camping flashlights that are used for providing light for general camping tasks.

Jack has two flashlights he takes on camping trips. He has a Petzl Tikka three-LED plastic headlamp that he uses most of the time. It is extremely light (2.5 oz), reasonably durable, and shines a very good general-purpose beam of light. It uses three AAA batteries that are rated to 150 hours of use. As a backup he has an all-metal CMG Infinity single-LED light, which is virtually indestructible and waterproof, weighs two ounces, and uses one AA battery that provides 100 hours of use.

Keep in mind that warm batteries work better than cold ones. This is particularly noticeable with all-metal flashlights like the CMG Infinity, which tend to conduct heat rapidly. If possible, keep the flashlight next to your skin during colder weather and you will notice your batteries last longer. Don't forget extra batteries for those times that they do finally give out.

What are LEDs and how do they work?

LEDs (Light Emitting Diodes) are tiny colored lights typically found in electronic equipment, household appliances, toys, and more recently in flashlights. Red, yellow, and green LEDs have been around the longest and thus are the most common. Colors such as turquoise, blue, pure green, and white are much newer and so are not as common, with the exception of white LEDs, which are now found in flashlights. Traditional light bulbs generate light by heating a filament. Over relatively short periods of time these filaments either break or burn out. LEDs are different because they have no filament, generate very little heat, and require less energy. Thus they are ideal for putting lights into battery-operated equipment like telephones, toys, portable computers, and of course flashlights.

An LED is just a fancy diode. What's a diode, you ask? The name diode comes from the Greek for two. Diodes have two electronic elements that only let electric current flow in one direction. LEDs are diodes that have the ability to produce light when electricity flows through them.

TECHWEENIE TIP: Shedding Some Light on LED Flashlights

LED Flashlights are as common as fireworks on the fourth of July, but why are they so popular and how do they work?

Quality LED flashlights have three distinct advantages over conventional flashlights:

1. The bulbs can last up to 100,000 hours. That's over 11 years of continuous use. Suffice to say that you can leave your LED flashlight as a family heirloom to your loved ones, and it will still not need a bulb replacement.
2. You will replace batteries less often. LED bulbs require much less electricity to light, saving you the need to replace batteries as often. Different flashlights vary in terms of energy needs; but even the relatively power-hungry ones will require battery replacement less frequently than conventional flashlights. In any event, battery life is frequently measured in days, not hours.
3. When the batteries do start to run down, the LED doesn't go out as a conventional flashlight does; it just gradually gets dimmer. In many cases the amount of light provided may still be useful for an extended period of time.

Games

Entire books have been written about games for the outdoors. Many games don't require equipment, but some do. We consider one or two portable games as luxury items that we like to bring along. The length and purpose of our trip determines what sort and how many games to bring. We've brought playing cards, backpacking-sized board games, hacky sacks, a small ball, and flippy flyers (a cloth version of a Frisbee). Don't overdo it, but don't be afraid to bring along something.

GPS Receiver

Global Positioning System (GPS) receivers have become less expensive and more common. In addition, the number of features available has increased tremendously. We consider a GPS receiver an extremely convenient but nonetheless optional item. Jack believes, however, that it is just a matter of time (perhaps 20 years or more) until GPS receivers become dependable enough to replace the current compass and paper map. Beam me up, Scotty.

For more specific information on GPS receivers see Chapter 6 *Wilderness Travel: Finding Your Way*.

Hydration Systems

Pack hydration systems allow you to carry a small bladder of water accessible by a drinking tube, which provides you with a hands-free means to walk along the trail and not have to pause to take a drink. While we think they have many practical applications (soldiers, police officers, and joggers all find them useful), in general for backpacking we think they are overrated and complicate what is supposed to be a relatively simple camping experience. If we don't have time to stop and take a drink, much less take in the view and smell the roses, then what is life coming to? Nonetheless, since they do have their place, we want to clue you in on these ingenious devices.

A recent survey of a popular online camping store showed no less than 139 items related to backpack hydration systems. Complete systems range in price from 17 dollars to over $100. Is a hydration system right for you?

Advantages
- Allows you to carry more water than two water bottles can handle in relative comfort.
- Allows you to have hands-free continuous access to water.

Disadvantages
- Extra cost.
- Relatively high maintenance to keep them clean.
- In some parts of the country you may be inclined to carry more water than you need to. Keep in mind that a pint of water weighs 1 pound.
- Before you decide, borrow one from a friend and give it a try.

Knife

Knives are another one of those very personal items that can trigger arguments regarding the best, sharpest, most durable, and functional type of knife. We prefer small, multipurpose knives with locking blades. In our opinion, the locking blade is the most important component. A locking blade saves your knuckles and palms from being sliced by unpredictable closing blades. Multipurpose tools such as the well known Leatherman described below are another form of knife that we find extremely useful.

Jack has a number of knives. His favorite is a Wenger Swiss Army knife with a locking large (2-in.) blade, small blade, can and bottle opener, slotted screwdriver, awl, the essential corkscrew, and the rarely used toothpick and tweezers. In order of frequency, the tasks we use our knives for are cutting pepperoni, cheese, and cord; cleaning fish; gutting deer; and, of course, opening bottles of wine. A 2-in. blade is plenty big to do all those jobs well.

Eric has a slightly larger Victorinox Swiss Army knife with a locking 3-in. blade, can and bottle openers, small and large screwdrivers, awl, saw, toothpick, tweezers, and the ever-essential corkscrew.

Don't spend a fortune on your knife. As outdoor writer Patrick McManus says, people do four things with their first knife soon after they get it. They whittle a stick, cut themselves, sharpen the blade, and, finally, lose the knife. That has happened to both of us more than we care to admit!

 **BOTTOM-LINE TIP: Knives**

Look for a relatively small locking blade (2–3-in.) knife with no more attachments than you think you will really use. A knife is an essential but sometimes overrated item. Learn to sharpen it on a whetstone or buy a simple sharpening system.

Lash Straps and Cord

A pair of straps to lash on a sleeping bag or other occasional item that won't fit into the pack is extremely handy. Straps also are useful on the rare occasion that you have to build a litter out of native material to carry out an injured camper. We prefer the old-fashioned metal ladderlock buckle for superior strength and durability. Unfortunately, this type of strap is nearly impossible to find any more. Instead, you can find good quality, although heavy, spring-loaded metal cam buckles. Most common, however, are plastic Fastex buckles, which we find have a higher failure rate. Get straps at least 4 feet long, as they are handier and more versatile than shorter straps.

Don't forget 20 feet of multipurpose 1/8-in. cord for all sorts of camp needs. If you're in bear country, you'll need about 40 feet of 1/4-in. rope. See Chapter 4 for more information about protecting your food.

Licenses and Permits

Be sure to have fishing, hunting, driving, or other licenses you may need. More and more, areas require permits as well. Be sure to contact the management agencies in the area you are traveling well in advance to find out what you will need.

Maps

Like your American Express card, don't leave home without it. The number of times we have come across people who have no idea where they are in a wilderness area is astounding. Remember, outdoor travel is about being independent and responsible for the well-being of you and your group. You are negligent if you don't have a map of the area you are traveling in and know how to use it. See Chapter 6 for a thorough discussion on where to get maps and how to use them.

Matches and Lighter

Another essential item is a means to light a fire, stove, or candle. We always carry a waterproof film container of matches along with a lightweight disposable lighter. Although lighters are very handy, they aren't as reliable as matches and have to be kept warm in cold weather in order to function properly.

In addition to matches and a lighter, we like to bring some kind of homemade or commercial fire starter. When a fire is essential and the weather and fuel aren't cooperating, fire starters provide an excellent means of providing a reliable heat source to get the tinder started. See Chapter 5 for more information on starting fires and the preparation and use of homemade fire starters.

Multi-Tool

In 1983 when Tim Leatherman and Steve Berliner founded the Leatherman Tool Group, Inc., and started producing the original Leatherman tool, a new industry was created. Today there are more than 10 different Leatherman tool models and dozens of Leatherman "multi-tool" copycats on the market. They are heavier than the traditional Swiss Army knife but include much more functional versions of the Swiss Army knife tools as well as pliers, wire cutters, and other unique tools.

Jack likes to make sure there are at least one or two multi-tools per group and that everyone else has a jackknife.

Notebook and Pencil

Another essential item is a means to provide written communication in case of emergency. A small notebook and reliable pencil allow you to leave messages, send out messages, or make note of important information. There are a number of convenient and serviceable waterproof notebooks available, but a good waterproof plastic storage bag works nearly as well.

Repair Kit

A repair kit is invaluable on long and short trips, because with all the modern technology represented in our equipment, it is rare that something doesn't fail or break down. You should develop a repair kit that meets your own personal needs, but some items we like to bring include a large needle and polyester thread (cotton thread breaks easily and rots); rip-stop repair tape for patching holes in your rain gear, tent fly, and other nylon material; a Therm-a-Rest Repair Kit if you have a Therm-a-Rest sleeping pad; rubber bands; spare stove parts; epoxy putty for repairing any number of broken items; duct tape, which has a million and one repair uses; an extra Fastex buckle for your pack waist belt; a small pair of vice grips, pliers, or Leatherman tool; extra pack parts (e.g., clevis pins and split rings); extra cord toggles; an extra washer for your fuel bottle; and appropriate screwdrivers for your stove (if you don't have a screwdriver on your knife).

Shovel or Trowel

Shovels rank with axes as one of the most maligned pieces of equipment taken into the outdoors due to the damage inflicted digging trenches and pits. However, we would take a shovel or trowel (Figure 3.9) over an axe nearly every time. Some sort of tool is necessary to bury human waste in most environments. A small plastic trowel may do for small groups while a small metal shovel may be more appropriate for larger groups. Although in many cases a small hole for human waste can be dug with the heel of the boot or by hand, we rank a trowel or small shovel very high on the necessary equipment list.

Shovels are also indispensable when baking over an open fire. They are used to shovel hot coals onto the Dutch oven. In this case, a plastic trowel just won't cut it.

Keep in mind that shovels and trowels should not be used for digging trenches or any other environmentally unsound activity.

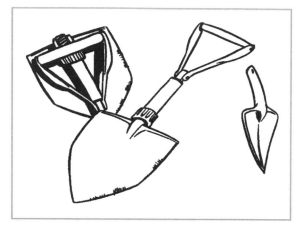

Figure 3.9
A shovel (left) or trowel (right) can be indispensable in the outdoors.

Stuff Sacks and Dry Bags

Stuff sacks are invaluable for stowing sleeping bags, clothes, and other odds and ends. When hiking in particularly wet areas or participating in water sports, a heavier-duty dry bag may be just the ticket. Stuff sacks range in their waterproof ability from barely waterproof to nearly completely waterproof. Check the description and look for factory-sealed seams, which help avoid seepage. Dry bags are designed specifically to do what their name implies—keep things dry. They work well, but are more expensive, bulky, and less convenient to work with.

Water Bottle

Canteens retired along with Roy Rogers and Dale Evans. Their weight and bulk make them impractical compared with the readily available alternatives. The least expensive alternative is to recycle the plastic bottle your favorite drink comes in. Many now even come with the convenient pop-up opening. They won't last as long as commercial water bottles, but you can't beat the price. The most common plastic water bottle is made of rigid, Lexan plastic by companies like Nalgene. They are relatively inexpensive and come in a variety of sizes and shapes. Eric likes the 1-quart narrow-mouth bottle, because the narrow mouth is easier to drink from. Jack likes the 1-quart wide-mouth, because it is easier to put water or powdered drink mixes into the large opening. If camping in semi-arid areas where water is scarce, you may want to bring more than one bottle per person. Desert campers may want to bring as much as 1 to 4 gallons of water per person if water sources are uncertain.

There has been an increased concern about plastic containers and their potential for causing cancer. While some concerns seem to be overblown, our research has demonstrated that there is some legitimate cause for worry. Plastic numbers 2, 4, and 5 appear to be the safest plastics. Be sure to use your plastic containers for what they are designed for. Avoid freezing water in plastic bottles; do not use them in microwave ovens. Clean them regularly but avoid using harsh detergents.

There is an alternative to plastic water bottles. The Klean Kanteen is a stainless-steel water container that is strong, lightweight, and easy to Klean . . . uh, we mean clean. We expect to see more and more alternatives to plastic water bottles in the future.

Water Sack or Carrier

Using a 2- or 3-gallon water sack or foldable water carrier (Figure 3.10) minimizes the number of trips to your water source. This not only saves your back, but is kinder on the environment, because the more trips you make to the stream or pond's edge, the more you cause shoreline erosion and affect the water source. Also, water holders make convenient portable water faucets that you can hang on a tree near your cook area. We highly recommend bringing either a water sack or a foldable water carrier.

Figure 3.10
A water carrier (left) or sack (right) is a must when camping.

Water Treatment

Whatever means of purifying the water you intend to use, don't leave it behind. See Chapter 5 for more information on the different water treatment options.

Whistle

Eric once had a wooden whistle but it "wooden" whistle. Then he got a steel whistle and it steel wooden whistle. Then he got a tin whistle; now he tin whistle. You wish we wood stop our bad jokes.

Whether wooden, steel, tin, or plastic, a whistle is an important essential item for that rare instance when you or your companion gets lost.

PERSONAL CARE ITEMS

The final category is the dozen or so things that help you maintain a little sanity and decorum in the areas of sanitation and health. Listed below in alphabetical order is our list of personal care items.

Comb and/or Brush

A comb and brush are valuable because they can maintain your personal appearance with a minimum of effort. Taking a little time to spruce up goes a long way in promoting good expedition behavior. (See Chapter 8 for further discussion of expedition behavior.)

Hand Lotion

Life in the outdoors has a tendency to dry and chap your hands. Some feel dry hands are a badge of outdoor living. However, anyone who has had the tips of their fingers dry out and develop deep, painful cracks knows better. Get a high-quality hand lotion and use it religiously. Vegetable oil will do very well if you run out or forget the lotion.

We have found Bag Balm, originally designed for protecting chapped cow udders, is very effective for extremely dry hands. Seriously!

Insect Repellent

Repellents work as their active ingredients evaporate and confuse and disorient insects. Each type has distinct advantages and disadvantages. "Natural" repellents usually use low concentrations of plant derivatives such as citronella and are considered by many to be safer than the synthetic, extremely effective formula called DEET. "Natural" formulas, however, have been proven to be considerably less effective than DEET-based formulas.

It should be noted when it comes to DEET that more is not necessarily better. Newer "controlled release" DEET-based formulas with as little as 20% DEET in them are considered most effective because the active ingredients are designed to remain on the surface of the skin longer, not only increasing their effectiveness but also minimizing the absorption of the DEET. (See the safety tip below).

Research has shown that "controlled release" formulas can stay effective for over 20 hours in certain conditions. Keep in mind that lotions always last longer than sprays, but sprays work well on clothing. DEET is a nasty chemical that can have a harmful effect on some synthetic fabrics. Read the label, and if in doubt, test it on a hidden portion of the fabric before you use it elsewhere.

Keep in mind that sunblocks and insect repellants are not always compatible. That is, neither may work as effectively as when they are used alone. According to Sawyer Products, the manufacturer of a line of insect repellants, if you need both, then you should put the sunblock on first, wait at least 10 minutes, then put on an insect-repellent lotion.[4]

SAFETY TIP: DEET Health Risks

While DEET does the trick in making the mosquitoes "bug off," it is absorbed rapidly into the skin and in extreme cases can cause health problems. Ten to 15% of each dose of DEET can be recovered from the urine. In some cases, brief exposure to high concentrations of the substance has caused serious reactions, including anaphylaxis and grand mal seizures. Ingestion of DEET can be fatal. New York State tried to ban 100% DEET products, but the ban was overturned in the courts.

PERMETHRIN

Permethrin is a synthetic insecticide. Permethrin doesn't work when applied to your skin, yet is very durable on clothing and gear. When a tick or insect comes into contact with permethrin it gets a lethal dose. It is relatively easy to use; is particularly effective against ticks, which carry Lyme disease; and holds up well to exposure to light and even to multiple trips through the washing machine. If you are in tick country you may want to treat your clothes with permethrin.

Bottom line is that using insect repellents is complex stuff. Experiment with different brands, read the directions, apply accordingly, and see what works best for you.

TECHWEENIE TIP: What's the Dope on DEET?

Developed for the military in the 1950s, DEET (diethyltoluamide) is very effective against mosquitoes and ticks and less effective against flies, gnats, and other insects. However, 100% DEET is not necessarily the most effective insect repellent. Composite formulas provide more effective insect repellency with less DEET through the use of a synergist that "activates" the DEET so it works as if present in greater potency. In addition, composite formulas can contain additional ingredients effective against additional insects. We're big fans of Sawyer Products' DEET PLUS composite formula.

To get an idea of how effective one of the new composite formulas is, the U.S. Air Force conducted a research study in an area of Alaska with a large mosquito population. (Is there any area of Alaska without a large mosquito population?) The results were reported with typical military understatement. "The DEET formulations provide greater than 99

continued

percent protection for more than eight hours (a mean of four mosquito bites per person per hour), while a permethrin-treated uniform alone provided 93 percent protection (78 mosquito bites/hour), compared to 1,188 bites per hour with no protection."[5] How would you like to have been a volunteer for that study?

Lip Protection

Just as the rigors of outdoor living require hand lotion to care for your hands, your lips also need protection. We've found Carmex and similar brands to be very effective. We have found the stick lip balms to be less effective. If you are in particularly sunny areas, make sure your lip balm has PABA or another sun protection ingredient in it.

Nail Clippers

Regularly trimming your toenails reduces the incidence of painful ingrown toenails.

Powder

Baby powder comes in very handy to keep your feet healthy, minimize chafing caused by clothing and your backpack harness, and can also serve as an excellent low-impact substitute for deodorant.

Soap

We recommend a biodegradable soap such as Sawyer Products' Camp Soaps. Keep in mind that there is no industry standard to measure biodegradability, and even if there were, all soaps have the potential to harm the ecosystem. Be sure to use soaps well away from the shorelines of your fresh water sources. See Chapter 5 for more information on using soaps in the backcountry.

Sunblock

Given the dire predictions for the tremendous increase in the number of diagnosed skin cancers in the coming decades, it is essential that campers take action to protect their skin while in the outdoors. A sunblock should ideally protect you from both UVB and UVA rays. Keep in mind that, unless you have extremely sun-sensitive skin, an SPF (sun protection factor) rating of 15 is the maximum protection anyone should need.

Sunglasses

A good pair of sunglasses is highly recommended. We have seen campers suffer from numerous eye-related problems (e.g., headaches, snow blindness) over the years due to not using sunglasses.

Tampons/Pads

Women should bring more tampons or pads than they think they need. There are few things worse than being caught unprepared. Our experience tells us that women occasionally start their periods earlier than usual when exercising strenuously. After once being with a student who was caught without tampons, we now carry them in our first aid kit. Maxi pads are also great as bulky wound dressings.

Disposing of tampons is serious business. Do not leave them strewn about the woods or even bury them, for they do not decompose readily and may get dug up. Wrap them up in toilet paper, place them in a plastic bag, and pack them out. Add a used teabag or aspirin to combat odors. We don't recommend disposing of them in fires, as it will take a very hot fire to burn them completely.

Toilet Paper

If you use toilet paper, be sure to keep it in a waterproof bag with a pack of matches. We recommend that you use toilet paper sparingly and use only plain white brands. It should either be buried thoroughly, placed in a plastic bag and packed out, or discreetly burned in a campfire. In some environments you can safely burn your toilet paper once it has been used. It is important, of course, to be aware of the local fire danger and use judgment in burning toilet paper. There was at least one case of a camper who started a forest fire by burning his toilet paper. If that wasn't humiliating enough, he also had to pay a hefty fine.

Did you notice that we said *if* you bring toilet paper? That's right, many people don't! They use "natural" toilet paper including leaves, smooth stones, snow, sticks, smooth bark, and other suitable natural substances. Again, use your judgment and avoid poisonous, prickly, or otherwise uncomfortable plants as well as rare or endangered species. Don't knock it if you haven't tried it. It takes a little getting used to, but natural toilet paper is definitely the low-impact way to go.

Toothbrush, Paste, and Floss

There's nothing like waking up in the morning, looking over at your tent partners, and seeing last night's dinner stuck between their teeth. Not only is brushing and flossing good for oral hygiene, but it's important for maintaining good interpersonal relations in the outdoors.

Towel

We've found that a good-size bandanna works as well as anything. Real towels have a tendency never to dry out and get mildewed. Cotton/poly towels are also heavy and bulky. The commercial camping towels are okay but hardly worth the expense, in our opinion. Over the years, we have made an amazing discovery: even if you don't have a towel, you still will eventually dry off. Don't be afraid to drip dry—it won't kill you.

CONCLUSION

Well, there you have it. You can now make your choices and head out. One last suggestion. Be a little analytical and don't bring an item because we or someone else says so—bring it because it works well for you. Try new things, and if they work well, use them. If they don't, leave them at home the next time you travel in the outdoors. Try to have a good rationale for everything you bring.

Big-Ticket Items

1. Backpacks (day packs)
2. Sleeping bags and sleeping pads
3. Tents
4. Cookstoves

Miscellaneous Items

1. Water bottle
2. Water treatment
3. Stuff sacks and waterproof bags
4. Food bag
5. Misc. cordage (knots?)
6. Lash straps
7. Knife
8. Multi-tool
9. Shovel/trowel
10. Saw
11. Flashlight and batteries
12. Candles and/or lantern
13. Matches and/or lighter
14. Notebook and Pencil
15. Licenses and permits
16. Sewing kit
17. Repair kit
18. Games (playing cards, small board games, Frisbee, hacky sack, etc.)
19. Books

Personal Care Items

1. Lip protection
2. Hand lotion
3. Sunblock
4. Foot and/or body powder
5. Soap
6. Toothbrush, paste, and floss
7. Towel
8. Nail clippers
9. Comb/brush
10. Sunglasses
11. Insect repellent
12. Toilet paper
13. Notebook and pencil
14. Licenses
15. Sewing kit
16. Repair kit
17. Games (playing cards, board games, flippy flyers, hacky sacks, etc.)
18. Books

Notes

[1]Maslow, H.H. (1954). *Motivation and Personality*. New York: Harper & Row.
[2]Petzoldt, P. (1984). *The New Wilderness Handbook*. New York: W.W. Norton.
[3]Brown, T. (1980). *The Search*. Berkley.
[4]Sawyer Products. (1992). *Sawyer Solutions*. Safety Harbor, FL.
[5]"Insect Repellent." (1989, May 19). *The Medical Letter on Drugs and Therapeutics, 31*(792), 45–46.

References

Drury, J., Ed. (2005). *The backcountry classroom: Lessons, tools and activities for teaching outdoor leaders*. Guilford, CT: Falcon Guide.

Petzoldt, P. (1984). *The new wilderness handbook* (2nd ed.). New York: W.W. Norton & Company. (Original work published in 1974.)

Simer, P., & Sullivan, J. (1983). *The National Outdoor Leadership School's wilderness guide*. New York: Simon and Schuster.

Internet References

http://www.kosa.com/staple/polarguard.htm
http://outside.away.com/outside/gear/gearguy/200406/20040610.html
http://www.backpacker.com/jargon/
http://ledmuseum.home.att.net
http://www.angelfire.com/electronic/funwithtubes/Basics_03_Diodes.html
http://www.equipped.com/led_lights.htm
http://www.kleankanteen.com/toxicplastics.html
http://www.checnet.org/healthehouse/chemicals/chemicals-detail-print.asp?Main_ID=275
http://www.sawyerproducts.com/index.htm

CHAPTER 4
Food Preparation and Planning

"One cannot think well, love well, sleep well, if one has not dined well."
—Virginia Woolfe

"Nothing says loving like something from the oven."
—The Pillsbury Doughboy

Topics:
- Food's Role in the Outdoor Experience
- Nutrition
- Food Planning
- Food Protection
- Introductory Cooking
- Cooking Tools
- Food Waste Disposal
- Dishwashing in the Backcountry
- Backcountry Frying and Baking

THE STUMPS' FOOD DILEMMA

Holly and Forrest had heard it all before. They had seen Moss, Willow, and Woody wolf down food in the wilderness and heard them say things like, "Food tastes better outdoors. You can cook anything and it tastes good." Meanwhile, what the kids were savoring was soggy Ritz crackers spread with mustard. Should the Stumps as food planners rely on this wide-eyed food idealism when they plan the family camping trip? Why shouldn't the Stumps bring boxes of Pop-Tarts and tubes of Pringles? Why shouldn't they just go easy and light, taking ready-to-eat foods that taste okay? Commercial snacks make fair food for an afternoon or overnight, but on longer trips, the Stumps will soon need more wholesome and tasty food for their physical and mental well-being.

We suggest that Holly and Forrest shouldn't rely on their hungry family's good nature. (You can guess how long that will last!) Instead, they and all campers should try to feed everyone easily prepared, nutritious, and good-tasting camp dishes made from quality ingredients.

We have seen people create truly gourmet dishes in the field, adding joy, creativity, and health to their wilderness experiences. For some people, nothing can improve a glorious sunset in the mountains with its beautiful colors, wildflowers, and serenity like a fresh-baked yeast dough pizza with a blueberry cobbler dessert!

WHAT ROLE DOES FOOD PLAY IN THE OUTDOOR EXPERIENCE?

In order to choose appropriate food items for use in backcountry settings, it is helpful to consider the benefits food gives to the camper. The first benefit of good food is that it allows us to maintain good health. If we are well nourished, we are more resistant to illness and disease and are much less likely to have our backcountry experience tainted or endangered by sickness. Another health benefit of good food is that it allows our bodies to maintain themselves by repairing damaged tissue and generating antibodies for systemic defense.

If we consider the "mind-body connection," in which what we eat affects what we think and feel, we see that quality, good-tasting food builds a positive attitude. Lack of certain nutrients (notably vitamin C) has been said to lead to irritability, listlessness, and depression. To some degree, lack of fresh fruits and vegetables was partially responsible for making sailors ornery in historic sailing expeditions. Nutrition also supports a consistently high energy level.

Consistent energy provided by nutritious food also helps backcountry campers when facing crisis situations and trying to make sound decisions. For this reason, good nutrition plays a critical role in overall safety and the prevention of risky situations.

WHAT WE NEED FOR GOOD NUTRITION

Calories

In this culture of Slim-Fast, diet frenzy, supermodels, and skin-deep beauty, many of us have been programmed to fear calories. On the other hand, the Centers for Disease Control have found that the U.S. rate of obesity has been rising for the past 20 years, now reaching epidemic proportions. Hmm. What's wrong with this picture?

In the outdoors, throw out your diet and start eating for warmth and performance. The most basic concept in nutrition is the calorie. A calorie is a unit of measuring heat. Specifically, 1 calorie of heat raises 1 gram of water 1° Celsius. That's right, 1 calorie isn't much. But how many do we need? A million?

Maybe a million over a couple of years. Most people with a sedentary, office-bound lifestyle need only about 1,800 calories a day. That's about five candy bars. Although the numbers vary widely, most wilderness travelers need between 2,800 and 4,000 calories per day in the summer and from 3,800 to 6,000 calories per day in the winter. That's a lot of food. You'll be surprised by how hungry you are in the woods and how much food you can shovel in. Few people, however, put on weight during strenuous wilderness traveling, so you can eat without worrying about your love handles!

Carbohydrates

Carbohydrates include simple and complex sugars and starches, forming the bulk of the backcountry diet. Since these nutrients are simple in structure, they break down quickly to provide short-term energy useful when climbing steep mountain slopes, cross-country skiing, and backpacking. If you think of your body as a woodstove, carbohydrates would be like tinder and small softwood twigs—fast lighting, lots of heat, but short-lasting in terms of food value. Carbohydrates should make up about 60% of the camper's diet by weight.

Many people are wary of carbohydrates in the wake of the many fad diets that minimize carbohydrate intake in favor of protein and fat. While these diets work for some people in suburban and urban front-country settings, we urge all backcountry travelers to leave their low-carbohydrate diets in South Beach. Hardworking backpackers, hikers, climbers, and paddlers need the benefit of short- and medium-burning calories found in breads, sugars, fruits, and trail snacks. Well-rounded *nutrition* is important in the wilderness; whether you are well-rounded is not!

Look for carbohydrates in
- pasta (spaghetti, macaroni),
- rice, and
- bread and crackers.

Fats

Fats are often maligned in supermarket tabloids but are much needed for nutrition in the outdoors. High-fat foods provide flavor and most of our long-term energy. In our internal wood stove, fats would be the slow-kindling, long-burning hardwoods that keep you warm through the night. If you feel cold, eat carbohydrates to warm you up quickly and fats to keep you warm for the long term. Fats should make up 20–25% of the calories in our diets.

Look for fats in
- cheese,
- nuts, and
- cooking oils.

Proteins

What's the beef with beef? As a good source of protein, it also has more than its share of unhealthy fats. The most significant problem with meat is the problems backpackers have in keeping it fresh. Many other foods can provide nutritious, easily preserved and lightweight protein for camping.

 ### ENVIRONMENTAL TIP: Beef Impact

One excellent way for campers to reduce their impact on global resources is to reduce consumption of commercially produced beef, which requires a disproportionate share of land, water, and vegetable resources for its production compared to alternative protein sources. Further, methane (a cow "end product") is a problematic greenhouse gas able to warm the atmosphere at a rate 21 times faster than CO_2. (Not to mention the cubic kilometers of solid waste produced annually by the bevy of bovine food processors.)

Proteins serve as sources for building materials within the body. As the body breaks down muscle fiber, skin, or other tissues, it uses the amino acids contained in proteins to construct new tissue. Proteins also play important roles in fighting diseases and regulating body processes as materials for antibodies and hormones. More complex than carbohydrates but faster burning than fats, proteins provide mid- to long-term energy.

Our bodies need all of the 22 amino acids found in most protein sources in order to synthesize new tissue. All but 8 of the 22 amino acids are produced within our cells. The eight leftovers must be found in food protein. Finally, proteins should compose 15–20% of the foods in our diets.

Complete proteins contain all eight of the essential amino acids necessary for healthy body function.

Look for complete proteins in
- meats,
- fish,
- soy products (soy flour, milk, nuts, tofu), and
- dairy products.

Incomplete proteins contain some but not all of the eight essential amino acids and so are not sufficient by themselves to provide full nutritional value.

Look for incomplete proteins in
- cereals and grains;
- greens, cabbages, and other veggies;
- legumes.

Combining Proteins for Complete Nutrition

By combining complete with incomplete proteins or two incomplete proteins in the same day, one can obtain all the amino acids necessary for optimum body function. Usually, this happens as a matter of course when meals are prepared, unless the camper has a single-item meal. Macaroni and cheese, beans and rice, pizza, chili and rice, nut butter with bread, hot cereal with sunflower seeds, and vegetable soup with cheese or soy products are examples of complete combinations of dietary proteins within meals. One of Eric's colleagues taught him this memory device many years ago: "Don't Get Love Sick." D=Dairy; G=Grains; L=Legumes;

S=Seeds. If you combine foods from adjacent letters (e.g., dairy with grains or grains with legumes), you can come up with complete proteins. In our example, a good dish could be cheese and macaroni (D+G) or rice and beans (G+L).

Vitamins and Minerals

As is the case with protein, variety in foodstuffs is the key to ingesting sufficient amounts of vitamins and minerals. Both vitamins and minerals are present in most foods chosen for the outdoors. If you choose liberally from our sample list of nutritious food, you can leave the Flintstones chewable vitamins back in Bedrock. Unless the camper has a special medical/ nutritional need for extremely high dosages of these trace substances, he or she will find excellent nutrition in a varied camp menu.

Water

We make a point of mentioning water in this section because it is often overlooked in the discussion of healthy eating. Many people walk around their offices, houses, and schools in a state of perpetual dehydration. We know Eric did! As a kid he thought urine was supposed to be yellow, and when his urine was clear he thought he was sick. In a normally hydrated person, urine should be clear and not darkened with salts and other wastes. Yellow or dark urine may indicate dehydration, which affects the outdoor person in many ways. Not only do continually dehydrated people strain their kidneys, they often suffer from dry skin, mouths, scratchy throats, and headaches. ("You say you've got a headache? Drink some water."—*Eric's Mom*, 1975)

Beware of water loss at high elevations and in cold weather through respiration. To maintain normal physiologic function, the well hydrated camper needs to consume between 2 and 4 quarts of water a day in summer and between 3 and 4 quarts in the winter. In his book, *Hypothermia: Death by Exposure*, Dr. William Forgey notes that as little as a 10% degree of dehydration reduces thermal efficiency by 30–40%.[1] Keep drinking! Mixers, flavorings, and carbonation are allowed. Leave alcohol, however, at home. It causes dehydration and affects sound judgment.

SAFETY TIP: The Danger of Drinking TOO Much Water

Just when you thought you couldn't miss by drinking water in the backcountry to stay hydrated, along comes a condition caused by (you guessed it) drinking *too* much water. *Hyponatremia* is the name of the condition caused by excessive water intake during exertion. What happens is that when you drink too much water, the plasma portion of the blood, which is the liquid part, becomes excessive, overreaching the body's ability to lose water through sweat. This excess plasma dilutes the level of salt and electrolytes in the blood just as the body is in the process of losing salt by sweating. The result is a rapid decline in available salts and potassium as electrolytes in the bloodstream. Hyponatremia can lead to apathy, confusion, nausea, fatigue, and even death. Experts recommend between 8 and 16 oz of water per hour during periods of high activity.

PLANNING FOR OUTDOOR PROVISIONS

Before they started to learn about nutrition and food planning, the Stumps would storm the local Piggly Wiggly with a convoy of shopping carts and buy enough food for Woodstock IV in preparation for their weekend camping trip. Not only is the expense of such an approach exorbitant, but think of the weight, bulk, and disposable packaging of a backpack stuffed with ready-to-eat, commercial snacks, lunches, and dinners! There must be an easier way to plan food for outdoor trips.

Where Do You Start?

When we started attempting to plan food for trips, we were hopeless! We had a fairly conventional lifestyle and rarely ventured away from beige, white, and pink food bought on double-coupon day at the local Shop 'n' Drop. We had trouble varying our diets beyond the occasional Fluffernutter sandwich at midnight and suffered migraine headaches when trying to plan tasty food for a camping trip. All we learned about food variety and nutrition came from cooking class in seventh grade. So when we first started, we had more questions than Socrates.

What foods do we buy? How much do we need for 3 days? Seven days? Can we realistically prepare a particular item 7 miles from the trailhead? What should we buy for good nutrition?

At the beginning, consider the length, difficulty, and goals of the trip when selecting food items.

Use these criteria to help:

- **Energy content.** Pick food that has high calorie-to-weight ratio.
- **Nutritional balance.** Cover all nutritional bases.
- **Weight and bulk.** Remember you have to carry all provisions on your back. Find a balance between weight and bulk (for example, a pillow-sized bag of potato chips is light but bulky—you wouldn't bring it on a backpacking trip). Choose dried items so you do not have to carry unnecessary liquid.
- **Spoilage.** Phew! 'Nuff said.
- **Expense and availability.** Can you afford costly dehydrated porterhouse steaks? Will pepperoni serve as well or better?
- **Packaging and handling.** Avoid heavy and bulky cans. Repackage foods in plastic bags and containers. Avoid terribly messy foods.
- **Variety.** Try oatmeal every morning for 10 days and you'll understand the importance of having a varied diet.
- **Ease of preparation.** How much time and energy do you want to spend cooking? Keep it simple. However, most "no-cook" or instant foods have little appeal. You should balance taste and food appeal with ease of preparation. You can do a *little* cooking out there! What else are you going to do in the evenings without cable TV?
- **Wild foods as supplements.** Do you have the knowledge and desire to safely eat wild greens, fish, mushrooms, or insects? Is it legal? Is your tent partner a "Survivor" wannabe who insists on eating grubs and toasted grasshoppers as a rite of passage? Make sure it's safe and has little environmental impact, and then *you* go first and tell us how you like it!

Menu Planning System

The most obvious option for planning provisions for camping trips is the menu planning system. In this straightforward approach, the food planner decides on a simple menu for each meal that the group will eat while in the backcountry, from soup to nuts. Well, we mean planning every aspect of each meal including beverages, snacks, and dessert—you can have more than soup and nuts.

The menu method requires the planner to estimate amounts of food each meal requires as well as to plan reasonably simple yet tasty food combinations for the backcountry.

We recommend many of the more basic and lightweight meals that are prepared at home. Using familiar ingredients minimizes expense, simplifies shopping, and enhances cooking results in the backcountry. It is not necessary to purchase the freeze-dried prepackaged meals widely available in camping supply shops. Not only are these meals quite costly, but many people are disappointed in the taste, nutritional value, and small portion size of the rehydrated meals.

Total Food Planning

If you seek an alternative to the potentially mind-numbing process of determining a menu for each meal, which increases in mind-numbingness as group size and trip length increase, look to Total Food Planning (TFP). TFP creates a backcountry pantry of foodstuffs from which campers draw supplies to make each meal. The process determines caloric needs and analyzes food calorie content to ensure that the group has enough food to meet its needs while staying within weight and budget constraints.

Planning Criteria

Caloric needs. In our experience, an average active camper consumes between 3,000 and 3,750 calories per day, depending on the person's metabolism and level of activity. For winter camping, we plan for 3,800 to 5,000 calories per day. In extreme conditions, mountaineers have been known to consume 6,000 calories per day or more during hard pushes. That's about 50 bowls of corn flakes!

Weight constraints. When using a wide variety of ordinary dried supermarket food, we have found that we can provide between 3,200 and 3,750 calories with about 2 pounds of food. In general, for the summer months we try to provide 2 pounds of food per person per day. For winter camping, bump the amount up to 2 1/4 or 2 and 1/2 pounds per day.

Budget constraints. For a healthy and tasty variety of foods, we've found that we can provide 2 pounds of food per day for between $3.00 and $7.00. Food costs can be greatly reduced by ordering food in bulk from wholesale suppliers, buying clubs, supermarkets, and co-ops. Ideally, the camper can set up a bulk food warehouse system, with sacks of staples such as oatmeal, flour, dried milk, and sugar. Most dried foods stay usable for several months when stored in cool, dry locations.

Using the three constraints and a calorie list of common camping foods, the food planner can figure the total pounds of each food item needed for the trip and buy in bulk. The bulk food can then be measured and repackaged for convenience and portability. When cooking any meal in the field, campers need only to look at what they have and create a meal from the contents of their "portable food pantries" that they carry on their backs.

Advantages of Total Food Planning

Before we look at how the process works from start to finish, consider the advantages TFP offers over the menu system. Most wilderness schools, such as the Wilderness Education Association (WEA), National Outdoor Leadership School (NOLS), and Outward Bound, use some form of TFP largely because of its systematic approach. TFP reduces food waste because of its pounds-per-day constraint. It increases the variety of each meal because the cook can incorporate many different ingredients. Creativity flourishes as cooks experiment with flavors, spices, textures, and "secret" recipes.

Perhaps most importantly, TFP saves frustration by eliminating the need to preplan each meal before the trip leaves the trailhead. Imagine planning each meal for a week-long backpacking trip. You'd soon find that it involves six or seven breakfasts, lunches, and dinners. That's about 20 different meals! Do you see yourself running out of ideas? Mac and cheese. . . cheese and mac . . . spaghetti . . . spaghetti and cheese . . .

How Total Food Planning Works

Let's look at how the Muskrat Pack uses TFP to help illustrate the process. When we last saw the group of paddlers, they were gearing up for a trip to the Drifting Paddle National Canoe Area (DPNCA). Juan, Anne, Stella, and you then had to tackle how to plan, purchase, and pack food for the 7-day trip. Somehow, you are left the responsibility of planning the food. You thought this was supposed to be a vacation. Take a deep breath. Here goes.

Calories. Multiply the number of people in the party (four total) by the length of the trip in days (7) by the number of calories you determine you need each day (3,300). Four people × 7 days × 3,300 calories = 92,400 total calories. Now you know you need to purchase food that has 92,400 total calories. You're on your way!

Weight. Multiply the number of people in the party by the length of the trip by the number of pounds of food to be brought per day (2 pounds). Four people × 7 days × 2 pounds = 56 total pounds. Now you've determined how many pounds your total food heap will weigh. To determine how many pounds of food each person will carry, divide the total (56) by the number of people (four). That's 14 pounds per person.

Cost. Multiply the number of people in the party by the length of the trip by the amount of money you want to spend per person per day on food (let's say $6.00). Four people × seven days × $6.00 per person per day = $168.00 total. Yikes! You have to spend $168 for a week's worth of camping food? Well, remember that it's $168 for four people for a week. That's $42 per person for a week of eating out. That's about five trips to the fast food joint or two dinners at a Red Lobster.

Creating Food List A: Total Trip Food Weights

Given your constraints (92,400 total calories, 56 total pounds, and $168 total food allowance), look at a calorie and price list for common camping food items and create a shopping list of pounds to purchase for each item. Pay attention to the mix of breakfast, lunch, and dinner foods. Make sure you buy enough ready-to-eat foods for trail lunches and snacks. Try to purchase items that can work for lunch, dinner, or breakfast, such as bagels, crackers, soup mixes, mashed potatoes, rice, and couscous.

As you can see, a list for even a weeklong trip can seem monumental. Once you get used to the system, it's really not that difficult. We used a computer spreadsheet program for this list, but you can also make one by hand, which takes a little longer. If you are interested in a copy of the spreadsheet, contact the authors through the publisher. As we stated above, Food List A (Figure 4.1) is used to plan overall amounts of food to buy for an entire group of people. The individual or cook group food list is presented in Food List B (see Figure 4.3).

The crucial information (who is going on the trip, trip dates, trip length, pounds of food needed per person per day, and calories needed per person per day) is listed on the heading. For convenience, we divided the food into eight categories: Bases/Veggies/Desserts, Breakfast, Cheese, Dinners, Flour, Staples, Sweeteners/Beverages, and Trail Foods. The columns include the amount of calories per pound for each food item, the number of pounds ordered, and the total calories for each food item. The Totals category is where you add the weights of food ordered and total the calories. You then compare the total weight and total calories with your overall goals (56 pounds and 92,400 calories).

You will also see that we included a percent of the total food weight for each category. For example, Staples are 8%, Trail Food is 25% and Flour is 8%. This is where judgment comes in. We have found that these percentages work well for three-season camping in moderate terrain for moderate itineraries. You can use these percentages as your starting point and then adjust them for your own nutrition and eating patterns and for trips that require more or fewer calories. You can also raise or lower the pounds of food per person per day and calories per person per day. By using the percentages we have supplied, adequate nutrition and balance between different types of food (Staples, Trail Foods, etc.) can be attained.

Organizing Cook Groups

You may also want to create a food list for the people who will cook together (Figure 4.2). Decide how you want to manage the cooking process on your trip. Do you want to prepare meals on a group-wide level, cafeteria-style? This way you cook large amounts of each item and everybody eats the same thing. The group can rotate cooking and cleanup crews, if desired. This arrangement has advantages and disadvantages. For instance, what if Chef Anne favors volcano-curry flapjacks for breakfast?

Small cook groups enjoy greater autonomy in creating their daily meals, can moderate portions according to hunger, and share the closeness of being a group within a group. Also, with separate cook groups, one cook doesn't assume sole responsibility for cooking disasters affecting an entire group. Lastly, small cook groups require more people to develop outdoor cooking skills, which might be a great goal for your trip.

Trip:	DPNCA, 4/12-4/18		Members:	Juan, Anne
Days:	7			Stella, Me
Pounds/Day:	2		Total people:	4
Total Pounds:	56		Calories/Day:	3300
			Total Calories:	92400

Staples

	cal/lb	lbs	tot. cal
Margarine	3387	1.5	5081
Powdered Milk	1650	1.5	2475
Vegetable Oil	4000	1.5	6000

Trail Foods

	cal/lb	lbs	tot. cal
Apples	1102	1	1102
Apricots	1081	1	1081
Cashews	2604	1	2604
Choc. Chips	1650	0	0
Coconut	2648	0	0
Crackers	1828	1	1828
Dates	1243	1	1243
Hard Candy	1751	0	0
M&M's	1650	1	0
Nut Mix	2694	0	0
Peanut Butter	2682	1	2682
Peanuts	2558	2	4510
Pepperoni	2255	1	2255
Prunes	1018	0	0
Raisins	1359	2	2718
Sesame Stcks	2454	0	0
Snflwr Seeds	2550	0	0
Trail Mix #1	2000	1	2000
Trail Mix #2	2000	1	2000
Bagels	1800	0	0
Walnuts	2950	0	0
Choc Raisins	1873	0	0

Flour

	cal/lb	lbs	tot. cal
Corn Meal	1610	1.5	2415
White Flour	1650	1.5	2475
Whole Wheat	1651	1.5	2477

Sweeteners/Beverages

	cal/lb	lbs	tot. cal
Brown Sugar	1700	1	1700
Cocoa	1628	1	1628
Fruit Drinks	1950	1	1950
Honey	1379	1	1379
Jello	1683	0.5	841.5
Tea	1 bag/person/day		
White Sugar	1700	0	0

Breakfast

	cal/lb	lbs	tot. cal
Cream/Wht.	1658	2	3316
Oatmeal	1672	2	3344
Pancake Mix	1615	2	3230
Pancake Syr.	1600	1.5	2400
Potato (Slice)	1624	2	3248
Wheatena	1618	0	0

Cheese

	cal/lb	lbs	tot. cal
Cheddar	1826	1	1826
Colby	1786	1	1786
Mozzarella	1270	1.5	1905
Muenster	1671	1	1671
Parmesan	2266	0	0

Spices (weight not included)

Baking Powd.
Basil
Chili Powder
Curry
Garlic
Ginger
Oregano
Parsley
Pepper
Salt
Soy Sauce
Vanilla
Vinegar
Yeast

Dinners

	cal/lb	lbs	tot. cal
Bulgar	1621	1	1621
Cous Cous	1709	0	0
Egg Noodles	1760	2	3520
Elbow Mac	1674	2	3348
Potato buds	1650	2	3300
Refried Beans	2667	0	0
Rice	1647	1	1647
Spaghetti	1674	2	3348
Soy Protein	1500	0	0

Bases/Veggies/Desserts

	cal/lb	lbs	tot. cal
Beef Base	1082	0	0
Brownie Mix	1828	1	1828
Cheese Cake	3500	1	3500
Chicken Base	1117	0.25	279.3
Dried Veggies	1600	0.25	400
Gingerbread	1928	0	0
Mshrm soupmx	2000	0	0
Onions-dried	1465	0.25	366.3
Peppers-dried	1000	0	0
Popcorn	1642	0.5	821
Pudding	1637	0.5	818.5
Sloppy Joe	1400	0	0
Tomato Base	1350	0.75	1013
Veggie Chili	1450	0	0

Totals (%)	%	need	actual
Staples (8%)	0.08	4.48	4.5
Trail Food (25)	0.25	14	14
Flour (8)	0.08	4.48	4.5
Sweets (8)	0.08	4.48	4.5
Breakfast (17)	0.17	9.52	9.5
Cheese (8)	0.08	4.48	4.5
Dinners (18)	0.18	10.1	10
B/V/D (8)	0.08	4.48	4.5
totals	1	56	56

Total Calories Needed
92400

Total Calories Actual
100979

Figure 4.1
Food Planning List A

Cook Groups:	Juan and Stella	Anne and Me

Figure 4.2
Sample list of cook groups.

Creating Food List B: Cook Group Food Weights

If you choose to have small groups or pairs of people cook together, you need to divide the total food accordingly. Use your formula to determine how many pounds of food need to be issued to each cook group. For example, Juan and Stella are a cook group for the seven-day trip. You've figured on 2 pounds of food per person per day. Two people × 7 days × 2 pounds = 28 pounds of food. Now you make a list of food items and weight for each item totaling 28 pounds.

In this case, we simplified the spreadsheet from List A. All we did was list the total amount of food ordered for each item and then figured out what share of the total should go to each two-person cook group. In this case, two people are one half of the total number of people on the trip. Therefore, each two-person cook group should get half of the four-person food total. We divided the total for each food item by two. Of course, this gets more complex when you have larger groups or cook groups of three and four people. When packing food, use the amounts from List B (Figure 4.3) for each cook group.

Purchasing Food

Most of the food items on the sample list may be purchased at a good supermarket. For longer trips or for stockpiling items, find a source of bulk food in order to minimize packaging and cut down on expense. Bulk food "shopping clubs" often have jumbo packs of staples. Generally, the least expensive route is to order bulk food from food co-ops in large quantities, usually from 10 to 50 pounds.

Food Packaging and Handling

Once all the food for the trip has been purchased, resist the temptation to simply load your pack willy-nilly directly from the grocery bags. We strongly recommend weighing and repackaging food items in plastic bags.

Plain, thin but sturdy, food-grade plastic bags work well for backcountry camping trips for several reasons. Plastic bags are much lighter than glass or cardboard packages, are safer than glass because they cannot shatter, are easy to pack into a backpack, and can be brought out of the woods easily when empty. Also, some plastic containers can be reused many times.

Zippered plastic bags work well on short trips to store anything from pasta to underwear, but fail on longer trips. The zippers become clogged with food particles and do not remain sealed inside your backpack. Exploding food bags will become an unpleasant reality at some point in your wilderness travel career.

After you've purchased suitable plastic bags, the next step is to weigh out proper amounts of each item on your food list. Use a dietary scale or a small beam balance. Wash your hands and wear plastic gloves or put a spare plastic bag on your hands when handling ready-to-eat items such as raisins and cheese. Cheese will mold in the spots where it is touched.

Trip:	DPNCA, 4/12-4/18		Members:	Juan, Anne
Days:	7			Stella, Me
Pounds/Day:	2		Total people:	4
Total Pounds:	56		Cook grp size:	2
			lbs/cook grp:	28

Staples

	Tot. lbs	2 pers
Margarine	1.5	0.75
Powdered Mlk	1.5	0.75
Vegetable Oil	1.5	0.75

Sweeteners/Beverages

	Tot. lbs	2 pers
Brown Sugar	1	0.5
Cocoa	1	0.5
Fruit Drinks	1	0.5
Honey	1	2
Jello	0.5	0.25
Tea	1 bag/pers/day	
White Sugar	0	0

Dinners

	Tot. lbs	2 pers
Bulgar	1	0.5
Cous Cous	0	0
Egg Noodles	2	1
Elbow Mac	2	1
Potato buds	2	1
Refried Beans	0	0
Rice	1	0.5
Spaghetti	2	1
Soy Protein	0	0

Trail Foods

	Tot. lbs	2 pers
Apples	1	0.5
Apricots	1	0.5
Cashews	1	0.5
Choc. Chips	0	0
Coconut	0	0
Crackers	1	0.5
Dates	1	0.5
Hard Candy	0	0
M&M's	1	0.5
Nut Mix	0	0
Peanut Butter	1	0.5
Peanuts	2	1
Pepperoni	1	0.5
Prunes	0	0
Raisins	2	1
Sesame Stcks	0	0
Snflwr Seeds	0	0
Trail Mix #1	1	0.5
Trail Mix #2	1	0.5
Bagels	0	0
Walnuts	0	0
Yogurt Raisins	0	0

Breakfast

	Tot. lbs	2 pers
Cream/Wht.	2	1
Oatmeal	2	1
Pancake Mix	2	1
Pancake Syr.	1.5	0.75
Potato (Slice)	2	1
Wheatena	0	0

Cheese

	Tot. lbs	2 pers
Cheddar	1	0.5
Colby	1	0.5
Mozzarella	1.5	0.75
Muenster	1	0.5
Parmesan	0	0

Bases/Veggies/Desserts

	Tot. lbs	2 pers
Beef Base	0	0
Brownie Mix	1	0.5
Cheese Cake	1	0.5
Chicken Base	0.25	0.125
Dried Veggies	0.25	0.125
Gingerbread	0	0
Mshrm soupmx	0	0
Onions-dried	0.25	0.125
Peppers-dried	0	0
Popcorn	0.5	0.25
Pudding	0.5	0.25
Sloppy Joe	0	0
Tomato Base	0.75	0.375
Veggie Chili	0	0

Spices (make own kit per group)

Baking Powd.	.
Basil	
Chili Powder	
Curry	
Garlic	
Ginger	
Oregano	
Parsley	
Pepper	
Salt	
Soy Sauce	
Vanilla	
Vinegar	
Yeast	

Flour

	Tot. lbs	2 pers
Corn Meal	1.5	0.75
White Flour	1.5	0.75
Whole Wheat	1.5	0.75

Figure 4.3
Food Planning List B

QUALITY CAMPER TIP: Beware the Death-Knot!
Tie off your plastic bags filled with food with a simple overhand knot. Scrupulously avoid the "death knot," which is the inscrutable wad of fused plastic that results from holding the top of the bag, spinning its contents to form a tight spiral rope of the bag's neck, and looping the neck several times. This complex and confounding knot prompts murderous exclamations when a hungry tent partner attempts to cook dinner in waning sunlight.

Figure 4.4
Avoid tightly tied knots.

Food Organization and Care

You can either impress or annoy your tent partner by taking the time to organize your food bags. For most extended backcountry trips, we recommend storing the individually bagged food items in a medium-sized duffel bag. In our example, Juan and Stella had 28 pounds of food between them for the weeklong trip in the DPNCA. If they decided to distribute the weight equally, they would each have carried 14 pounds of food in their food bags. But Juan said he was a light eater and didn't want much food. Stella remained open-minded, but insisted he carry a full food bag in case he changed his mind.

You and Anne had a squabble. Anne, the Muskrat Pack's most experienced outdoor person, wanted to divide the food alphabetically and wanted to carry items A through L. You, the outdoor novice, held up a hefty bag and said, "Do you call this pancake mix with a 'P' or Bisquick with a 'B'?" You advocated a color-based system where one person carries the whites, browns, and beiges while the other takes the brighter colors. Anne groaned and rolled her eyes.

Stella, based on her time backpacking in the Wyoming mountains, offered a two-person system divided by function. Breakfast, dinner, and baking make one group; lunch, drinks, dinner, and desserts make the other. Yeesh! What will you do? You'll figure it out!

Food Care Tips

- Keep food bags clean, not gooey.
- Promptly double-bag burst bags.
- Lift bags underneath the knot (so knots don't tighten).
- Double-bag potentially messy or pointy items (dry milk, spaghetti).
- Put plastic containers of liquids inside plastic bags (e.g., honey).
- Store food in the shade to avoid deterioration and melting.

FOOD PROTECTION

The Food Bandits Come by Night . . .

It was a dark and stormy night on your camping trip. You and your tent partner were lying in your warm sleeping bags after feasting on a wonderful Mystery Stew. Your luck was about to change for the worse. At about a quarter to midnight, the Woodland Welcome Wagon arrived in the form of a squadron of ravenous chipmunks, raccoons, and bears. Your thoughts flashed to your food bag, lying like a defenseless piñata on the ground near the stove. Who's getting up this time?

Instead of this chilling nightmare, we face a bright-eyed, furry reality when we set out to secure our food for the night. Mice, raccoons, porcupines, coyotes, bears, and squirrels, the scariest food bandits of all, compete with campers in the struggle for store-bought snacks.

One night years ago, one of our friends decided to sleep with his foodbag. Zak woke from a blissful sleep to find his foodbag slowly scuttling away. Jumping out of his sleeping bag, he was soon engaged in a tug-of-war with a brave raccoon the size of a basset hound. He managed to drive the raccoon away, but was hesitant to eat any of the food that the animal had torn into, recoiling from raccoon cooties.

Some people will say, "Well, that was a raccoon. Little critters like mice and chipmunks can't hurt. How much can a mouse or two eat anyway? Relax!"

When Human Food Isn't Eaten by Humans

What most campers will learn sooner or later is that one mouse can eat quite a bit and often brings its siblings or cousins. Invading chipmunks and squirrels chew through the thickest Cordura, nylon, or canvas. Porcupines gnaw the salt off of boots and pack straps. Coyotes and bears can abscond with entire food bags, leaving campers with little or no food.

On the other side of the issue, human items like candy bars, dried potatoes, dehydrated apples, chocolate chips, and toothpaste can cause indigestion, and sickness, or worse—habituation—for the animals that eat them. When wild animals learn that human campsites are a reliable and easy source for a food bonanza, they come to rely on their nocturnal runs to the woodland "convenience store."

While many backcountry campers thrill to the sight of raccoons and porcupines and think chipmunks and red squirrels are adorable, they lack the same enthusiasm for coyote and bear encounters. Animals habituated to human food soon lose their fear of humans and can no longer be counted on to be "more afraid of you than you are of them," as the saying goes.

Some experts maintain that a human-fed bear is a dead bear. They reason that a food-habituated and fearless bear becomes a potential hazard to humans and must be either relocated or shot by wildlife managers. Bears that are trapped and driven to another location have a very low rate of survival. Therefore, in a sense, if a bear gets into your improperly protected food, you are responsible for the chain of events that results in a dead bear.

BOTTOM-LINE TIP: A Fed Bear Is a Dead Bear

Campers are responsible for protecting their food from wild animal consumption. The consequences of animals eating human food range from disruption of natural feeding habits to animal death.

Principles and Methods for Food Protection

When Should You Bother to Protect Food in the Backcountry?

Campers should nearly always protect their food, especially where local policy or regulations dictate, as in the case of areas known for high levels of animal-human contact, such as Yellowstone Park. In general, the more popular an area is, the greater the likelihood of human-habituated animal contact.

Conversely, the more remote the setting, especially in off-trail sites, the less likely it is for animals to overcome their fear of humans to investigate human food.

Methods for Food Protection

As is the case with most camp chores, protect food bags with the aid of daylight. Campers attempting to struggle with ropes and heavy food bags after nightfall often degenerates into a not-too-funny slapstick comedy as the rope tangles around every tree like Charlie Brown's kite string.

Find a location for the protected food that meets the following criteria. To protect food from small mammals (squirrels, raccoons, mice, porcupine) the food bags should be 4 feet off the ground and 4 feet from the nearest tree. Raccoons need to build stepladders to reach items 4 feet up. To protect food from bears, hang food bags 12 feet off the ground and 6 feet from the nearest tree.

Figure 4.5
Forrest and Holly hang the food.

Most tree-based methods fall under three general categories: the Cadillac of food bag hangs is the two-tree method. The Chevy version is the one-tree method. The secondhand Yugo is the one-branch method. In the *two-tree method*, tie a weight (a rock or a plastic bag filled with gravel) to the end of the rope and wing it through a tree crotch about 15 feet off the ground. Take the weight off and secure that end. Leaving slack on the ground, do the same thing to the other end of the rope with a nearby tree crotch. Tie your food bag (via a butterfly knot and a carabiner) to the middle of the rope, between the two trees. Haul the far end of the rope through the second tree to lift the bag off the ground. If you've secured your food bag at the right spot on the rope, your bag will be neatly suspended 15 feet off the ground and 15 feet from either tree. Pretty slick!

The *one-tree method* calls for finding only one really excellent tree crotch. Throw your weighted rope end through the crotch. Take the weight off and tie the end to one handle of your food bag. Clip the other handle to the standing end of the rope. Haul on the standing (free) end of the rope until your foodbag is a sufficient height from the ground. Secure the free end of the rope to a nearby tree at an angle, thus pulling your foodbag away from the tree its rope runs around.

The *one-branch method* entails finding one branch roughly parallel to the ground. Throw your weighted rope end over the branch. Tie the end to your foodbag. Haul your foodbag off the ground to a height that will discourage all but NBA-bound bears. Tie the free end off on the trunk of the same tree. This might get you through the night, but will probably be raided shortly.

As most backcountry travelers agree, there is no one best method for food bag hanging. You must evaluate your resources at each location and solve a miniature engineering problem every time. Obviously, some methods are best suited for particular conditions or locations. Trees usually help the effort, but if no trees are available, caching food under rocks might be your best bet. The National Park Service recommends in treeless areas to store your food, double-wrapped in plastic, at least 300 feet downhill and away from camp. Make sure all "smellables" (toothpaste, gum, candy, trail mix, etc.) are kept with your food cache. You don't want your backpack to be chewed by those cute but pesky squirrels while you're dreaming of paradise!

QUALITY CAMPER TIP: Bear Canisters

A more recent development in the food protection effort is the advent of plastic cylinders designed to foil Yogi Bear and his posse. Bears just can't seem to get a grip on how to open these so-called bear canisters, which are shoebox-size, threaded barrels designed to accommodate up to 7 days of food. Designed to be odor-proof, watertight, and slippery, bear canisters don't have to be hung in the trees. In fact, you simply fill them with food, secure the latch (there are various versions of the closure device), and stash them under a bush somewhere within 50 yards of camp. Make sure you don't forget where you left it! If you keep them clean, you aren't likely to attract nosy critters. We have heard of occasions when bears simply bat them around, so make sure you don't stash your canister near a riverbank or lakeshore—you could be feeding somebody downstream. The only downside is the price. You can pay in the neighborhood of $75 for a bear canister, or rent them for $5–10 per day.

INTRODUCTORY COOKING IN THE BACKCOUNTRY

In order to avoid making exotic dishes like hand flambé and scalded loin of camper, we should take a look at safety. Adopting a set of safety procedures can be considered a sort of minimal-impact ethic for self-preservation, since cooking accidents outnumber all others in the backcountry.

Safety in the Backcountry Kitchen: Setup

Locate the kitchen and cooking area well away from the sleeping area in order to eliminate the chance of cooking spills and sparks damaging flammable and fragile tents and sleeping bags. Also, when campers keep the zone of intense food odor away from their sleeping area, they have fewer nocturnal encounters with hungry critters.

When using a campstove or a cooking fire, clear a 3- to 5-foot "safe zone" around the heat source. Remove flammable ground litter, plastic food bags, clothing, and any object that could be tripped over. It is especially important to move fuel bottles well away from the heat source in order to prevent accidental fireworks.

The cook should "guard" the safe zone vigilantly! Make sure nobody saunters through the area and inadvertently kicks over the stove. Keep all hacky-sack circles, Frisbees, and sumo wrestling matches well away from the safe zone. In other words, the cook should take care to keep anyone not involved in cooking out of the cooking area. High traffic breeds confusion and dangerous accidents, especially with campstoves and fires at foot level.

Sterilize your utensils before you eat! When they are at home, most people wash their dishes after they eat. In the backcountry, we do a quick cleanup after dinner and a scalding session of sterilization before digging in. At some point before eating, bowls, cups, and spoons should be sterilized to prevent bacteria and infectious germs from spreading through the camping party. We've seen intestinal bugs sweep through a group over the course of a few days, and the only people who remained healthy were those who took care to practice good personal hygiene and sterilize their utensils regularly. A simple method to kill all bacteria on utensils is to immerse them for 10–30 seconds in boiling water. Use pliers or pot grippers in this operation! Sterilization is often our first step in preparing a meal. Most importantly, make sure to wash your hands before you begin your food preparation activities.

Take care when using knives to prepare food. Cut and chop food on a hard surface rather than on your leg or in your hand. Also, cut away from yourself.

Safety in the Backcountry Kitchen: Burn Prevention Techniques

First and foremost: Use pot gripper or gloves or both when handling hot pots. Very few of us have mastered the mystic talents of walking on coals, eating fire, or lifting a hot pot off a roaring fire with our bare hands. Take the time to find a pair of non-meltable cotton gloves or pliers in order to spare yourself and your group the suffering and inconvenience of a burn.

Next, dress for success! We don't mean that cooks should don puffy hats, white aprons, and little mustaches, but that open flames present hazards for certain types of clothing. Heat is the worst enemy of nylon, synthetic fleece, and Gore-Tex. Sparks can land and eat holes in your $300 mountain parka quicker than you can say "American Express." Also, take care to tie up long hair.

In brief, many of the safety techniques are very commonsensical. They may echo parental maxims from our youth, like "don't run while carrying scissors." We repeat them as short reminders, not as scoldings:

- Pour hot liquids away from you, so spills don't end up in your lap.
- Pour hot liquids into containers resting on the ground, not held in someone's hand. (Ouch!)
- Stir food in hot pots with the pot resting on the ground, not perched on a precarious stove or in the fire.
- Remove pots from the heat source before adding additional food. This prevents burned food bags and hands.
- Avoid passing hot pots filled with food over another person. This may result in severe burns, especially to the ankles and feet.

- Keep a filled water bucket nearby when cooking over a fire.
- When using a stove, keep an empty pot or billy can nearby to place over the stove to smother a flare-up.

COOKING TOOLS FOR THE BACKCOUNTRY KITCHEN

1. Two 1- to 2-quart cook pots or #10 "billy cans."
2. Pot grippers.
3. Fry pan oven.
4. Stovetop oven or ring pan.*
5. Hard plastic or metal serving spoon.
6. Plastic or metal spatula.
7. Collapsible plastic water jug or nylon water sack.
8. Metal or hard plastic (Lexan) cup, bowl, and spoon.
9. Cotton gloves.
10. Pot and pan storage bags.
* optional item

Figure 4.6
Cooking gear for the backcountry.

Each cook group of two to four campers should have the following items (Figure 4.6) to prepare a full range of outdoor dishes. For expeditions concerned with traveling as lightly as possible, or for trips where boiling water is the most complex function needed, scale down the cooking paraphernalia as necessary.

1. **Two 1- to 2-quart cook pots or #10 "billy cans."** We recommend two for many applications, including use as water carriers, clothes washers, showers, and cookstove snuffers in the case of flare-ups. Buy a set of stainless steel camping cookpots or use the low-tech, economical alternative: "billy cans." These large tin cans used for commercial food service serve as convenient and disposable cookpots. Look for billy cans at restaurants, schools, or other institutional kitchens.

TRICKS OF THE TRADE: Pot Lids
Bring a lid to facilitate boiling; covered pots boil much quicker, consuming less fuel than with uncovered pots.

2. **Pot grippers.** Many companies make some sort of pot-handling pliers. Some are more functional than others. In a pinch, common pliers or some types of plumber's wrenches work well, although they add weight to your pack.
3. **Fry pan oven.** Take a fry pan with a nesting lid. Look for fry pans without handles—you can save weight by using your pot grippers. The lid should fit over the fry pan, clamshelling the bottom so that ashes from coals on the top won't spill into the food inside.

4. **Stovetop oven or ring pan** (optional item). Several excellent stovetop ovens are on the market now, allowing campers to bake bread, cakes, and pizzas without building fires. We have had good experiences with the Outback Oven and the Bakepacker. An alternative is the old-fashioned ring pan (Figure 4.7), which made Bundt cakes in the '60s and '70s. Make sure to bring a nesting cover and make an 8-in. diameter stabilizer ring out of aluminum flashing to provide a solid base on top of the stove burner. Cut a 1 1/2-in. hole in the center of the flashing to allow heat to rise through the center column of the ring pan. This heat circulation bakes the contents evenly.

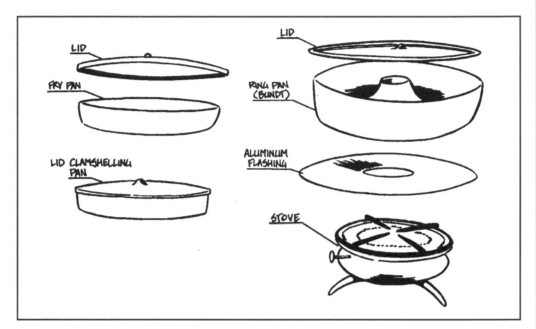

Figure 4.7
Use a stovetop oven (left) or ring pan (right) to cook delicious outdoor bread, cakes, or pizzas.

5. **Hard plastic or metal serving spoon.** A sturdy, big spoon helps to stir and serve food.
6. **Plastic or metal spatula.**
7. **Collapsible plastic water jug or nylon water sack.** This item helps in carrying and storing water from the water source to the campsite for cooking, bathing, and laundry. It should hold 1 to 3 gallons of water. The Mylar bags from inside wine boxes work well, although they retain memories of vino for months afterward.
8. **Metal or hard plastic (Lexan) cup, bowl, and spoon.**
9. **Cotton gloves.** These are to protect hands from burns and excessive drying when working around stoves and with fires.
10. **Pot and pan storage bags.** One or two cotton/polyester bags can be used to cover sooty billy cans and the stove.

QUALITY CAMPER TIP: Super Kitchen Organization

Meal preparation can be one of the most hazardous and frustrating times of the day. An organized approach saves headaches, streamlines the cooking process, and often results in better-tasting food.

- Keep the kitchen area distinct from the cooking area for safety.
- Lay out utensils, pots, and pans in an organized manner on ensolite pads, jackets, or stuff sacks. These "tablecloths" help keep everything clean and organized.
- Keep track of your utensils, especially when cooking with or near other cook groups. Pot grippers have a strange habit of disappearing and reappearing in someone else's food storage bag.
- Lay out food ingredients for the meal on "tablecloths" similar to those used for utensils.
- Open all food bags before starting to cook so that each may be readily added to the pot.
- Some incredibly (obsessively?) organized cooks arrange the opened bags of ingredients in the order they will be added to the pot. We're not sure why they really do this; they say it prevents them from accidentally doubling ingredients. You can be the judge.
- Finish all special preparations for the meal, such as mixing up tomato paste, rehydrating milk, or preparing pancake batter, before firing up the stove. This saves fuel and prevents a rushed atmosphere around a lit stove.

The Five Deadly Sins of Cooking

Well, they're not exactly deadly, but they could lead to poor cooking self-esteem or even invite revenge from hungry tent partners. We refer here to common mistakes in cooking that can occur to otherwise well-meaning outdoor chefs.

Thou Shalt Not Burn Food

The first and biggest bummer in outdoor cooking is burned food. You can only go so far with the line, "It's Cajun-style!" Save your stroganoff by

- cooking on low heat,
- stirring constantly,
- making sure there is enough water in the pot, and
- cooking with clean pots (old burned food on the bottom taints the new food).

Too Much Spice Is Not Nice

Just your luck. Your tent mate won the national Hot Chili Cookoff in Terlingua, Texas, for the last 3 years. And it's her turn to cook. Over-spiced food, whether too hot, too salty, too sour, or too sweet can be at best unpleasant and at worst inedible. Be considerate of your tent partners when cooking by:

- **Keeping spice levels relatively bland.** You can add more spices to individual portions if necessary.
- **Measure spices by the capful or pinch.** Do not pour spices directly from the bottle.

- **Be aware that spices often intensify during the cooking process.**
- **Experiment with one spice at a time.** Don't add five spices and wonder which one is out of balance.
- **Taste the food before adding any spices.** Adjust incrementally.

Not Enough Is Worse Than Too Much

Make sure that you've planned for the proper amount of cooked food. Accurate estimation of food amounts is difficult at first but should come with experience and careful observation of food levels on cooking pots. Generally, it is a slightly greater sin to cook too little food than too much. Can you imagine hiking 7 miles with a full pack and being served one cup of spaghetti? You'll be filling up on lunch food at that rate. On the other hand, if you cook too much, you can always pack away the leftovers to reheat for the next day's breakfast or dinner. Roughly speaking, one half of a 2-quart cook pot is enough food for dinner for two. Two thirds should be good for three people.

No Mush Is Good Mush

We refer here to the sin of overcooking food. Pasta that cooks too long, or sits undrained in a pot of water becomes pasty and gooey. Try to plan for the cooking times of the different ingredients accordingly. For example, barley or rice takes much longer to cook than does elbow macaroni, so add the noodles near the end of the cooking time for excellent noodle soup. Rehydrate dehydrated food items first for 10–15 minutes before cooking with them.

Leave Your Lumps Behind

The last cooking sin involves little balls of undissolved dry milk, tomato crystals, and flour or other powder floating like miniature islands in the dinner. Take a bite, and you'll see why we try to avoid them. Thoroughly mix powders in a cup or bowl before adding them to food on the stove. Use water sparingly—add a little at a time, since it's easy to add more water, but impossible to take it away when your sauce is too thin.

Cooking Suggestions

For a list of recommended cooking items and suggestions for turning them into great outdoor meals, see the food preparation list in the appendix section of *The Camper's Guide to Outdoor Pursuits*.

FOOD WASTE DISPOSAL

Now that you've cooked a pot of volcanic ash stew, which didn't go over well with the crowd, what do you do with it?

Not too long ago, it was an accepted practice to cast leftovers into the woods or water. Campers often thought that dispersal into the elements would disintegrate the food in short order. Today, with millions of visitors to wild areas, such actions are no longer viable. If we retained these food waste disposal methods, the woods would come to resemble a compost pile.

Improperly disposed-of food affects wildlife feeding patterns in the same way that inadequately protected food does: animals develop a taste for human food and may become habituated to it. Human food is often not good for animals as it introduces nutrients and chemicals not found in their ordinary fare.

Food waste contaminates water sources with nutrients, contributing to cultural eutrophication. (See "Water Treatment and Purification" in chapter 5.) In many cases, leaving food behind is illegal. Finally, rotting food near campsites and in the water causes a very negative aesthetic impact for subsequent campers. Who wants to look at soggy corn flakes in the eddies of a clear mountain creek?

Methods for Food Waste Disposal: Solid Food

Once you've finished eating and you're faced with solid leftovers, you have three choices for what to do with the leftovers. You can walk over to Juan and Stella's campsite and offer it to them, counting on the axiom that campers are always hungry. You can toss the food in an empty bag and eat it the next day; or you can bag it and pack it out to the trailhead, carrying it as a wet memento for the rest of the trip. It's that simple.

Some may argue that you could burn the leftovers in the fire. This is a good solution, providing the fire is hot enough and you don't have several gallons of soggy food to burn. Burning works well with small amounts of food and a very hot fire. Make sure that the fire burns solid food completely—unburned food can attract animals who may later dig up the firesite. Along the same lines, don't put food into a firesite if there is no fire burning. Animals will come!

Methods for Food Waste Disposal: Cooking Water and Food Particles

Minimal impact campers should be careful to remove all particles of food from waste-water. After a cookpot has been scrubbed, the dishwater usually is filled with particles of solid food. How can you remove these particles from the water? We recommend straining the particles with a wire or nylon mesh screen, and then packing out or burning the solid waste. The water itself may be scattered through the bushes at the edge of camp or poured into the corner of the fireplace. Make sure you are at least 200 feet from a trail or water source before scattering wastewater.

ENVIRONMENTAL TIP: Making Food Strainer Bags

If you haven't brought a screen, a strainer bag may be easily rigged up using twiggy or pine-needle-filled ground litter. Place a small amount of this pointy material in a thin plastic bag and squeeze it so that the twigs and needles inside puncture the bag. Now you can pour particle-filled wastewater into the bag; the water will flow out of the holes while the particles will be trapped in the twig-needle matrix (Figure 4.8). Pack out or burn the litter inside the bag.

We discourage the use of sump holes, or holes in which wastewater is poured, because our experience shows that they get dug up by animals. Unless you are very careful to strain all particles out of the waste-water, you are quite likely to cause a disturbance in animal feeding patterns when the critter smells the buried food scraps.

Figure 4.8
Food strainer bag using natural litter.

The Camper's Guide to Outdoor Pursuits

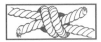

BOTTOM-LINE TIP: Food Disposal
When making decisions about food waste disposal, remember, "When in doubt, pack it out!"

DISHWASHING IN THE BACKCOUNTRY

Contrary to the traditional practice of scrubbing soapy dishes in the water source, our minimal-impact ethic tells us to wash dishes well away from water sources to prevent pollution. It can be a great challenge to resist letting the stream carry food scraps and soap suds away, but alternative methods are just as effective and simple.

First, clean off and properly dispose of solid and liquid food waste. Next, move to an area well away from the water source to clean the dishes (at least 200 feet is recommended). Fill the pot with a small amount of clean water and scrub with your fingers, mineral soil, ground litter, pine needles, pine cones, or other dead and down abrasives. In the winter time, snow makes an excellent scrub brush! Any natural litter used to scrub pots should be burned or packed out to prevent animal attraction.

Just like at home, tough, burned-on food in pots can be soaked overnight. In the morning they should be much easier to clean. In bear country this practice is not advised. Make sure to clean up thoroughly before going to bed at night.

Did you notice how we never mentioned using soap? This may be hard to swallow at first, but soap is not necessary to achieve a clean and hygienic pot. By cleaning utensils daily to remove cooking grease and clinging food, bacteria growth is inhibited. Sterilizing utensils and pots with boiling water just before cooking completes the hygienic circle. Soap can cling to pots, especially when rinsed with cold water, and cause diarrhea if ingested.

Either broadcast (disperse) rinse water at the edge of the campsite or pour it into a lit firesite, if bears are a concern.

BACKCOUNTRY FRYING AND BAKING WITH THE MUSKRAT PACK

One last hill. Shrugging on your day pack one last time, you are thankful that the day hike up Blueberry Hill in the DPNCA is almost over. Stella is hiking just ahead on the path and changes course at the bandanna that marks the turnoff to the campsite. You know that the site is a 2-minute walk at a 67-degree bearing off the main trail. The two of you make sure not to walk the same path to and from your wilderness campsite. The air is warm and fresh, and the sun casts pools of radiant light onto the rich forest floor. A dozen blue butterflies flutter in the sunshine nearby.

Just before you enter the campsite, you catch a delicious and incongruous scent. Warm, sweet, and comforting, you swear that the incredible odor belongs in an old-fashioned bakery. It must be bread! How can this be?

Drawn on by your nose, you float back toward camp, magnetized by the amazing fragrance of food. You've never felt this hungry! You desperately hope that you aren't imagining the scent and don't want to be awakened if you are dreaming!

Stepping through the bushes and into the sunlight of the campsite, you wearily take off your pack and swab at your forehead.

"Hey, Anne, where did you go?" you say. At once, you see that everyone is gathered around the campfire to watch Juan work at something. Everyone is eating pieces of something warm, white, fluffy—Bread!

"That's what I was smelling! How did you get bread out here?" you say.

"It was easy!" says Juan. "If you're interested, take a seat. I'm making another loaf."

Food for the Soul

Back to reality, folks. Juan and company aren't enrolled in a Chef Emeril correspondence course for culinary wizards. Baking bread, pizza, biscuits, cinnamon rolls, and wonderful desserts need not be a threatening undertaking. Almost anyone can do it! All you need is patience, skill, organization, and a little luck.

Some might ask, "Why bake in the backcountry? Isn't it too much trouble?" Baking does take a little extra effort, skill, and time. But we think the payoffs are worth it. Firstly, fresh-baked bread provides nutrients usually in short supply on an extended wilderness outing. Carbohydrates, protein, and B-vitamins come with each biscuit or brownie. Secondly, baked goods add variety and flavor to otherwise routine camping meals.

Perhaps most important is the positive effect on group attitude and morale that bread or a pizza brings in the deep woods. Homesick or uncomfortable campers get a big lift from the familiar presence of baked goods. Nothing shows loving care like a freshly baked cake. Try it!

Using Baking Powder

Baking powder is the relatively simple alternative to yeast that causes baked goods to rise. Cinnamon rolls, brownies, cakes, and some varieties of bread call for baking powder. Usually, you mix the dry powder in with flour and other dry ingredients before adding water, milk, or other liquids. Try using baking powder for your first adventures with backcountry baking, and then go for the challenge of yeast baking!

Quality Camper Tip: Bannock Bread Recipe

If you want to bake a quick and tasty pan bread, try this field-tested recipe, used for decades on WEA expeditions across the country.

Ingredients:
- 3 to 4 cups white flour
- 1/2 to 1 cup powdered milk
- 1/2 to 1 tbsp. baking powder
- pinch of salt
- 1 cup cold water
- optional spices and add-ins

Instructions
1. In a large fry pan or billy can, combine three quarters of the total amount of flour with all the salt, powdered milk, and baking powder. Mix dry ingredients thoroughly.
2. Use remaining flour for dusting your hands, dusting the pan, and adding to dough later.
3. Add small amounts of water to the dry mix and stir with a serving spoon. Continue adding water and stirring until the dough thickens to a point where stirring is difficult.
4. Add any items you wish for additional flavor and texture. Cinnamon, sugar, honey, raisins, sunflower seeds, cheese cubes, garlic, and the like make interesting additions.
5. Dust hands with flour and sprinkle about a handful of flour on the dough. Using fingers, fists, and knuckles, knead the dough so that all flour mixes thoroughly into the dough.
6. Continue adding flour and kneading until the dough can be picked up and manipulated by hand without sticking to fingers. The dough should be full of lumps but relatively smooth to the touch.
7. Form the dough into the desired shape for baking or frying (balls, loaf, flat breads, etc.). All dough should be completely prepared before starting the baking or frying process.
8. Bake or fry on a greased pan until light brown. Cool before eating.

Tools for Backcountry Baking: The Fry-pan Oven

Simplicity and multiple uses guide our selections for backcountry bakeware. The fry-pan oven, or the "tote" oven, can be used for either baking or pan frying food. The fry-pan oven consists of a 10-in. Teflon-coated frying pan and a nesting 10-in. lid. The lid should fit over the fry pan, completely covering it up so that ashes cannot fall into the food within. The lid should also have a lip around its rim to hold hot coals. Ideally, take a fry pan with no handle; the pot grippers suffice to manipulate hot pans.

Place the dough inside the oiled or cornmeal-sprinkled pan and cover. Make sure you fill the pan only half full, as baked goods rise. If the baked good touches the top of the oven, it will burn. Next, place the oven on a heat source. You can either use a stove on its lowest setting or a cooking fire. If you choose a fire, make sure the coals are completely level and stable. If you set the oven on sticks or logs, make sure they won't burn through and spill your cake into the fire!

The next step is to provide a heat source for the top of the oven. If you don't cook the dough from all sides, you'll get sticky goop instead of bread. Place glowing coals from the fireplace onto the top of the oven, and replace them when they cool down. If available, use hardwood coals, as they heat more evenly and for a longer period of time. Heat rises, so the top needs to be good and hot for about 20 minutes to cook the bread. Many campers start a small fire from pencil-sized branches. Make sure this fire is well tended. This type of fire dies out quickly and tends to drop burning embers onto the ground nearby.

Suggestions for Baking on Fires

- **Select hardwoods for baking fires, if possible,** since they provide the hottest, longest lasting coals. Make sure you have enough wood.
- **Many backcountry bakers choose to bake in one corner of the firesite.** They will enlarge one corner, in a keyhole pattern, to serve as the baking area. Others will pile a baking mound of mineral soil and bake on top of it off to the side of the fire.
- **Baking goes much more smoothly if two people help out.** One person can make and tend the fire while another makes and bakes the baked goods.
- **Use a small shovel and gloves** when transporting coals and moving hot ovens.
- **Regulate and check the heat of the coals** before and during baking. When holding an open hand 6-in. above the coals, an ideal temperature should feel hot, not searing. If you can't hold your hand 6-in. above the coals, they are too hot! Replace coals beneath and on top of the oven as they cool down.
- **Do not roast or attempt to cook baked goods by holding them directly in the fire.** This almost always ensures burned food!
- **Minimize lifting the lid off of the oven to check the baked goods.** The resulting cool air can cause the baked goods to "fall."

Suggestions for Baking on Stoves

- **Make sure you use the stove's lowest heat setting.** It's best if your stove has adjustable heat settings.
- **Rotate the stove top oven around the burner to ensure even cooking.**
- **Grease or flour the oven to keep food from sticking.**
- **Make sure the oven is completely level** so that batter or dough does not bubble out of the sides.

Yeast Baking in the Backcountry

We know it sounds ambitious to some—why not try neurosurgery in the woods? We admit that neither of us had ever touched yeast until the baking class on a wilderness expedition. (We mention this fact to show how easy it is to bake in the backcountry, not to illustrate our lack of initiative.)

If we may return to the "why bother?" theme, yeast-baked bread is to baking-powder bread as a Mozart symphony is to a limerick. Well, maybe that's a bit strong. Quick bread is good. Yeast bread is much better.

Yeast baking is an excellent leadership activity. The smell of yeast bread quickly wins the baker supporters, confidantes, and chums willing to agree to just about any issue brought up by the baker. A successful loaf of bread, properly donated to the masses, gains the baker respect, prestige, and good standing in any outdoor group. The spell usually lasts 2 days, or until somebody else bakes bread.

One of the reasons for the peerless power of fresh-baked yeast bread in the backcountry is its rarity. Few people find the time or patience to bake on most outings. Yeast baking takes several hours, good weather, and a good command of basic baking techniques.

How Yeast Works

To produce a high-quality loaf, the baker should have a working understanding of the science of yeast. First, what is it? Yeast are one-celled organisms that exist in a dormant state in the powder we buy in the store. They come alive when mixed with warm water and fed with sugar or starch.

Yeast need a warm environment to flourish, yet not so warm as to kill them. Generally speaking, the ideal temperature for yeast activity is 110°F or 43°C. People have many tests for determining whether water is warm enough. We suggest that you touch the water. If you can just feel the heat of the water, it lies somewhat above your body temperature of 98°F, or in the 100–110°F range. Add a little sugar or starch to give the yeast some food.

As the yeast eat the food, they release carbon dioxide gas as a by-product. As the bread rises in a warm environment, carbon dioxide is trapped in the bread. The yeast are sacrificed in the baking process, dying to give your bread its distinctive, warm flavor and adding nutrition as well.

QUALITY CAMPER TIP: Whole Wheat Pastry Flour

Use whole wheat pastry flour for good-rising bread. Whole wheat is high in gluten, which forms elastic fibers in dough. These fibers trap rising CO_2 bubbles, causing the bread to rise as well.

Use any good yeast bread recipe, whether found in a domestic cookbook, outdoor cookbook, or from friends. The NOLS Cookery provides several great yeast recipes.

QUALITY CAMPER TIP: Simple Yeast Bread Recipe

Basic yeast dough
Ingredients:
1. 3 to 4 cups flour (1/2 wheat and 1/2 white is fine)
2. 2 tsp. salt (a small spice cap equals about 1 tsp.)
3. 2 Tbsp. sugar
4. 1 Tbsp. butter or oil
5. 1 3/4 cup warm water
6. 1 Tbsp. yeast

Instructions:
1. Organize the kitchen area and ingredients. Be sure everything is readily accessible.
2. Heat water on the stove. Pour into a cup or bowl, and let it cool until it is warm to the touch. Add the yeast and 1 tsp. of sugar and stir gently. Allow this yeast solution to stand for about 5 minutes. The solution should show gas bubble formations within a few minutes and become frothy if the yeast is fresh and properly metabolizing. (Remember, the yeast will die if the water is too hot.)
3. If there are no signs of gas activity, you will need to start over.

4. Mix one half of the flour with the salt, remaining sugar, and butter or oil in a mixing pot.
5. Add the yeast mixture to the dry ingredients and mix thoroughly to develop gluten. The batter should become stringy.
6. Add the remaining flour, and continue to mix until the dough is thick.
7. Remove the dough from the mixing pot and place on a flat, clean surface where you can knead the dough.
8. Knead the dough by using the palms of your hands. Press the dough out and fold it in half. If the dough is sticky, add a small amount of flour.
9. The dough will be smooth and springy when done.
10. Shape the dough into a loaf and place in a well-oiled fry pan. Cover the pan with a plastic bag or a moist bandanna and let it rise for 1 hour or until it doubles in size. If it is a cold day, place the pan on top of a pot of boiling water.
11. Once the dough has risen, bake the bread for 30–50 minutes using the flip method, a twiggy fire on the fry pan lid with the stove on low heat, or on a fire. The bread is done when the surface is golden brown, crisp, and sounds hollow when thumped with a finger.
12. Cool for 5–10 minutes before cutting and serving.

A FINAL COMMENT

Never underestimate the power of food! It can raise a weary camper from seeming death, calm an anxious 12-year-old, soothe tensions between quarreling mates, and boost the joy and feeling of well-being of an outdoor adventure. Quality food and quality cooking take quality planning. The techniques are simple and just require time, willingness, and creativity. Think of cooking as part of your adventure!

Notes
[1]Forgey, W., MD. (1985). *Hypothermia: Death by Exposure*. Merrilville, IN: ICS Books, Inc.

References

Bird, P. (2000). *You Can Drink Too Much Water. Keeping Fit.* (725) University of Florida College of Health and Human Performance. Retrieved Dec. 14, 2005 from http://www.hhp.ufl.edu/keepingfit/ARTICLE/toomuchwater.htm

Boy Scouts of America. (1984). *Fieldbook* (3rd ed.). Irving, TX: Boy Scouts of America. (Original work published in 1944.)

Drury, J. (1986, Fall). Idea notebook: Wilderness food planning in the computer age. *Journal of Experimental Education, 9*(3), 36–40.

Drury, J., Ed. (2005). *The backcountry classroom: Lessons, tools and activities for teaching outdoor leaders.* Guilford, CT: Falcon Guide.

National Park Service. (2003). *Denali National Park and Preserve Bear-Human Conflict Management Plan.* United States Government Department of the Interior. Retrieved Dec. 14, 2005, from http://www.nps.gov/dena/home/resources/Wildlife/Bearmgmt/Appendix%20D.pdf

Medical College of Wisconsin. (2002). *US Obesity at an All-Time High.* Medical College of Wisconsin. Retrieved Dec. 14, 2005, from http://healthlink.mcw.edu/article/1031002183.html

Richard, S., Orr, D., & Lindholm, C. (Eds.). (1988). *The NOLS cookery: Experience the art of outdoor cooking* (2nd ed.). Lander, WY: National Outdoor Leadership School.

Simer, P., & Sullivan, J. (1983). *The National Outdoor Leadership School's wilderness guide.* New York: Simon and Schuster.

CHAPTER 5
From Soup to Tent Pegs:
Basic Camping Skills

"It is easier to stay out than get out."
—Mark Twain

> **Topics:**
> - Historical Perspective
> - The Case for Minimal Impact
> - Selecting a Campsite
> - Camping Cookstoves
> - Campfires
> - Human Waste Disposal
> - Water Treatment and Purification
> - How to Degrime in the Woods

WASHING CLOTHES

The Muskrat Pack in Paradise

Juan, Anne, and Stella chat quietly about loons and politics as the afternoon sun wanes on your canoe trip in the Drifting Paddle National Canoe Area. Paddling in the bow of Stella's canoe, you wear a weary smile as you round the last point on the lake and approach your night's destination: a beautiful wilderness campsite. As your canoes glide up to the shore, you see that you have neighbors. The Muskrat Pack is not opposed to sharing nature's beauty with other groups, but you sense you are in for a wild night as you walk to your site.

Passing the neighboring campsite, you dodge Frisbees and runaway Chihuahuas and re-coil from a campfire that could be seen from the space shuttle and is fueled with half-burned Paul Bunyan-sized logs. You shrink away from the shrieks of battling radios. Finally, you reach your site only to find a backcountry slum left by the last campers with cut pine boughs for sleeping and dish soap suds and food scraps fouling the water's edge. Fat, brazen squirrels loiter around the shelters like a street gang shaking down campers for nuts. You see what might be the aftermath of tropical storm Yogi with pizza boxes, diapers, broken lawn chairs and assorted bottles strewn around the shrubs nearby. Not entirely an appetizing prospect.

"Well," says Juan. "We seem to have lost paradise."

Defining Paradise

Although this scenario may sound extreme, most outdoor people have witnessed aspects of it at various times during their wilderness travels. If we are to experience the outdoors with minimal signs of human use while maintaining the integrity of backcountry ecosystems, we need a collective vision of what a quality outdoor experience should be. This vision will help us develop the skills and values to support it.

Picture instead an alternative scene for the ideal backcountry camping experience. To many campers, the ideal backcountry campsite gives us quiet and solitude, since we do not see or hear other campers. The campsite is fringed with healthy plant life and an absence of axe marks, human-made paths, filthy fire rings, litter, soapsuds, human waste, and trampled veg-etation. Birds chirp in the distance and the local critters are not overly friendly and are unused to human presence.

This chapter describes methods to maintain and restore such naturalness to a wide range of campsites. It also addresses the formation of an ethical standard for backcountry use behaviors that has a deep regard for the integrity of life in the wilderness along with reasonable and livable standards for human impact.

HISTORICAL PERSPECTIVE OF CAMPING

After World War II, many Americans enjoyed increases in disposable income and leisure time and had access to new technology, such as nylon and other synthetic fibers, welded aluminum pack frames, plastic products, and freeze-dried foods. These factors made camping easier and more enjoyable. As people flocked to the backcountry in growing numbers, they realized that the effects of traditional destructive camping practices were magnified because of the exponential increase in backcountry use.

In the last 10 years, people have slowly improved their stewardship of campgrounds and the backcountry. Congested campgrounds with traffic lines, high-impact practices, and crowds of semi-tame animals are fading into the past, as campers seem to value solitude and natural settings. More and more people turn to backcountry or "pristine" camping in order to rediscover the unspoiled beauty that their parents experienced in roadside campsites. However, these new users expand the circles of human impact into previously untouched spots. For these reasons and others, there remains much room for improvement in the methods and standards backcountry visitors employ in their day-to-day living in outdoor settings.

Figure 5.1
Islands of wilderness.

 PHILOSOPHY TIP: Human Impact
Much has been written about the phenomenon of "loving our parks to death" or the effects of the booming interest our culture has developed over the past quarter-century for our wild and protected lands. These wild areas are small in comparison to developed lands and the hundreds of millions of people living on them, and they become islands of wilderness in a sea of human-affected landscapes. How are these lands to retain natural wilderness ecosystems and interrelationships, or even to survive as refuges for wildlife? These are questions that wild land users cannot pass off to the experts and scientists; our impacts and sheer numbers loom too large.

THE CASE FOR MINIMAL IMPACT

Have you ever seen people play tennis with 19 people on the court? When you go to the movies, do you take off your big hat, lower your voice, and say "excuse me" if you spill your root beer on your neighbor? Should people throw out their empty popcorn boxes and light up their cigars after they leave the theater? Most people would say that tennis is not tennis with 19 people and that common courtesy should guide our actions in social settings like movie theaters.

Virtually all activities require standards, rules, and courtesies. We all use social skills to minimize our "impact" when attending a movie, play, or sporting event, so why not apply the same thinking to outdoor experiences?

We call the standards, rules, and courtesies of outdoor living "minimal-impact" camping techniques. As millions of outdoor recreators place increasing demands on limited outdoor resources, minimal-impact techniques have become essential for the health of natural ecosystems and the preservation of quality outdoor experiences for campers. In the movie theater or on the tennis court, lack of common courtesy may be a source of irritation, while in the backcountry, courtesy violations may decrease our enjoyment of the experience and scar the land for many years.

The standard bearer for minimal-impact camping is the Leave No Trace Center for Outdoor Ethics, a nonprofit program that teaches awareness and respect for natural areas. The center has established a nationally recognized set of skills and ethics and provides training for their application in a variety of ecosystems and many of the numerous outdoor activities we engage in.

There are seven principles of Leave No Trace (Table 5.1):

1. Plan Ahead and Prepare
2. Travel and Camp on Durable Surfaces
3. Dispose of Waste Properly
4. Leave What You Find
5. Minimize Campfire Impacts
6. Respect Wildlife
7. Be Considerate of Other Visitors

Table 5.1
Leave No Trace Principles with a Brief Description

Plan Ahead and Prepare
- Know the regulations and special concerns for the area you'll visit.
- Prepare for extreme weather, hazards, and emergencies.
- Schedule your trip to avoid times of high use.
- Visit in small groups. Split larger parties into groups of 4–6.
- Repackage food to minimize waste.
- Use a map and compass to eliminate the use of marking paint, rock cairns, or flagging.

Travel and Camp on Durable Surfaces
- Durable surfaces include established trails and campsites, rock, gravel, dry grasses, or snow.
- Protect riparian areas by camping at least 200 feet from lakes and streams.
- Good campsites are found, not made. Altering a site is not necessary.

In popular areas:
- Concentrate use on existing trails and campsites.
- Walk single file in the middle of the trail, even when wet or muddy.
- Keep campsites small. Focus activity in areas where vegetation is absent.

In pristine areas:
- Disperse use to prevent the creation of campsites and trails.
- Avoid places where impacts are just beginning.

Dispose of Waste Properly
- Pack it in, pack it out. Inspect your campsite and rest areas for trash or spilled foods. Pack out all trash, leftover food, and litter.
- Deposit solid human waste in catholes dug 6 to 8 in. deep at least 200 feet from water, camp, and trails. Cover and disguise the cathole when finished.
- Pack out toilet paper and hygiene products.
- To wash yourself or your dishes, carry water 200 feet away from streams or lakes and use small amounts of biodegradable soap. Scatter strained dishwater.

Leave What You Find
- Preserve the past: examine, but do not touch, cultural or historical structures and artifacts.
- Leave rocks, plants, and other natural objects as you find them.
- Avoid introducing or transporting non-native species.
- Do not build structures, furniture, or dig trenches.

Minimize Campfire Impacts
- Campfires can cause lasting impacts on the backcountry. Use a lightweight stove for cooking, and enjoy a candle lantern for light.
- Where fires are permitted, use established fire rings, fire pans, or mound fires.
- Keep fires small. Only use sticks from the ground that can be broken by hand.
- Burn all wood and coals to ash, put out campfires completely, then scatter cool ashes.

Respect Wildlife
- Observe wildlife from a distance. Do not follow or approach them.
- Never feed animals. Feeding wildlife damages their health, alters natural behaviors, and exposes them to predators and other dangers.
- Protect wildlife and your food by storing rations and trash securely.
- Control pets at all times, or leave them at home.
- Avoid wildlife during sensitive times: mating, nesting, raising young, or winter.

Be Considerate of Other Visitors
- Respect other visitors and protect the quality of their experience.
- Be courteous. Yield to other users on the trail.
- Step to the downhill side of the trail when encountering pack stock.
- Take breaks and camp away from trails and other visitors.
- Let nature's sounds prevail. Avoid loud voices and noises.

For more specific information for the area you will be traveling in, visit http://www.lnt.org

 PHILOSOPHY TIP: Outdoor Ethics

Ethics are the attitudes and behaviors you choose because they are the right things to do, even when no one is watching. Minimal-impact skills are the application of an outdoor ethic that values the integrity of existing wilderness life processes. Developing your personal outdoor ethic is a dynamic process; you may change your attitudes and actions after talking with people and observing the effects of common practices in the wilderness.

How to Do It (In the Woods)

We've divided the basic minimal-impact camping skills into six sections. Most of these skills can be used by outdoor enthusiasts in campgrounds and untouched backcountry sites.

A Note on Camping with Recreational Vehicles

Many outdoor people choose to use drive-in campgrounds and thereby greatly simplify the task of selecting a campsite. Some car campers need only consider if the campsite has hookups for the RV and whether the neighbors play bridge. We will see, however, that most of these skills can be used in established campgrounds as well as primitive backcountry sites.

SELECTING A CAMPSITE

People venturing away from the roadhead have two basic choices for camping: established campsites and pristine campsites. *Established campsites* are either designated by management agencies or show signs of frequent use. These campsites typically have firesites, level and bare tent sites, and sometimes an obvious means for food protection (discussed in Chapter 4).

Established, heavily impacted sites are generally considered to be good choices for most users of the backcountry. Since they are known by management agencies, they provide some security, and as they are already highly impacted, they are resistant to more user damage. Most decisions, such as where to tent, cook, and go to the toilet, are fairly obvious due to the setting and the various paths around the campsite. For these reasons, as well as comfort, established campsites are ideal for beginning campers, children, or anyone who wants a simple and safe place to sleep for the night.

On the other hand, *pristine campsites* are well off established trails and show no sign of human use. They should be used with care and left with as little evidence of human habitation as possible in order to discourage future use. For the adventurous types who desire the challenge, beauty, and solitude of the wilderness, proper use of pristine campsites demands a clear backcountry ethic and the discipline, patience, and expertise to adhere to these ethical standards.

A third category, *medium-impact campsites*, should be scrupulously avoided. These sites show signs of use, but are not as "blighted" or impacted as established camping areas. With further use, medium-impact sites become as scarred and trampled as established sites, thereby expanding the scope of human impact on natural settings.

When choosing a campsite of any type, ask yourself these questions:

- **Esthetics**—Is your group out of sight and sound of shorelines, trails, and other groups? Privacy affords the highest quality experience for you and others, and in many places, space between groups is the law!
- **Water**—Are you near enough to use a water source yet far enough away not to pollute it or drive animals away from it? (Check local regulations—usually 150–200 feet)
- **Ground cover**—Are you trampling delicate plants, or is the ground cover resilient? (Hardy surfaces are grass, sand, rock, or gravel bars.)

- **Firewood**—Are you near enough to appropriate campfire fuel (dead and down), if fires are legal and desired?
- **Wildlife**—Will your presence adversely affect wildlife feeding or travel habits?
- **Slope**—Will you roll downhill in your sleep or cause slope erosion with your feet?
- **Weather**—Are you exposed to wind in insect season or protected from it during cold weather? Are you protected from precipitation, lightning, and floods?
- **Overhead hazards**—Are dead trees, limbs, or loose boulders overhead? These become nasty wake-up calls in the middle of the night.
- **Aspect**—Is your campsite facing the appropriate direction to optimize sun and weather exposure according to your needs?

Always try to camp before everyone in your group becomes exhausted and before night-fall. Minimal-impact decisions and techniques tend to take a back seat when exhausted campers have spaghetti for legs and need to be poured into their sleeping bags. Stop early so that you have time to relax and enjoy the sunset. You earned it!

While You're in Camp

After you've set up your tent and are enjoying your night's lodging, keep a few things in mind. Avoid using the same paths over and over to get to your kitchen, your neighbors, the water, or your firesite. You quickly wear paths in pristine vegetation that may take a long time to heal and may attract other campers in the meantime. Also, *make no lasting changes to the campsite*. This may be a hard habit to break, but trenches around tentsites, nails and axe marks in trees, cut pine boughs for bedding, and native material stools and benches are not consistent with minimal-impact camping ethics. Extend this thinking to such temptations as a small patch of beautiful wildflowers. Look, but don't pick! This may be the toughest guideline, but it does make a difference in keeping floral species viable in the wilderness.

Breaking Camp

The final aspect of campsite selection is breaking camp and moving on. The Boy and Girl Scouts tell us to leave a site neater and better than we found it and typically leave a mountain of stacked firewood and raked fireplaces. Lacking the Scouts' enthusiasm, youth, and Merit Badge motivation, we civilians should nonetheless walk through every area of the campsite, including the kitchen, sleep area, water access, and toilet area and look for signs of impact.

Try to restore the natural appearance of pristine sites and the neat and litter-free condition of established sites. Pack out food wrappers, garbage, and anything you packed in. Leave deer antlers, arrowheads, Anasazi vases, and buried treasures. All of these are protected by federal law and the minimal-impact ethic. Just before leaving a pristine campsite, make it a personal challenge to camouflage all signs of your presence by sprinkling leaves on disturbed soil, "fluffing up" trampled pathways and tossing a stick in high-use areas to give the appearance of nature's chaos.

CAMPING COOKSTOVES

What type of stoves do we mean and when should one use them? The most efficient backcountry camping stoves are single-burner and lightweight and burn liquid fuels. The camper carries both stove and fuel. For a more detailed discussion of particular stoves and fuels, please see Chapter 3.

Stove Location

First things first. You arrive to your safe, comfortable and environmentally friendly campsite and now want to cook dinner. Where should you set up your cookstove at mealtime?

Choose a site that is

- level, to prevent stove tip-overs;
- stable, not balanced on the family dog's back;

- free of flammable materials—clear away pine needles, fuel tanks, and so forth; and
- protected from the wind.

Lastly, cook outdoors! Only cook inside a tent when you are in a blizzard on Mt. Everest or in similar conditions! In such close quarters, the dangers of fire or asphyxiation are extreme.

Stove Operation

How should you run your stove without blowing yourself up or burning down the woods? Read the operations manual for your particular model carefully, and keep in mind these general guidelines.

- Always refuel the stove well away from the cooking area as fuel fumes linger in the air, presenting a flare-up hazard.
- Extinguish open flames and cigarettes before handling stoves and fuel.
- Make sure that the top to the fuel bottle is securely threaded to avoid spills on the ground or in your backpack.
- Light match or lighter BEFORE turning on the fuel to avoid the camper's Big Bang.
- Tie back long hair; avoid loose, flammable nylon clothing.
- Crouch down when lighting the stove to be prepared to spring away from the stove if it flares up.
- Smother a flared-up stove with a pot or fire blanket. Do not use water, as it spreads the flames.
- Use cotton gloves and/or pot grippers when handling hot pots.
- Let the stove cool off before refueling or packing.

When to Use a Stove

Choose to cook over a stove rather than a campfire when you want time efficiency, simplicity, and almost no wilderness impact. Even though stoves are easy to use, they are the single most dangerous aspect of the backcountry outing besides the car that you drive to the trailhead. Imprudent techniques can result in fuel burns, hot pot burns, exploding stoves, and burned clothing and hair. Try to avoid these types of wilderness adventures.

QUALITY CAMPER TIP: Conserving and Storing Cookstove Fuel

When cooking, have your pot of water or food ready to place on the burner before you light the stove. This saves fuel and earns you the Efficient Camper merit badge. When you are ready to pack the stove, turn the fuel valve off and loosen the fuel cap to let pressure escape. Tighten the fuel cap and pack away in your pack. These actions minimize the risk of fuel leaking out in your pack. Remember to always pack both stove and fuel away from food in your pack to prevent fuel or fuel vapor from contaminating the food while you're in transit. Few things are less exciting than a white gas belch.

CAMPFIRES

When should you use a fire in the backcountry? It's up to you, and local regulations, to decide if a fire is appropriate.

Campfires and Safety, Environment and Comfort

Outdoor experts tell us that except in the case of an emergency, such as warming a hypothermic camper or signaling rescuers, fires are a luxury reserved primarily for cooking and atmosphere. Most people on short (1 to 5 days) trips probably don't need to use fires at all, especially since cookstoves have become simpler, lighter, and less expensive over the years.

When deciding whether to have a fire in the backcountry, consider safety and environmental consequences. In terms of safety, ask these questions: Will the duff catch on fire? Has the weather been exceptionally dry? Is the nearby vegetation exceptionally flammable? Will the firesite itself contain the fire?

In terms of environmental impact, additional questions must be answered. Can you find adequate fuel lying on the ground within a 2-minute walk of the campsite? If not, the area has been over-stripped of firewood and you should use your stove instead. Will the area naturally replenish the fuel you use in a reasonable amount of time (or is the area too heavily used)? Can you build and dismantle the firesite with no visual scars?

In most cases, an existing firesite at an established site greatly reduces both wildfire hazard and the potential for environmental damage. Use existing firesites before attempting to construct your own firesite.

ENVIRONMENTAL TIP: Selecting Firewood

We tell our students on backcountry expeditions that dead and down wood, which is the only acceptable fuel in most cases, plays an important part in the life cycle of the forest and should not be completely depleted. In other words, don't pick the forest clean; leave some down wood, especially close to the campsite.

The Stumps Select a Firesite

Let's return to the Stumps at their campsite in the mountains. They wanted a fire to make hot, sticky s'mores for dessert. Answering their safety and environmental questions, they found they had chosen to camp at a pristine campsite, there was little danger of forest fires, they had found ample fuel, the area was ecologically resilient, and fires were legal. However, there was no existing firesite. No s'mores for the Stumps? No way! Didn't everyone deserve a treat for hiking all day? Of course. But they shouldn't start a fire just anywhere.

If there is no existing firesite, in order to be safe and avoid sparking wildfires, build your firesite

- out of direct wind;
- away from flammable vegetation, such as grass and overhanging tree limbs;
- away from other flammable objects, such as tents and scarecrows; and
- near enough to water to put the fire out.

ENVIRONMENTAL TIP: Gravel Bar Campfires

One of the lowest-impact methods for building a firesite is to find a gravel bar at a river's edge. Choose an area completely devoid of organic soil or plant life well below the high-water mark. Scoop out an area and reserve the pile of gravel. Make your fire and scatter the ashes as normal. Return your original pile of gravel. When spring floods come, all remaining traces of your fire will be swept away.

Soil Composition and Campfires

In addition, look at the layers of soil to help you determine the best placement for a campfire. Generally speaking, soil has three layers, something like the strata in a layer cake. The uppermost layer is the *litter*, which contains fallen leaves, twigs, and natural organic matter. The litter layer can be highly flammable and should be protected from open flames and heat. The middle layer is the *duff*, which is decomposing and compressed organic matter on its way to becoming regular old dirt. Dark, woody, and rich, duff is also flammable and may smolder underground for days before bursting into flames. The duff must also be protected from fire. *Mineral soil*, inorganic and sandy, is not flammable and makes an ideal base for fires.

Firesite Construction

If there is no existing firesite and you haven't brought your backpacking hibachi, you'll need to construct a safe, fireproof, and minimal impact firesite that avoids scarring rocks with smoke and ashes.

The Mound Firesite

Dredge up mineral soil from a stream bed, the base of an overturned tree, or other exposed sources to construct an oval, raised mound. You may build this mound on a flat rock, a boulder, or on the ground. This leveled mound of soil should be at least 3 in. thick and 18–24 in. in diameter. Since mineral soil will not burn, you can build the fire on the mound, keeping the flames away from the edges (Figure 5.2). The site can be easily reclaimed by thoroughly soaking the remains, scattering the ashes, and returning the soil to its original location.

Figure 5.2
The mound firesite.

Zen and the Art of Fire Building

The Stumps had dug their fire pit, were ready to build the fire, and Forrest was beginning to yearn nostalgically for his s'mores. How do the Stumps build their evening campfire? Never fear, because Holly had brought a copy of this book. (She didn't burn this chapter, though, at least until she had a good bed of coals.)

The first step of fire building is to collect firewood. First, take a 15-minute walk away from the vicinity of your campsite to look for wood. You want to avoid depleting the area around your campsite of firewood, which would affect the ecosystem as well as possibly alert future campers to your presence. Generally, take what you find, as long as it's dead and down. Forrest Stump's lumberjack cousin, Buzz Stump, preaches: "If you need a saw, the wood is too big for a campfire." He's right. Wood of larger sizes is very difficult to burn down to ash in one or two nights. In the spirit of minimal-impact camping, we try to leave as little evidence of our fire behind as possible. Charred stumps and hunks of partially burned firewood contribute to the wilderness

"IF YOU NEED A SAW, THE WOOD IS TOO BIG FOR A CAMPFIRE."

Figure 5.3
Take it from Buzz Stump . . .

slum scenario we're trying to avoid. A second reason is that smaller-diameter wood is easy to break and eliminates the need for a saw. Collect wood of different sizes, ranging from toothpick-sized twigs to those an inch or so in diameter.

We call the different sizes of materials tinder, kindling, and fuel wood (Figure 5.4). *Tinder* is any material that ignites readily, such as dry tiny twiggies from nearby downed evergreen trees, downed birch bark, spruce pitch, dried grasses, belly-button lint, and paper. *Kindling* is small-diameter branches (less than 3/4 in.) that can ignite from the heat of burning tinder. *Fuel wood* is the larger pieces that provide heat for longer periods and generally should not be much larger than your wrist. If you can't break it into smaller pieces, it is too large.

TRICKS OF THE TRADE: Fire Fuel

If you have a choice of firewood, take softwoods (conifers, pine, spruce, cedar) for kindling, since these resin-filled woods burn hotly and quickly. For long-term heat, choose hardwoods (maple, yellow birch, cherry).

Collect what seems to be more wood than you need. Control your wood-collecting frenzy, however, or you may illustrate a classic but outdated old Scout adage. It goes something like this: "When you think you are finished collecting wood for a fire, look at the pile. Now go back and double that amount." What those busy little campers mean is that fires burn rapidly and can consume a pile of wood the size of a hay bale in an hour or so. However, use your judgment when collecting wood and then stack the fuel according to size within easy reach of the fire.

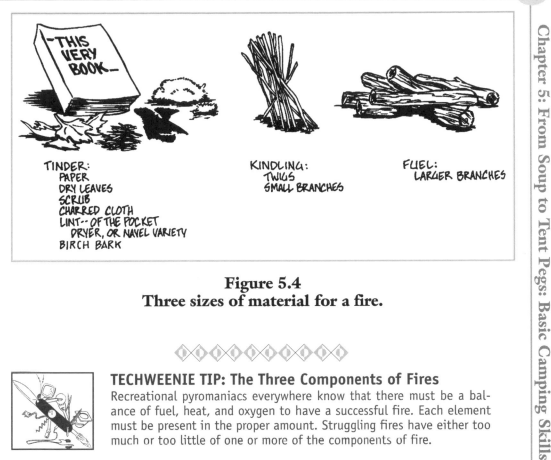

Figure 5.4
Three sizes of material for a fire.

TECHWEENIE TIP: The Three Components of Fires

Recreational pyromaniacs everywhere know that there must be a balance of fuel, heat, and oxygen to have a successful fire. Each element must be present in the proper amount. Struggling fires have either too much or too little of one or more of the components of fire.

Fuel: Wood provides the fuel in campfires. The key is to have the correct size of fuel for the amount of heat available. For example, 4-in. logs will not ignite from the heat of matchsticks. Rather, tiny bits of tinder will.

Heat: Heat ignites the fuel and must be balanced with it. Large fuel will not ignite until the heat of the fire rises to a temperature sufficient to heat the wood to the core. Water vapor generally lies close to the ground and will inhibit combustion; for this reason, ignite the fire a few inches off the ground.

Oxygen: The fire structure must have room for oxygen, yet be sheltered from smothering air currents.

Building the Fire

We suggest three basic methods of laying tinder and kindling to construct a fire (Figure 5.5). You may choose to mix the methods or use alternate means depending on fuel and weather conditions.

Figure 5.5
Three basic methods of building a fire.

In the *lean-to method*, lay a nest of tinder next to a larger piece of kindling or fuel. Lay a slanting roof of tinder and kindling over the highly flammable nest and ignite carefully. Make sure nobody sleeps in this lean-to.

The *teepee method* calls for stacking wood upright in an inverted cone around the nest of tinder. After lighting the nest, carefully add larger and larger kindling and fuel. The teepee will eventually collapse, usually after the fire has grown large enough to sustain itself. Teepees work well in rainy conditions, as the outer branches shelter the burning core and dry off from the rising heat.

The *log cabin method* is how Abe Lincoln built campfires as a kid in Illinois, according to local lore. For this method, lay a bed of medium-sized fuel wood 12–18 in length, then criss-cross additional pieces of fuel to form walls in a rectangular fashion. Lay your tinder nest within and partially enclose with a kindling roof. Young Abe would then ignite the tinder and do his homework by firelight, thinking about his 6-mile walk to school the next day. Log cabin fires provide excellent support for pots and pans with their stable right angles and flat tops.

◈▷◈◁◈▷◈◁◈▷◈◁◈

TRICKS OF THE TRADE: Homemade Fire Starters

Paper and homemade and commercial fire starters should not be scoffed at. These are valid and useful aids in wet or emergency situations. Even this book is not exempt from service as campfire tinder!

Eric has used two seemingly off-the-wall recipes for fire starters (Figure 5.6) that proved to work very effectively in cold, rainy situations. You can make *fireballs* by scraping the leftovers from old jars of petroleum jelly into a tin can and melting the jelly over a low heat on your stove at home. Add cotton balls to the melted petroleum jelly, cool, and store in film canisters. The cotton balls are impregnated with water-repelling

continued

petroleum jelly and burn hot and long, even in the rain! Just pinch a little wick in one of the fireballs, light, and place within your teepee or other fire shell.

You can also make *wax bombs* at home by filling paper egg carton cavities with 3/4 in. of sawdust and pouring melted candle wax on top. The wax seals the sawdust and soaks the egg cups. When cool, cut the cups into small pieces, bring into the woods and light them up. They burn cheerfully, even in the drizzling rain, and provide enough steady heat to dry and ignite small twigs to start your campfire.

◇◇◇◇◇◇◇◇◇◇

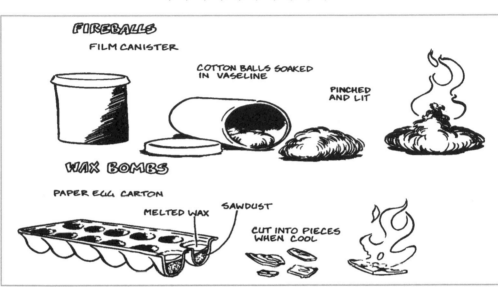

Figure 5.6
Making homemade fire starters is easy and inexpensive.

LIGHTING THE FIRE

Remember that heat rises, so hold the lit end of a match down, allowing the flame to grow large and burn up toward your fingers. (Watch it!) Some outdoor folks will ignite their tinder nest in the air, rotating it to allow the flame to burn upward into the center, and then they deftly insert the nest into a kindling cage. This takes practice. Also, light the fire from the upwind side of the fuel, so the wind blows the flame into the rest of the stack.

Keeping the Moths from the Flame: Safety Around the Firesite

Once you have your fire up and burning, you should consider some of the finer points of fire maintenance, management, and use. The most basic point is that fires consume fuel quickly and require careful and constant feeding. Beware that you don't feed the fire too much! It is amazing how quickly a small circle of flame-fascinated firebugs can build a cheerful little blaze into an inferno. Discourage those folks who would like to use "push fuel," or mammoth logs that can be burned a bit at a time and pushed further into the firesite as they are consumed. Not only are these burning trees a fire hazard, but they lead to either very large fires or lengths of charred timber when the fire is finished.

If you are concerned with the level of people traffic in and around the campfire, especially if your group is using the fire for cooking, appoint someone as a manager of the fire. One of Eric's groups gave one person the power to regulate traffic around the cooking fire by moving cook pots on and off makeshift grills and keeping a hazard- and people-free fire area. This "flame lord" saved people from unlucky burns, kept cook pots from upsetting, and fed the fire strategically.

Finally, dry boots and clothes with the greatest of care around a campfire. Snapping, popping, lively campfires regularly send out showers of sparks that can burn holes in expensive gear. Also, the intense heat of a fire can shrink and ruin boot leather, melt soles, and weaken the glue that keeps boots together. The best way to dry clothes in nonemergency situations is to wear them until they dry.

The Fire Aftermath: Extinguishing the Fire and Reclaiming the Site

The Stumps finished the s'mores and everyone came down from their sugar high. The fire snapped and crackled cheerfully as it burned some of the larger pieces of firewood. Holly stretched, gave a staged yawn, and suggested that everyone go to bed.

At this point, she could take a bucket of water and douse the fire, creating a wet, rolling fog reminiscent of a visit to a Turkish steam bath, but also leaving a black soup of soggy log ends and ashes. What would have been wrong with that? Well, the Turkish steam baths aren't the problem, but we can do without the ash soup. The Stumps thought about environmental and social consequences and chose a different course of action.

Our goal for minimal impact is to burn all wood down to ash so that no unsightly hunks of half-burned wood remain. These remnants tip off other visitors that there has been a fire in the area. Remembering our fundamental camping ethic in which we try to minimize signs of human use, we disguise all signs of our fires as a critical step in maintaining the natural quality of outdoor experiences. Another consequence of leaving evidence of our fires is that it encourages others to do the same, resulting in more wood being consumed, more fire scars, and the perpetuation of a damaging cycle of repeated use.

"THE FIRE IS SAFELY OUT WHEN YOU ARE WILLING TO RUN YOUR HANDS THROUGH THE ASHES."

Figure 5.7
Smoky Stump says . . .

All fires must be completely extinguished before the party leaves the campsite. Thoroughly douse the area with water until no steam arises. The Stumps' cousin, forest firefighter Smoky Stump, says, "The fire is safely out when you are willing to run your hands through the ashes."

The next morning, gather the sodden ashes and scatter them throughout the surrounding area, distributing them evenly so that the next campers cannot notice them. Scatter the ashes and return the mineral soil to where it was found.

Fires are a dangerous but central aspect to many campers' backcountry experiences. Unkempt and scarred fire areas left behind by irresponsible campers really disappoint and disgust many backcountry travelers. Ethical and safe firesite management is one of the most relevant and important skills one can gain from this book. Good luck, and save a s'more for us!

HUMAN WASTE DISPOSAL

"Uh-oh, Mom. Gotta go! Gotta go! Where's the potty?"

Sooner or later, you will hear this urgent statement, either from your children, someone else's children, your tent partner, or yourself. From our experience, it's amazing how much energy people put into worrying about or repressing this wonderful fact of life when in the woods, consequently damaging their health and risking the safety of others. We urge you to "Just do it!" and enjoy the simple pleasure of a little solitude in the wilderness.

But what an obvious conflict! In this society of convenience where we strive to flush our troubles away with the flick of a wrist, we're conditioned to find quick and easy solutions to waste disposal. The backcountry traveler must look at human waste disposal both as a natural process and one that requires an ethical commitment to proper disposal techniques.

Like most aspects of minimal-impact camping skills, human waste disposal involves a number of situational variables and requires decision making and judgment. In other words, you don't do "it" the same way every time.

Reasons for Human Waste Disposal (In Days of Old, When Knights Were Bold . . .)

Not very long ago, human waste disposal was not an issue. People urinated and defecated wherever the need arose. With increasing human pressure on wild areas, especially those that offer spectacular scenery, backcountry advocates recognize that the concentration of human waste has caused a variety of health, ecological, and esthetic problems.

Unfortunately, it is common to find human waste in odd and repulsive backcountry locations. In his research, expert scatologist T.P. Stump reports finding human waste on mountain peaks, the middle of trails, on rocks in stream beds, and even in trees several feet off the ground! Yuck! Unfortunately, people who should know better don't show it through their actions. Too many campers pick human waste disposal sites out of self-centered convenience and walk away without thinking of the consequences of their choices.

Esthetic Impact of Human Waste Disposal

Many people go to undeveloped natural areas for an experience of beauty, solitude, and little evidence of human activity. Human waste is one of the rudest reminders of human presence. Wild area users need to adopt attitudes and actions consistent with the preservation of natural beauty, both out of respect for the wilderness and other people.

Ecological Impact of Human Waste Disposal

Human waste carries with it profound potential for tainting water supplies with waterborne diseases such as cholera, typhoid, intestinal viruses, and giardia. Humans can contract these diseases by drinking contaminated water. Some animals, such as coyotes, bighorn sheep, beavers, and cattle may also carry these waterborne organisms spread by human waste.[1]

Figure 5.8
Dr. T.P. Stump, expert scatologist.

Methods for Human Waste Disposal

Existing Toilets and Outhouses

Just as you would build a fire in an existing campfire ring in preference to building a new firesite, we suggest that campers use existing toilets and outhouses whenever possible. This concentrates and contains waste matter in one area. Especially in heavily used areas, we strive to avoid scores of individual deposits of human waste both for esthetics as well as to decrease the chance of water source contamination. You need not dig a hole when urinating; just observe the guidelines for water source protection; for example, 200 feet from a water source.

Cathole and Latrine Use in the Backcountry

When you have to go and no outhouse is within sprinting distance, you'll need to use the most widely accepted method for depositing human solid waste, the cathole. Catholes, located at least 200 feet from the nearest water source, are small holes dug into the ground, usually 6 to 10 in. deep and 5 to 10 in. in diameter, located in an inconspicuous spot where others are unlikely to walk or camp. They can be dug with a small shovel or trowel and are designed to be used only once. Be sure to replace any soil you have dug out and camouflage the site after you have used it

If catholes aren't practical because you will create too many during your stay or are camping with young children, then latrines are a wise choice for human waste disposal. A latrine, like a cathole, is basically a hole in the ground, but with creativity and ingenuity can provide a comfortable, odor-free, hygienic means of answering nature's call. Dig them 8–16 in. deep, 18 in. or more square. Properly constructed and used, latrines save the local environment from an ever-widening circle of human waste sites and instead concentrate the waste in one area. Of course, this concentration creates other problems, as the area surrounding a latrine takes much longer to recover. You'll have to weigh the issues with each situation.

QUALITY CAMPER TIP: Catholes versus Latrines

In high-use areas, outdoor experts suggest that concentrating waste is preferable to dispersing impact, since we can't always rely on people to disperse the impact acceptable distances away from high-use camp-sites. Aside from the "sudden call of nature" scenario, you might choose to use catholes when you are with experienced campers in a light- to moderate-use area. Experienced campers are more likely to choose re-sponsible human waste sites, and in a pristine setting you won't worry as much about creating a waste-filled mine field, such as that which develops when catholes are used in highly camped areas.

Soil Layers and Human Waste Disposal

For the construction of the cathole and latrine, we need to review the information about soil layers that we introduced with fire pits. Soil's top two layers, the litter and the duff (humus), contain organic matter, while the bottom layer, the mineral soil, contains inorganic ("not living") materials.

While in the case of fire pit construction we seek to avoid and protect the organic layers from combustion, with human waste disposal we seek to place solid waste where it will decompose most quickly. Leaving human waste on the surface where it is exposed to the elements leads to the most rapid decomposition, but for obvious reasons this is only appropriate in some remote regions. The soil level with the most bacteria and organisms that break down waste is the organic or duff layer. For this reason, bury human waste within the duff layer.

PPPD: Three Ps and a D

These four letters can help you remember critical factors when constructing catholes and latrines.

Pollution

Make sure all catholes and latrines are located at least 200 feet away from water sources and are situated in well-drained soil. Avoid places that could be flooded during wet spells.

Proximity

When constructing a latrine, choose a site close enough to the campsite that group members will find it easily and quickly. Otherwise, people may use multiple or inappropriate sites. It is a good idea to show people the way to the latrine site and to mark the site with a bandanna or hat.

Privacy

Choose a latrine site that affords a reasonable amount of privacy, especially when camping with young people, new campers, or new acquaintances. If the site affords insufficient privacy, people will either delay relieving themselves or they will reject the latrine and choose their own little hideaway off in the forest.

Depth

Dig latrines and catholes into the duff layer (Figure 5.9), but not so deep as the mineral layer. Usually this translates as somewhere between 8 and 16 in. deep depending on where you are. Campers need to find a balance between digging shallow holes, which provide for the fastest decomposition, and holes that are too shallow, since waste sites can be dug up by animals.

Figure 5.9
Dig catholes and latrines no deeper than the duff layer.

QUALITY CAMPER TIP: Building Super Latrines and Catholes

In addition to PPPD, the quality camper will strive ever onward into the airy heights of latrine and cathole refinement. Consider these points:

- Choose a comfortable site (next to a downed log or boulder to lean on).
- Make sure the latrine site isn't so comfortable as to be chosen as a tent site or kitchen by next campers.
- Shape: Square, rectangular (easy to straddle), oval, star, be creative!
- Cut out the duff layer and set aside.
- Leave a pile of soil next to the hole with shovel.
- Close the latrine when the waste reaches 3 to 4 in. from top.
- Replace the soil and duff layers; blend into surroundings.

Using Catholes and Latrines

All right. We know everybody knows how to fill catholes and latrines, but what are the techniques for making them as simple and hygienic to use as our homebound porcelain?

- **Sanitary practices**—Wash hands after use—this is extremely important in maintaining good health and preventing the spread of intestinal illness; keep waste off shovel; keep waste in latrine. It's hard to put enough emphasis on maintaining the highest standards for sanitation. Many trips have ended because group members did not adequately wash their hands after using the latrine, causing diarrhea and other gastrointestinal illnesses to spread through the camp. Be sure to wash your hands with soap after using the latrine!
- **Toilet paper**—Use only the amount of toilet paper that is absolutely necessary, and use only plain, white, non-perfumed brands. To properly dispose of your used toilet paper, it should either be thoroughly buried or placed in a plastic bag and packed out. Experiment with natural toilet papers such as leaves, sticks, stones, and snow, as they can be very hygienic and pose no environmental problems; just don't use the poison ivy.
- **Covering up**—Completely cover and camouflage your cathole, and if using a latrine, sprinkle soil on waste after each use. This helps speed decomposition and keeps flies and odor to a minimum.
- **Place only human waste in latrine.** Food waste, tampons, and trash attract animals and may not decompose readily and should never be placed in an outhouse, cathole, or latrine. Pack out or thoroughly burn these items.

The Final Message: Deal With It!

The issues surrounding human waste disposal are sometimes awkward, but are universal, eternal, and always require attention from campers and good judgment. Ethical and consistent human waste disposal policies distinguish experienced and conscientious backcountry users. Nature calls us to deal with these issues, so have fun with them! Relax, dig in, and deal with the issues!

WATER TREATMENT AND PURIFICATION

As a logical step after human waste disposal we turn to water treatment. How well you take care of human waste has a direct bearing on the water supply that you and others in the outdoors depend on. In other words, as our water purity expert, Dr. Flo Stump, says, we're all

downstream. We're downstream from decaying organic matter, dead fish, closed mines, campfire sites, upstream bathers, and improperly disposed-of human waste. Guess what? It's time to fill up our canteens!

 **ENVIRONMENTAL TIP: Where Does Our Water Come from, and Where Does It Go?**
We're all part of the water cycle and are connected to other users and abusers of water quality. Make sure you are a clean and responsible user of water in the backcountry, your homes, and workplaces.

Our goal is to acquire clean, clear drinking water that doesn't make us ill. There are several methods to reach this goal; each has distinct advantages and disadvantages.

When Should We Purify Water in the Backcountry?

Although the evidence is becoming clearer that, in the backcountry, most infectious illnesses are transmitted by poor hygiene rather than by the consumption of contaminated water, we still advocate that you take steps to purify water whenever you have doubts about the water's purity. If you suspect animal, geological, or human contaminants upstream, purify the water. Unfortunately, as human presence in the backcountry increases, so does the risk of ingesting contaminated water. As a rule, there are few places in the world free of contaminants such as pathogenic bacteria, protozoans, and enteroviruses.

 **BOTTOM-LINE TIP: Staying Healthy in the Outdoors**
Three practices will go farther in assuring your health in the outdoors than anything else. They are:
1. Washing your hands thoroughly and often.
2. Not sharing water bottles or letting people reach into your snackfood bags.
3. Treating your water for all common microorganisms (bacterial, protozoan, and viral).

What Is in the Water That We Have to Treat For?

The first group of contaminants, bacterial and protozoan pathogens, are single-celled, microscopic organisms that can multiply and cause sickness. The little beastie with the baddest backcountry reputation is *Giardia lamblia,* which can cause the gastrointestinal illness giardiasis. This critter lives in a dormant phase as a cyst carried by all mammals, including humans. Mammals defecate in or near water sources, which releases millions of cysts into the streams and ponds. Scientists have found that a single stool can contain up to 300 million giardia cysts. Ingesting as few as ten cysts can cause the disease.

Although most infected individuals with giardia (75%) do not develop symptoms, it is not uncommon for individuals to develop the disease and require professional medical treatment. The symptoms of giardiasis are diarrhea, sharp abdominal cramps, flatulence, nausea, sulfurous belching, and an eventual nutritional deficiency due to malabsorption of nutrients.

A second category of waterborne pathogens includes enteroviruses or intestinal viruses. These pathogens are simpler and smaller than bacteria and cause rapid-onset, flu-like illnesses that usually subside in 24 to 48 hours. Other microorganic illnesses are prevalent in developing countries other than the United States and are of great concern for travelers there. We recommend consulting Dr. William Forgey's book, *Travel Medicine*, before traveling abroad.

Figure 5.10
Dr. Flo Stump, water purity expert.

How Do I Purify Drinking and Cooking Water?

Boiling

Although scientists, experts, and woods sages give a wide range of information about the temperature of the water or boiling time to ensure pure water, our sources indicate that simply bringing water to a boil will kill all major pathogens found north of Mexico, including giardia.[2] Boiling is cheap and 100% effective, but takes some time and consumes wood or stove fuel. For these reasons, boiling is not convenient for purifying drinking water along the trail. Water used in cooking need not be otherwise treated if it comes to a boil.

Chemical Purification

Here's a twist: we go deep into the woods for an experience of solitude, simplicity, and clean living, and we're ADDING chemicals to our drinking water? Something's wrong with this picture. Or is it? Many backcountry old-timers and programs choose chemical purification over other methods, hands down. Why?

Crystalline iodine products such as PolarPure work when water is added to a bottle containing iodine crystals. The crystals dissolve a tiny bit to supersaturate the water with iodine. When added to untreated water, the iodine solution kills all microorganisms, including viruses.

The advantages of crystalline iodine products are that, if used correctly, the method is completely effective, is relatively inexpensive, has an unlimited shelf life, and each bottle can purify thousands of liters. On the flip side, the water must sit for 20–60 minutes to become purified, which poses a challenge, especially for people who have difficulty anticipating their water needs and waiting the necessary time for the water to be purified. Be advised that the colder the water, the longer you need to wait for complete disinfection. Also, treated water has a slight chemical taste, and some people may be intolerant to iodine in their systems.

Iodine and chlorine tablets work on the same principle as crystalline iodine: they form a chemical solution that kills microorganisms. Usually this involves dropping one or two tablets into a water bottle, disinfecting the bottle threads by inverting the loosely capped water bottle and allowing a bit of treated water to seep out of the threads, and waiting the recommended time period. Iodine tablets are a good choice for infrequent campers because they are simple to use, inexpensive, and completely effective. The tablets have the same disadvantages as crystalline iodine; plus, the iodine tablets have a limited shelf life, becoming inert after several months, especially after the bottle is opened. In addition, chlorine's effectiveness against giardia has been questioned.

Filtration

You've heard the pitch. The Super Aqua Gizmo with Secret Adapter B52 will purify 10 gallons of water a whack and turn sludge into champagne. At only $399 for the base model plus $299 for each disposable Secret Adapter, you can't miss. Now just wait a second. The Gizmo would be a bargain for the military, but should we take out a second mortgage to buy it?

TECHWEENIE TIP: Filter Comparison Chart

Table 5.2 presents the information you need to compare current water purifiers that treat protozoa, bacteria, and viruses. Thanks to the people at Moontrail for compiling this information.

Water Purifiers Table - Water purification systems designed to eliminate protozoa, bacteria, and viruses

Water filters + purifiers: eliminate protozoa, bacteria, viruses

Manufacturer	Model	Weight min (max) oz	Flow Rate (quarts per minute)	Price	Extra filter	Cost per gallon*	Filter life (gallons)
Exstream	Orinoco	7.7 (7.7)	1.0 qpm	**$39.95**	$30	$1.15	26 g
Exstream	Mackenzie	7.8 (7.8)	1.0 qpm	**$49.95**	$30	$1.15	26 g

Water filters + purifiers + "structured matrix": eliminate protozoa/bacteria, bad taste, organic chemials, viruses

Manufacturer	Model	Weight min (max) oz	Flow Rate (quarts per minute)	Price	Extra filter	Cost per gallon*	Filter life (gallons)
General Ecology	First Need Deluxe	13.3 (15.6)	1.8 qpm	**$85.95**	$36	$0.29	125 g
General Ecology	Base Camp	64.8 (80.6)	high	**$480**	$72	$0.13	500 g

Water filters + activated carbon + purifiers: eliminate protozoa, bacteria, bad taste, organic chemicals, viruses

Manufacturer	Model	Weight min (max) oz	Flow Rate (quarts per minute)	Price	Extra filter	Cost per gallon*	Filter life (gallons)
MSR	Sweetwater Purifier System	9.9 (14)	1.3 qpm	**$74.95**	$34.95 (filter) $8 (ViralStop) *combined:*	$0.18 $0.10 $0.25	200 g 80 g

Water purifiers: kill/inactivate protozoa, bacteria, viruses

Manufacturer	Model	Weight min (max) oz	Flow Rate (quarts per minute)	Price	Replacement batteries	Cost per gallon*	Battery life (gallons)
MSR	MIOX	3.5 (8.0)	no pumping	**$129.95**	2 x CR123	$0.40	50 g
Hydro-Photon	SteriPEN	3.7 (8.0)	no pumping	**$149**	4 x AA	$0.75	Li: 18 g Alkaline: 8 g

*Cost per gallon = price of replacement filter divided by filter life

Compiled by: Moontrail (http://moontrail.com/)
http://moontrail.com/hydration/filters.html

Chart information used by permission.

Well, it depends on when and how often you need drinking water. Most filters work by screening particles and bacteria from water by using ceramic or microporous filters. By pumping the filter you force water through the filter. Slowly. Most filters take 1 to 3 minutes to pump a liter of water. Some filters speed up the process by combining a larger screen and an internal method of iodine treatment. These filters provide the advantages and disadvantages of each method.

The advantages of filtration are that it does not adversely affect water taste, it can be used quickly alongside the trail (compared with other methods), and the method is generally effective. Disadvantages of filters are the initial cost, the cost of replacement cartridges, the fact that most filters are ineffective against viruses, and that pumping takes time and energy. Users of filters must take care when handling and storing the filter since untreated water may easily come off the filter intake and contaminate the outflow end or the drinking water bottle. Unfortunately, it seems that the higher the complexity of the water filter, the more likely it will break down and need daily maintenance. If you are not the type of camper who will take painstaking care to clean your water filter and keep track of a dozen tiny parts, choose another way to spend your money.

SUMMARY

In recent years Jack and his family have joined with two other families on a series of canoe trips in the desert southwest. Each family seemed to have at least one member come down with a case of giardiasis within a couple of weeks after the trips, even though we all used the same methods to treat our water. We couldn't figure it out until Jack attended a presentation by Dr. Tom Welch, whose research indicates that it is not the water that is transmitting these illnesses but poor personal hygiene practices. When someone is a carrier of an infectious illness and he or she handles water bottles or other containers (bug repellant and sunscreen) or shares bags of trail food, the infection can be spread to others who touch these items. Thus, it is even more important to practice good personal hygiene (i.e., wash your hands) than to treat the water. Armed with this information we were much more careful to wash hands regularly, and snack foods were stored in recycled Gatorade bottles. That way people couldn't reach into and contaminate the snack foods; they had to pour them out directly into the hand. Lo and behold, on our most recent 2-week trip on the San Juan River, no one got ill.

Know that you can always depend on boiling water in order to provide drinkable water, but since that isn't always convenient, what should you buy? If you can tolerate the taste, have no adverse reactions to iodine, and have budget constraints, our recommendation is to choose a crystalline iodine product, such as PolarPure. If you can afford it and want a more comprehensive system, go with one of the systems in the table above. Note that the cost of the purifier isn't just in the initial cost. You have to figure in the cost of replacement filters, or, in the case of the electronic systems, the cost of replacement batteries.

RUB-A-DUB: CLEAN LIVING IN THE GREAT OUTDOORS, OR HOW TO DEGRIME IN THE WOODS

"Oh, darling. The mountains are rapturous and the air is divine, but I can't wait to get back to Fifth Avenue and my bathtub."

Has this happened to you? How many times have you felt that the only thing missing from your week in the Grand Tetons was a hot shower? How many times have you left only footprints in the wilderness but took back pictures, memories, and an inch of body dirt? Never fear—there are ways to wash up in the woods that preserve ecological integrity, personal health, and self-respect.

On the other hand, Woody Stump and his circle of grungy go-getters hold that excessive cleanliness, with the exception of clean hands and face, has been overrated by Madison Avenue and the soap industry. Jack agrees, citing his so-called Drury Dirt Scale, which traces the increase in body grime over the course of a backcountry trip. Many wilderness old-timers say that over the first 4 days you get really dirty, and after that you don't get much dirtier. Some

Figure 5.11
Some people say you can only get so dirty.

people maintain that your body begins to "clean itself" after several days and the layer of body oil helps maintain body moisture and heat and provides a barrier against sickness. Or it can make you sick. This depends on your point of view. The point is that good personal hygiene is important but not necessarily as much as Madison Avenue would lead you to believe.

So What's the Big Deal About Bathing?

Why don't we just soap up in the lake, have a swim to rinse off, and call it a day? Most backcountry users don't need to have had the experience of dipping a cup of soap suds downstream from a bather to appreciate the reason we suggest not bathing in water sources. Yecch!

Biodegradable Soaps

A few years ago, most soaps and shampoos contained phosphates and other chemicals toxic to stream life because they broke down too slowly or not at all. More recently, manufacturers have marketed new soaps as "biodegradable." These products break down into simple compounds that are nutrients to water system organisms or are inert. Unfortunately, even biodegradable soaps pose an impact to water systems because they act as nutrients for plant life.

Figure 5.12
The Stumps take turns rinsing off the grime.

TECHWEENIE TIP: Eutrophication in Wilderness Water Sources

Soaps, acting as nutrients to aquatic plants, contribute to a phenomenon known as cultural eutrophication, the human-induced acceleration of lake and pond life cycles. In this process, plant life blossoms with the increased food supply (provided by soaps and other nutrients of human origin) and makes the water cloudy. The algae-filled water cuts off the sunlight that aquatic plants need for photosynthesis. The absence of photosynthesis kills many aquatic plants. As they die, bacteria and microorganisms feed on the dead plants, consuming much of the available oxygen. The decreased availability of oxygen kills many oxygen-dependent species, including insects and fish. We don't know the extent of the effects wilderness users have on eutrophication, but we maintain that every effort should be taken to avoid the process.

Steps for Backcountry Bathing

We recommend a three-step method for minimal-impact bathing in backcountry settings.

1. Preparing for the Bath. Fill two or more containers with fresh water from the water source. (We use #10 cans from restaurants known as "billy cans.") Optionally, you may heat one or more over a stove or fire. Select a site at least 150 feet from the water source where soapy water will be absorbed by the soil.

2. Bathing Cycle. Take a dip in the water source in order to get wet. Walk to your bathing site and apply biodegradable soap.

3. Rinse Cycle. At the bathing site, have a partner carefully pour water over your head and body to rinse off soap. If necessary, have your partner run down to the water source to refill the buckets. Once there is no visible soap on your body, take another swim in the water source for a final rinse. Voila! You're now squeaky clean, invigorated, completely awake, and the stream or lake is still as clean as when you started!

The Brand X Challenge: Washing Clothes in the Backcountry

Now that you're dirt-free, how about the grimy togs you're wearing? Usually, polypropylene underwear smells worse than the person wearing it. Many of the same principles used in human bathing apply to washing clothes.

1. Soak Cycle. Soak clothes in water source. Fill two containers with clean water and go to a washing site identical to a bathing site.

2. Washing Cycle. Wash clothes in one container, using soap as necessary. Some campers choose to use warm water instead of soap. The results are sometimes as good as when using soap.

3. Rinse Cycle. Rinse clothes in the other container, replacing water until all suds are removed from the clothing. Make sure the clothes are completely free of suds, since soap can cause skin irritation. Do not rinse the clothes in the water source. Dispose of the dirty water at a well-drained site approximately 150 feet from the water source.

Try to bathe every day for good hygiene, health, and spirits. If this is impossible, try to spot-wash face, hands, armpits, and crotch regularly.

A FINAL THOUGHT

Backcountry minimal-impact camping skills require practice and discipline in order to protect the environment and a commitment to a personal environmental ethic to help guide individual actions. Usually, one's standards and skills increase side by side, and you may find that the practices you use this summer will change the next year as you witness the increasing effects of recreators in the wilderness. Lastly, keep personal and group safety first and foremost in your mind as you set about cooking, hanging food, starting fires, or engaging in any of the many backcountry camp tasks. You want this trip to be the first in a long series of safe, exciting, and rewarding ventures into the wilderness.

Notes

[1]Hampton, B., & Cole, D. (1988). *Soft Paths*. Harrisburg, PA: Stackpole Books.
[2]Forgey, Wm., MD. (1994). *Wilderness Medicine* (4th ed.) Merrilville, IN: ICS Books, Inc.
[3]Ibid.

References

Backer, H. (1989). Field water disinfection. In Auerbach & Geehr (Eds.), *Management of wilderness and environmental emergencies*. St. Louis: C.V. Mosby.

Boy Scouts of America. (1984). *Fieldbook* (3rd ed.). Irving, TX: Boy Scouts of America. (Original work published in 1944).

Cole, D.N. (1986). *NOLS conservation practices*. Lander, WY: Author.

Drury, J., Ed. (2005). *The backcountry classroom: Lessons, tools and activities for teaching outdoor leaders*. Guilford, CT: Falcon Guide.

Hammitt, W.E., & Cole, D. (1988). *Wildland recreation: Ecology and management* (p. 34). New York: John Wiley & Sons.

Hampton, B., & Cole, D. (1988). *Soft Paths*. Harrisburg, PA: Stackpole Books.

Hart, J. (1977). *Walking softly in the wilderness*. San Francisco: Sierra Club Books.

Kahn, F.H., & Visscher, B.R. (1977, April-May). Water disinfection in the wilderness: A simple method of iodination. *Summit, 23*(3), 11–14.

Jacobson, C. (1986). *The new wilderness canoeing and camping*. Merrilville, IN: ICS Books, Inc.

Mason, B.S. (1939). *Woodcraft*. New York: A.S. Barnes & Company.

Meyer, K. (1989). *How to shit in the woods*. Berkley, CA: Ten Speed Press.

National Outdoor Leadership School. (1994). *Leave no trace: Outdoor skills and ethics: Rocky Mountains*. [Manual]. Lander, WY: National Outdoor Leadership School.

Peacock, D. (1990, October). A practical guide to grizzly country. *Backpacker, 18*(6), 80–85.

Petzoldt, P. (1984). *The new wilderness handbook* (2nd ed.). New York: W.W. Norton & Company (Original work published in 1974).

Philips, J. (1986). *Campground cookery: Outdoor living skills series* [Instructor manual] (2nd ed.). Jefferson City, MO: Missouri Department of Conservation. (Original work published in 1983).

Schimelpfenig, T., & Lindsey, L. (1991). *NOLS wilderness first aid*. Lander, WY: National Outdoor Leadership School.

Simer, P., & Sullivan, J. (1983). *The National Outdoor Leadership School's wilderness guide*. New York: Simon and Schuster.

Vivian, E. (1973). *Sourcebook for environmental education*. St. Louis, MO: C.V. Mosby.

Wilderness Education Association. *Instructor's Manual* [Manual]. Unpublished.

CHAPTER 6
Wilderness Travel: Finding Your Way

"I'm also good at dematerialization. Once, using only a map and compass for props, I made myself and two companions vanish for three days in a Montana wilderness area. I have attempted to repeat this feat several times since and have succeeded."
—*Patrick McManus,* They Shoot Canoes, Don't They?

Topics:
- Navigation
- Maps
- The Compass
- Combining the Map and Compass
- Route Planning and Guideposts
- Triangulation
- Trail Techniques

Although wilderness travel implies different methods for different folks, we have decided to limit ourselves to backpacking, the basic form of self-propelled transportation. We have left water-based travel, mountain biking (excluded in virtually all wilderness areas), and animal-based travel (horses, donkeys, burros, llamas, camels, yaks, and other beasts of burden) for other texts. Since travel by foot is the most common and fundamental form of land travel, we focus on the basics of navigation and trail technique. Also, many land navigation principles transfer readily to water-based activities.

NAVIGATION

Anyone who has traveled extensively in the outdoors has more tales to share of their adventures with navigation than they care to admit. Getting lost never seems to be the problem, but getting found without outside assistance is often the hard part. Good navigation skills are essential, for not only do they add enjoyment to our travels, but they make us truly independent in the outdoors. When backcountry travelers have the skills to use a map and compass, they can make decisions based on their abilities and are no longer dependent on the trail builders and trail signs to guide their travel.

Just as it would be foolish to venture out into the wilderness without checking the weather forecast and bringing a raincoat even if it were sunny and warm, it would be foolish to venture out without a map and compass even if there are trails and trail signs. But we know, however, that people do it all the time. Just as a sunny day turns to rain and we're glad we have our raincoats, we sometimes lose the trails or take the wrong intersection and are grateful for our maps and compass.

PHILOSOPHY TIP: Maps and Wilderness

Some argue that once an area has been mapped, it is no longer true wilderness. This rings true in that map users are no longer true explorers of uncharted country as the earliest pioneers were. However, if maplessness were the criteria for defining wilderness, then there would be virtually no wilderness left on earth. We recognize maps as an essential tool for most wilderness users to assist in safe backcountry adventures.

Maps

By definition, a *map* is a miniaturized representation of a portion of the earth's surface. All of us use maps of one sort or another, whether as a sketch you make to help your friend find your house, a blueprint of your home, road maps, or a map of the mall complete with a "you are here" arrow (which always places you at the most distant point from where you parked your car). Jack once spent 2 weeks sailing with his uncle in the British Virgin Islands. The sailboat charter company told the happy vacationers no navigational charts were available but that they could give them a plastic-coated restaurant placemat that was a reduced version of the actual chart. The brave sailors cautiously made their way around the islands by placemat! The moral of the story: don't leave home without your map!

Topographic (sometimes shortened to topo) maps are most useful for land-based wilderness travel. Topographic maps differ from others in that they represent the three-dimensional aspects of the earth. That means they represent not only distance but also elevation.

TECHWEENIE TIP: Roots of the Word "Topographic"

The term topographic comes from the Latin "topo," which means place, and "graphein," which means to write or draw. Thus, topographic means "the drawing of the place."

The United States Geological Survey (USGS), the primary source for land maps in the United States, publishes topographic maps based on exhaustive survey work. These maps are continually being updated and provide the foundation for virtually all topographic maps in the country. In addition to USGS maps, some publishing companies and regional hiking organizations create hiking maps based on the USGS surveys. These maps can be readily found in outdoor sporting goods stores in the region in which you are traveling. This doesn't help much if you live in New Jersey and are planning a hiking trip in Wyoming's Grand Teton National Park. One option is to call or write to the state or federal land management office or the chamber of commerce of the area you will visit, requesting a list of appropriate map names and where you can purchase them. Be sure to check alternative maps, such as those provided by the United States Forest Service (USFS), the Bureau of Land Management (BLM), the National Park Service (NPS), local hiking clubs, and both state and county maps.

TRICKS OF THE TRADE: Map Sources

If you want to go to the original map source, you can websurf to www.usgs.gov, write to the United States Geological Survey at USGS Information Services, Box 25286, Denver, CO, 80225, or telephone 1-888-ASK-USGS and ask for a map index for the state to which you are going. You can then order the maps from the USGS. Plan ahead, as it takes a while for the maps to be delivered.

Map Features

Be aware that cartographers divide each of the 360 degrees that make up the sphere of the Earth into 60 minutes and each minute into 60 seconds. These subdivisions of degrees make it easier to locate ourselves on maps and in relation to the rest of the world. We use a ' to indicate "minutes" and a " to indicate "seconds."

The map features described apply to USGS maps and may vary on maps published by others. We like to break down the map into two parts: the margins and the map itself. The margins provide essential information necessary to understanding the features of the map. Most of the information listed pertains to the 15' x 15' (fifteen minutes by fifteen minutes) series and 7 1/2' x 7 1/2' series of USGS maps. The 7 1/2' x 15' series maps (1:25,000 scale) have a slightly different layout, although it is simple to understand.

Map Margins

This marginal information—marginal in location and not importance—provides such information as

- name of the map and relative location by state,
- names of adjacent maps,
- location of the map on the earth's surface by longitude and latitude (Figure 6.1),
- date of the map's survey and printing,
- map scale, and
- map series.

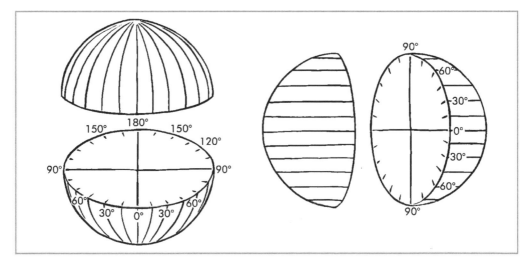

Noel J. Hotchkiss. *A Comprehensive Guide to Land Navigation with GPS*. Herndon, VA: Alexis U.S.A.

Figure 6.1
Latitude and longitude.

Map Name and Location

On most USGS maps (7 1/2' and 15' series) the names of the map and of the state it is located in are on the top and bottom right margin. The date the map was compiled is printed on the bottom left margin. On the bottom margin just to the right of this information is an outline of the state the map is located in with a black block representing approximately where in the state the quadrant lies.

Adjacent Maps

As you study your map late into the night deciding your route and anticipating what the surrounding countryside will look like, you suddenly find your route leading off the map's edge. How do you know what the name of the adjacent or bordering map is? The USGS provides this information in parentheses in small print along the map margins. Typically there are eight maps bordering one map, but depending on the scale, there could be more or fewer.

Map Location

Although you don't need to remember the difference between longitude and latitude to keep from getting lost in the backcountry, the information can be helpful. Longitude or meridian lines are the imaginary lines running north and south on the earth. They intersect at the poles and are measured by degrees, minutes, and seconds. Latitude or parallel lines are the imaginary lines going around the earth parallel to the equator and are also measured by degrees, minutes, and seconds. Sixty seconds equal a minute and 60 minutes equal a degree—this sounds like a watch crossed with a thermometer! In any event, by measuring where these imaginary lines intersect, we can determine our location anywhere on earth.

TECHWEENIE TIP: Remembering Latitude and Longitude

People remember longitude and latitude in different ways. Jack remembers that latitude lines are horizontal because "latitude" sounds like "ladder." Further, latitude lines look like the rungs of a ladder, since they run from side to side. Eric remembers longitude as the "long" lines; that is, they all intersect at the North and South poles. Longitude lines all have the same length as opposed to lines of latitude, which have different lengths.

USGS maps list the longitude and latitude at each of the four corners of the map as well as under the map name on the bottom right side of the margin. This information isn't often used, but when you need it, as in the case of search and rescue, it's essential. It allows people to locate themselves very precisely. As the high-tech gadgetry of the Global Positioning System (GPS), which determines location via satellites, has become affordable to the masses, knowledge of longitude and latitude has become more valuable.

Map Dates

Information regarding when the mapped area was surveyed and when the information was compiled is in the lower left margin. The year the map was printed, along with the most recent date that the map may have been updated, is in the lower right-hand corner under the map name.

SAFETY TIP: Maps Change Over Time

Remember that topographic features on maps change very little through the decades, unless of course bulldozers have leveled mountains to create a parking lot, volcanoes have recently erupted, or an asteroid has crashed nearby. On the other hand, human features, more commonly called cultural features (e.g., trails, shelters, roads, campsites), can change radically during the lifetime of the map. Wet areas also change. Beavers may dam up a brook or a beaver dam may break and dry out a previously flooded pond. In addition, open meadows may be reclaimed by the surrounding forest.

What's the point? In backcountry areas you can almost always trust the topographic features represented on your map, but be very skeptical of cultural features. This isn't to say that you shouldn't use cultural features to confirm your location, but that you should not be surprised if a trail has been relocated, a lean-to removed, or in worst-case scenarios, a housing development has been built along your favorite fishing stream.

Map Scale

The map's scale, indicated on most USGS maps on the bottom margin in the center, provides a means of measuring distance on a map and is a way of determining the relationship of the size of things on the earth to their relative size on the map. Falling back on our seventh-grade math skills (which was the last year either of us passed a math course), we remember that ratios are a fraction providing measurements in standard units around the colon. In other words, if the scale is 1:62,500, then whatever you're using as a standard of measurement on the right side of the colon must be the same standard on the left side of the colon. For example, one thumbnail width on the map equals 62,500 thumbnail widths on the earth. You can use pencil lengths, compass widths, inches, or any other form of measurement, knowing that one unit of measurement on the map equals 62,500 units of those measurements on the earth (Figure 6.2).

How does that help us? Well, if we figure out how many inches are in a mile (5,280 feet × 12 = 63,360 in.) we find that 1 in. on our map equals just 72 feet short of a mile. As Forrest Stump's orienteering champ cousin West Stump always says, "In backcountry travel, you should always know where you are within the length of a football field." In this case, we are close enough for us to say that 1 in. on a 1:62,500 scale map equals 1 mile on the earth.

Choose the Right Map!

What does this mean to you when you're out in the woods? The lower the numbers on the scale, the more detail will be represented on the map. Conversely, the higher the scale numbers, the less detail. A map of the world found in an atlas may have a scale of 1:115,000,000 (1 in. = 1,800 miles). This map is not much help in planning your hiking route, but if you're flying to New Zealand, you can see where your flight path will take you. On the other hand, you may decide to design a floor plan for your hunting cabin using a 1:12 scale (1 in. = 1 foot). This provides great detail and can even show where you'll put all your trophy mounts. If you tried to use a map of this scale to travel outdoors, you would need a piece of paper the size of a billboard to represent Central Park. Like everything in life, finding the perfect map is like finding the perfect love: it's an illusion. (Just ask our spouses!) The challenge is to find the right map for your purposes.

Map Series

The map series, indicated on the top right-hand side of the margin, refers to the size of the area covered by a particular map. USGS maps measure the area they cover in degrees of longitude and latitude (Figure 6.4). A 15' series map represents 15' of longitude and 15' of latitude, while a 7 1/2' series map represents 7 1/2' of longitude and 7 1/2' of latitude or only 25% of the area represented by the 15' series map. What does this mean to you when you're out in the woods? Basically, you will need four 7 1/2' series maps to cover the same area as a 15' map. Due to the scale, the 7 1/2' series map will show much more detail than the 15' map. Each map has distinct advantages and disadvantages, depending on what you're looking for.

Figure 6.2
West Stump, orienteer.

"IN BACKCOUNTRY TRAVEL, YOU SHOULD ALWAYS KNOW WHERE YOU ARE WITHIN THE LENGTH OF A FOOTBALL FIELD."

SCALE	INCHES PER MILE	CM PER KM	SERIES
1:62,500	1 = 1	1.5 = 1	15'
1:50,000	1 1/4 = 1	2 = 1	N/A
1:25,000	2 1/2 = 1	4 = 1	71/2' × 15'
1:24,000	2 1/2 = 1	4 = 1	71/2'

Figure 6.3

Some of the most common scales and their relative inches to a mile, centimeters to a kilometer, and their series.

SAFETY TIP: Perfect Practice Makes Perfect

Having a compass and map in your backpack is not enough; you must know how to use them. Learn how to use these essential tools from a friend, hiking club, adult education program, or from this book. Once you learn the basics, get out and practice, practice, practice. The more time you spend outdoors reading your map and using your compass, the better you will get.

Map Features

As you look at a map, one of the first things you will notice is the variety of colors. Green, blue, brown, white, black, and red are the most common colors. Colors help distinguish the different map symbols (Figure 6.5). Black usually indicates cultural or human symbols like

7½×15' (1:25,000)

7½' (1:24,000)

15' (1:62,500)

Figure 6.4
Map scale comparison.

COASTAL FEATURES

Foreshore flat	
Rock or coral reef	
Rock bare or awash	
Group of rocks bare or awash	
Exposed wreck	
Depth curve; sounding	
Breakwater, pier, jetty, or wharf	
Seawall	

BATHYMETRIC FEATURES

Area exposed at mean low tide; sounding datum	
Channel	
Offshore oil or gas: well; platform	
Sunken rock	

RIVERS, LAKES, AND CANALS

Intermittent stream	
Intermittent river	
Disappearing stream	
Perennial stream	
Perennial river	
Small falls; small rapids	
Large falls; large rapids	
Masonry dam	
Dam with lock	
Dam carrying road	
Perennial lake; Intermittent lake or pond	
Dry lake	
Narrow wash	
Wide wash	
Canal, flume, or aqueduct with lock	
Elevated aqueduct, flume, or conduit	
Aqueduct tunnel	
Well or spring; spring or seep	

SUBMERGED AREAS AND BOGS

Marsh or swamp	
Submerged marsh or swamp	
Wooded marsh or swamp	
Submerged wooded marsh or swamp	
Rice field	
Land subject to inundation	

BUILDINGS AND RELATED FEATURES

Building	
School; church	
Built-up Area	
Racetrack	
Airport	
Landing strip	
Well (other than water); windmill	
Tanks	
Covered reservoir	
Gaging station	
Landmark object (feature as labeled)	
Campground; picnic area	
Cemetery: small; large	

ROADS AND RELATED FEATURES

Roads on Provisional edition maps are not classified as primary, secondary, or light duty. They are all symbolized as light duty roads.

Primary highway	
Secondary highway	
Light duty road	
Unimproved road	
Trail	
Dual highway	
Dual highway with median strip	
Road under construction	
Underpass; overpass	
Bridge	
Drawbridge	
Tunnel	

RAILROADS AND RELATED FEATURES

Standard gauge single track; station	
Standard gauge multiple track	
Abandoned	
Under construction	
Narrow gauge single track	
Narrow gauge multiple track	
Railroad in street	
Juxtaposition	
Roundhouse and turntable	

TRANSMISSION LINES AND PIPELINES

Power transmission line: pole; tower	
Telephone line	
Aboveground oil or gas pipeline	
Underground oil or gas pipeline	

Figure 6.5
United States Geological Survey symbol index.

roads, railroad tracks, churches, trails, buildings, cemeteries, bridges, schools, quarries, and mines, although some roads and populated areas may be represented in red. Control stations, frequently referred to as benchmarks (BM), are reference points placed by the surveyors to help in determining elevation and distance. They are marked in black with an X or BM along with the measured elevation.

Natural features round out the limited rainbow hues found on the map. Blue represents water. Lakes, ponds, and larger rivers are solid blue. Smaller streams are marked with a single blue line, while swamps are indicated by little tufts of blue lines, which, with a little imagination, might look like tufts of swamp grasses.

TECHWEENIE TIP: Telling River and Stream Width from the Map

On 7 1/2' maps, stream widths of more than 40 feet (12 m) are drawn showing both shores of the stream. On 15' maps, stream widths of more than 80 feet (24 m) are drawn showing both shores. This information can be helpful when planning canoe explorations (those 7 1/2' maps can be helpful) and when backpacking, in order to anticipate whether you may or may not be able to cross or navigate a river.

The color green indicates some type of vegetative cover. Most commonly, green represents trees, but if your backcountry ventures take you into orchards, scrub, or vineyards, they too will be indicated by the color green.

Contour Lines

Arguably the most valuable color of the map is brown. Brown indicates elevation change in the form of contour lines. *Contour lines* are imaginary lines along which the elevation above sea level is constant. In other words, if you were to take a hike and stayed exactly 100 feet above sea level for the entire trip, you would have hiked along the 100-foot contour line.

When you look at a topographic map, you see that some lines are darker than others. These *index contour lines* indicate a standard increase in elevation and are usually located every 100 feet in elevation. They also have the elevation written in brown somewhere along the line. Lying in between index contour lines are *intermediate contour lines*, which aren't marked with elevation. So how do you tell how much elevation change takes place between any two adjacent contour lines? Look at the contour interval.

The *contour interval*, one of the most important pieces of information found on your map, indicates the change in elevation between contour lines. Usually located in the center of the bottom margin, it is measured in feet or meters and may range from 5 feet in flat country to 80 feet or more in mountainous country. Maps in the northeast typically have a 20-foot contour interval, while maps in the west may have a 40-foot contour interval.

Interpreting contour lines, that is, imagining what the countryside looks like in real life, is something of an art. The skill seems to come easier to some than others. The process is a bit like looking at computer-generated 3-D images that you see for sale in poster boutiques in malls (Figure 6.6). These images don't seem to make any sense; then all of a sudden a picture jumps out at you. With practice, contour lines will do the same thing.

Roaming the countryside while interpreting maps is a wonderful form of physical and mental exercise. Don't forget, just as an Olympic-class athlete or concert pianist must practice, so must an aspiring outdoor navigator. Now get out there and do it!

The Compass

The various types of compasses for sale are like automobiles in some ways. Any working auto will get you to the grocery store, but some get you there inexpensively, while others allow

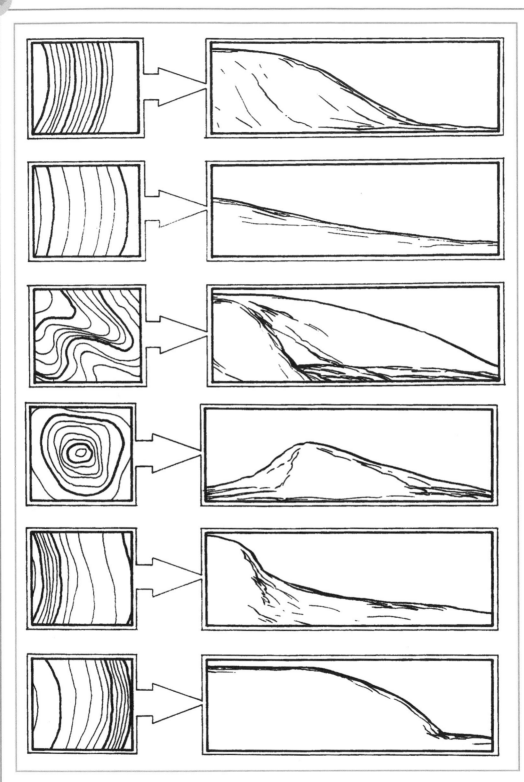

Figure 6.6
With practice, you'll be able to interpret contour lines with ease.

you to listen to Rush Limbaugh and provide air-conditioned, leather-bound interior comfort. Some come in four-wheel drive and can drive off-road, while others can cruise down the interstate at 70 miles per hour in luxury. The bottom line is, regardless of the fancy options, they all get you there.

Think of compasses the same way. You might say that we recommend the pickup truck version of compasses: the orienteering compass. Like a reliable truck, a good compass shouldn't cost a ton of money, should take you anywhere inexpensively, and should be very reliable. The only essential characteristic we think a compass must have is that it be liquid-filled. The liquid dampens or slows down the movement of the magnetic needle. This style of compass does everything you need, and the lower-priced models do it as accurately as the higher-end ones. There are three major manufacturers of orienteering compasses: Silva, Brunton, and Suunto. They all provide a reliable product, but the Silva Polaris 177 compass is our favorite for teaching and learning navigation skills at beginning and intermediate levels.

BOTTOM-LINE TIP: Purchasing a Compass

There are many good quality compasses. Whatever compass you buy, make sure it is liquid-filled. We recommend you purchase an orienteering compass from either Silva, Brunton, or Suunto.

SAFETY TIP: Mirrored Compasses

The fancy compasses with mirrors have a definite purpose. The mirror helps take more accurate sight bearings. In addition, they are an excellent safety device, as they can be used for signaling for help in an emergency; getting foreign objects out of eyes; and, of course, checking to make sure your mascara hasn't run.

The Legend of the Compass

How did the compass come to be? We have an idea of how it might have been discovered in the Stump universe. Forrest Stump's Neanderthal predecessor, Zak Stump, stepped out of the cave into the sunlight one morning and realized that his clan had killed all the mastodons within an easy walk of the cave. The clan then had to venture farther from the cave, and they weren't sure if they could find their way home.

As Forrest's primal grandfather pondered this problem, he paced back and forth in front of the cave. In this pensive state, he didn't see the small boulder of magnetite (a naturally magnetized ore) in front of him and cursed loudly as he stubbed his toe on it. Like many serendipitous discoveries, he didn't immediately realize the significance of this monumental event.

Upon impact with Zak's hammer-like big toe, the rock cracked, propelling a small piece of magnetite away from the boulder and onto a small stick floating in a large puddle nearby.

In his contemplative mood, the perceptive Neanderthal started spinning the stick around in the puddle. Suddenly, he exclaimed, "Eureka!" which was the first spoken word in history. Zak had discovered that no matter how many times he spun the magnetic stick, it would always end up in its original position. He at once realized the magic stick's potential in helping him find his way to new mastodon turf in the search for fresh meat for his clan. More importantly, he guessed it would also help him get back to the cave. He had discovered a tool that pointed to the same reference point no matter where it went. Thus, the first compass was invented when primordial Zak put the magnetic stick in a big pottery bowl and carried it wherever he went. Well, at least that's how Forrest told us it happened!

Figure 6.7
Zak Stump with the first portable compass.

It Points to *WHICH* North?

The compass of today, of course, is much lighter and more compact, but works on the same principle. A floating magnetized strip will always point to magnetic north. But wait a minute, what is magnetic north and how does it differ from true north, or Oliver North, for that matter? *Magnetic north* is where the compass needle points to, about 1,000 miles northwest of Hudson Bay. *True north* points to the North Pole. The difference between magnetic and true north, measured in degrees, is called *declination*. Is this difference important? You bet it is, but we'll get to that a little later.

Not Another Stump Compass Story!

To understand compasses, you need to understand direction. In the historic days of ocean exploration, Christopher Columbus, or Cristoforo Colombo for you Italian aficionados, hired Forrest Stump's Spanish forefather, Silva Stump, as navigator on the *Santa Maria*. Now the *Santa Maria* had a state-of-the-art 15th-century liquid-filled ship's compass, but during this time direction was based on the 32 cardinal points of the compass. In other words, Silva had to memorize North, South, East, West, along with Northeast, Northwest, Southeast, Southwest, North by Northeast, North North by Northeast and the remaining 22 cardinal points. What a headache!

Before the explorers set sail, Queen Isabella asked Silva where Columbus was so that she could kiss him goodbye. Silva responded, "South, South by Southwest of Cleveland." Silly Silva thought she meant Columbus, Ohio, and not *Christopher* Columbus, who was down at the shipyard. The queen was rightfully miffed and considered canceling the expedition. After some well timed groveling and ring kissing, Silva managed to regain the queen's favor and so the ships shoved off for terra incognita.

After months at sea, Chris Columbus, or Cristóbal Colón for you Spanish aficionados, bumped into the New World with Silva Stump by his side. On the return voyage, Silva discovered that if he broke down the cardinal points on the compass into 360 degrees with 0° or 360° being North, 90° being East, 180° South, and 270° West, he could give detailed directions without having to memorize the 32 cardinal points. Unfortunately, young Silva Stump disappeared from history when Captain Columbus asked Silva what direction they were heading and he yelled back, "97°!" Thinking the smart-alec lad was giving him the air temperature rather than the direction of travel, Columbus had Silva walk the plank. Poor Silva—he wasn't even a footnote in history!

Figure 6.8
Know the proper name and function of each tool you use.

Parts of the Compass

Now we have the modern compass (Figure 6.9) with a floating needle and directions broken down into 360°, typically marked in 2° increments. Learning the parts of the compass is as important as learning the parts of your car. Can you imagine what would happen if you confused the gas cap with the tire's air valve? You would spend a lot of time trying to force gasoline into your tire and filling your fuel tank with air. The same can be said about your compass. If you don't know the parts of the compass, you'll get confused about how to use it.

These compass parts are based on the Silva Polaris 177 and other similar orienteering compasses.

Base Plate—The rectangular, transparent piece of plastic upon which all compass parts rest. The base plate's sides are parallel to the "direction of travel arrow" engraved on the middle of the base plate. Typically, the base plate has millimeter and inch markings along the edge for measuring distances on the map.

"Direction of travel" arrow—The direction of travel arrow is an engraved arrow on the base plate that runs from the edge of the compass housing to one end of the base plate. Compass bearings are read where the base of the direction of travel arrow touches the numbers on the edge of the compass housing. The direction of travel arrow should always point toward the intended destination.

Compass housing—The compass housing is the circular rim found in the middle of the base plate that has the initials of the four cardinal points, N, S, E, and W, and degree lines marked. Many compasses have lines representing increments of 2° with every 20th degree numbered.

Magnetic needle—The magnetic needle is the floating arrow suspended on a bearing in the middle of the liquid-filled compass housing. The magnetic needle points to magnetic north when the compass is held steady and level.

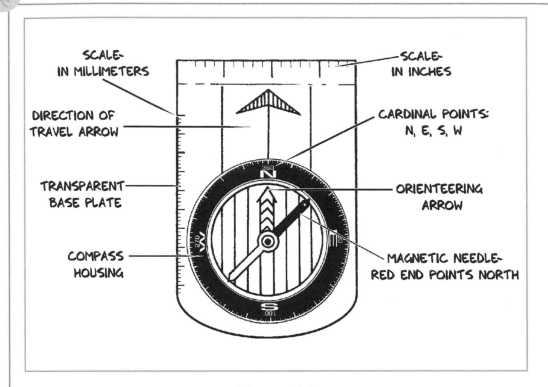

**Figure 6.9
The modern Compass.**

Orienting arrow and orienting/meridian lines—Frequently blue or white, these are represented by the outline of an arrow and parallel lines on the base of the compass housing. The compass is said to be "oriented" or "boxed" when the compass housing is turned so that the magnetic needle lies directly over the orienting arrow, and both the arrow and needle simultaneously point to north on the compass housing.

Compass Functions

The compass has two main functions. It points to north and measures angles. You're probably thinking, "Oh no, they're getting into math again!" Rest assured that we promise to stick with basic math. To get an idea of how the compass works, think of it as a big protractor. Whenever we want to figure what direction to travel, all we do is measure an angle from north to the direction of our destination.

Using Figure 6.11, think of your present location as A and where you want to go as B. This forms one line of your angle, the other being formed by your present location (A) to north. In this example, the angle created by these two lines is 45° or Northeast. Every time we determine what direction we want to travel, all we do is measure an angle from 0° to 359°. This angle is called our *bearing*, or the intended line of travel to our destination.

Sight Bearings

While visiting relatives in New York's Adirondack Park, the Stump family took a drive through the Lake Placid region, which was the site of the 1932 and 1980 Winter Olympics. Forrest saw a small hill with an apparently beautiful vista about a mile from the road poking out of the surrounding wooded countryside about a mile from the road. The kids were sick of riding in the car, and Forrest and Holly were sick of hearing them threaten each other with bodily harm. Forrest got the grand idea, since parents are notorious for grand ideas, of taking the family up that small hill for a picnic lunch.

Figure 6.10
Forrest takes a sight bearing.

Woody was eager to give it a try, while Willow and Moss would rather have been taking the elevator to the top of the Olympic Ski Jump. Holly wondered if the crazy idea would create headlines in the Stumps' hometown newspaper announcing that the family was the subject of an intensive search and rescue operation. With some fundamental compass skills, it shouldn't.

One of the simplest uses of a compass is taking sight bearings. A sight bearing is the line of travel established when the compass is used alone to sight a destination. Forrest and the family parked on the side of the road and stared up at the small hill with the beautiful vista. Forrest dreamed of a warm breeze and a great picnic while gazing at the natural surroundings. Holly decided to practice her rusty compass skills. She pried the compass out of the dog's mouth and took a sight bearing on the hill by pointing the "direction of travel" arrow at the top of the hill.

Now, holding the compass level, she turned the compass housing until the compass was oriented; that is, the orienting arrow "boxes" the magnetic needle (Figure 6.12). The magnetic needle and the orienting arrow both pointed north while the "direction of travel" arrow pointed to "picnic hill," the family's

Figure 6.11
Figuring a map bearing.

destination. The "direction of travel" arrow also indicates the bearing in degrees where it says, "read bearing here." It's not a bad idea to jot down the bearing for later reference. In this case, Holly measured a 344° bearing.

GPS: Compasses of the Future, Used Today

It may not be long until a GPS unit might be as common in your backpack as a first aid kit. GPS was developed in the 1970s for the U.S. Department of Defense as a highly accurate navigational system. GPS units (Figure 6.13) lock on to high-frequency radio signals from some of the 24 GPS orbital satellites and calculate the exact location of the user through triangulation. Originally, this powerful and costly technology was reserved for military purposes, and civilian GPS units received intentionally degraded or somewhat inaccurate signals in order to prevent misuse of the signals by hostile forces. On May 1, 2000, President Clinton removed this program, called Selective Availability, in order to allow all civilian GPS units to receive signals with the same accuracy as those used by the military. This improved accuracy has benefited the many public and private-sector uses of GPS, including air, road, rail and marine navigation; emergency response; telecommunications; and other activities. Now, your GPS unit receives signals that are accurate to 50 feet or less.

Figure 6.12
Point the direction of travel arrow at the destination. Turn the housing until the magnetic arrow needle is boxed. The result is a "sight bearing."

How Does GPS Compare to the Standard Compass?

Before you toss your compass into the dustbin or send it to the Smithsonian Institution's Silva Stump Collection of Quaint but Obsolete Camping Gizmos, consider the limitations of the GPS. First, it's more expensive than a compass (always an issue for most of Woody Stump's low-budget backpacking buddies). Second, you can't guarantee that when you push the "on" button, you'll be rewarded with the soft, comforting glow of the digital screen. Sometimes—not often—GPS doesn't work. The units can be sensitive to extremes of climate (winter use drains batteries and desert heat might cause unit failure) and local moisture (read: "Whoops! Well, I just dropped your new GPS into the lake!"). Furthermore, you also have to have the interest or ability to read the GPS manual in order to understand how to use the thing. This comes more easily to some people than others.

Some other limitations hinder both GPS and handheld compasses. When you're in dense cover by forest, shrub, or canyon, the GPS signal might not come through. Likewise, your line of sight might be restricted. However, you can trust that your standard compass needle will still be attracted to magnetic north, day or night, through fog, freezing rain, or impenetrable forest.

The following list summarizes some of the features that a serious backcountry traveler should consider when choosing a new GPS unit. Consider each one, and then think about the setting in which you plan to use your GPS. Also, try to project how you might use it when you get more and more comfortable with the features. In other words, the gizmos that you don't understand when you buy the GPS might just come in very handy once you become a GPS whiz!

Figure 6.13
The Garmin GPSMap 60CS and the
Magellan Meridian Gold GPS receivers.

1. Make it waterproof—The better units are capable of being submerged for short periods of time.
2. Make it small and handy—Remember, you're going to be lugging it with you, taking it out, and putting it back with a pack on your back!
3. Beam me up! Look for a 12-channel parallel receiver system and possibly an external amplified antenna (if available). These features will help you read signals even under forest cover or through rainclouds.
4. Power-packed—Make sure the battery life is as long as possible. Compare units.
5. Downloadable maps—Make sure your GPS can be loaded with topographic maps in addition to the standard waypoints.
6. Routes and waypoints—Look for storage capacity for at least 20 routes and 500 waypoints. Routes are essentially linked waypoints, which are highlighted points in space, such as campsites, mountain peaks, trailheads, and other essential features.
7. Can you see me? Make sure the screen is as large as is practical. Black and white screens are fine, while some color screens are hard to read in daylight. Look for the Trans-Reflective color screens on some GPS units.

Current prices of $130–$600 make GPS affordable for committed backcountry travelers. GPS is available in wristwatch-sized units, wrist-strapped units, handhelds, and automobile dash-mounted units. If history is an indicator and mass production gears up and prices continue to go down, the day will come when the compass as we know it goes the way of the slide rule.

Following the Compass Bearing

With day packs on their backs, the Stump family was ready to head into the woods and anticipated a short hike to the top of "picnic hill" (actually Little Burn Mountain on the map). Of course, Forrest might have underestimated the distance, and rather than a half a mile, the trip was more like 5 miles.

Following the compass, Holly kept them heading toward their goal even after they entered the wooded countryside and Little Burn Mountain disappeared from sight. Keeping the compass oriented (the needle "boxed"), they traveled in the direction of their "direction of travel" arrow. There were, however, a couple of things they needed to keep in mind. They had to remember that the compass needle is only a piece of magnetized metal and so can be pulled off course by exposure to metal objects. We've seen hunters follow their rifle barrels through the woods thinking that they were following their compass bearings the whole time. To avoid magnetic malfunction, make sure you take off your suit of armor before you head into the woods.

As they started off, Holly looked for a landmark in line with her destination: a large boulder, distinguishing tree, or similar feature. By moving from one known landmark, checking the bearing, then moving on to the next sighted landmark, she proceeded along the line of travel without following the exact path indicated by the compass. This "leap frog" method of travel allows the traveler to circumvent hazards or obstacles while still holding to the correct line of travel.

Before they knew it, the Stumps made it to the top of Little Burn Mountain. Unfortunately, the scene was less than idyllic for a picnic lunch. The wind was gusting to 40 miles an hour, and in between the gusts the mosquitoes were so bad that their bodies felt like goalies on a dart team. Remember what we said about parents getting great ideas?

While Holly and Forrest took great satisfaction in finding their destination, how did they get everyone back to the car before the kids formed a lynch mob? The return route was easily established by adding or subtracting 180° to or from the original bearing. This "back-bearing" reverses the original line of travel and allowed the Stumps to proceed back along the original route to the awaiting car and the bug repellent they had left in the trunk.

Figure 6.14
Make sure you don't take compass bearings near metal objects.

 SAFETY TIP: Trusting the Compass
Trust the compass. If we had a dime for every person who told us the reason they got lost was because the compass was wrong, we could take a vacation to the Bahamas. Although it is not impossible for the compass to be wrong, the odds are about the same as being hit by lightning. Be wary, but if in doubt, trust the compass.

Combining the Map and Compass

Maps and compasses can be used independently, but like the axiom, "The whole is greater than the sum of the parts," combining the map and compass makes for much greater accuracy than using the two separately. Working with the map and compass together provides a wonderful opportunity to practice decision making and use judgment. The challenge is determining when to rely more on the map and when to rely more on the compass. The map will show you how to improve the route and keep you out of swamps and away from cliffs, while the compass is the one point of reference you can trust. Interpreting the map is subjective, while following the compass is objective. You're either following the bearing or you're not. The compass is what you fall back on when all else fails.

Let's look back on the Stumps' adventure up Little Burn Mountain. Forrest and Holly felt elated about the off-trail hike because the family was successful in traveling to the summit and back. However, other than Woody, the rest of the family didn't share their enthusiasm. They understood that Willow and Moss had difficulty putting the off-trail hike into perspective. They understood that the kids couldn't let go of their idea that a picnic doesn't include gale-force winds and mosquito sandwiches. They understood that the kids didn't want to forgive them. They knew the two would come around. Eventually.

What Is Bushwhacking?

By some miracle, perhaps through a promise to stay at a five-star theme park on the way home, the Stump family decided to venture out once again. Forrest told them they were ready for a real bushwhack. Bushwhacking, the art of off-trail hiking, may be an appropriate term. If the word conjures up an image of beating your way through vegetation thicker than King Kong's eyebrows, then you're getting an idea about how much fun it can be in some cases. It may sound like torture, but that's where the decision making and judgment comes in.

Bushwhacking should not invoke thoughts of slashing through the wilderness with no regard for vegetation and the rest of the environment. Some people think the term bushwhacking should be avoided because of its negative environmental connotations. We feel that it is an appropriate term, especially when used with what we call The Scale of Bushwhack Nastiness. The Scale of Bushwhack Nastiness consists of three off-trail hiking conditions: thick, thicker, and thickest. Only a few select areas in North America qualify for a thickest rating. Anyone hiking in the Northeast's softwood thickets has an idea—ah, you gotta love spruce-fir forests. Hikers in the Smokies understand the meaning—ah, remember those rhododendrons. Our five-star award goes to the Pacific Northwest and Alaska. Bushwhacking through the painful spikes of devil's club holds a special place in our hearts (and bodies).

Figure 6.15
The Scale of Bushwack Nastiness: thick, thicker, and thickest.
(Be sure to leave your machete at home!)

Off-Trail Hiking With Map and Compass

The next day, the Stumps purchased a couple of "topo" maps of the area and planned their first off-trail hike. Woody and Forrest decided to start at a parking lot near Whiteface on the edge of Lake Placid and planned to hike about 2 miles to a small pond called Bartlett Pond. Of course, the only reason there is a small pond with no trail to it in a populated region is probably because there is absolutely no redeeming human value to the pond. In fact, it would probably remind the Stumps of the summit of "picnic hill," minus the gusts of wind. But let's forget that for a moment and look at how the Stumps figured to get there.

First, they planned to hike up the McKenzie Pond Trail until they reached the highest point on the trail. Then, using the compass as a protractor, Forrest needed to measure the bearing from the height of land to Bartlett Pond. To do this, he placed the compass on the map with one of the long sides of the base plate connecting the spot where they planned to leave the trail to Bartlett Pond. He had to make sure the "direction of travel" arrow was pointing in the direction of their destination, Bartlett Pond (Figure 6.16).

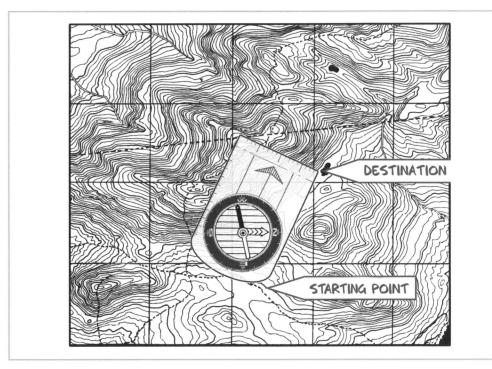

Figure 6.16
Step 1: Place one edge of the compass base plate so that it connects your starting point with your destination.

Next, he twisted the compass housing until the orienting arrow and the orienting lines were parallel with the north–south longitudinal lines on the side of the map. He made sure the orienting arrow pointed North (Figure 6.17).

Forrest read the map bearing from the compass housing where it says "read bearing here." This number was his *map bearing*, or the angle measured in degrees formed by a line of travel on a map in relationship to true north (the top of the map). In this case it was 34°.

Compensating for Declination

After Forrest took a map bearing, all the Stumps had to do was follow that bearing to get to Bartlett Pond. Right? Not quite. Remember declination, the difference between True North and Magnetic North as measured in degrees? Now is the time to take declination into account. Hold on, because this can be a little confusing.

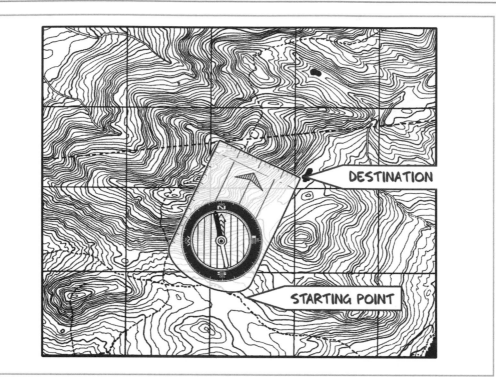

Figure 6.17
Step 2: Twist compass housing until orienting lines point north (top of the map.) The result is called a map bearing.

Using Figure 6.18 as a reference, imagine a line running down from Magnetic North through Lake Michigan, across portions of Michigan, Indiana, Ohio, Kentucky, Tennessee, North Carolina, along the South Carolina-Georgia border, and out into the Atlantic Ocean at Savannah, Georgia. This line is where true north and magnetic north line up and where there is no difference between the two. As you go east from 0° declination, magnetic north lies west of you, so the angle measured is called "west declination." As you go west of 0° declination, magnetic north is east of you, so the angle measured is called "east declination."

How did this information help the Stumps hike to Bartlett Pond? They had to convert their map bearing to a field bearing. They did that by adding or subtracting the declination listed in the legend of their map. It isn't as difficult as it sounds. Although some people suggest mnemonic devices (e.g., "east is least," therefore subtract), we suggest you develop a thorough understanding of the topic. This eliminates the need for cute phrases that sometimes confuse more than they clarify.

According to Forrest's map, the declination was 14° west. In other words, magnetic north (or the Agonic Line) is 14° to the west of him. Since the map bearing doesn't take into account

TECHWEENIE TIP: The Line of No Declination
The Agonic Line is the area where declination is 0°; that is, where there is no difference between true north and magnetic north. The word agonic means "no angle."

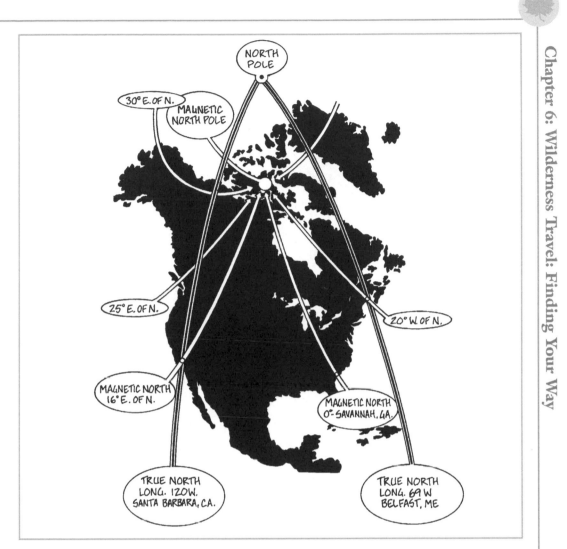

Figure 6.18
Declination map of North America. Note the agonic line, or line of 0° declination.

declination, using Figure 6.19 we see Forrest had to increase the bearing in order to account for west declination. If declination were east of him, as it would be in the western United States, he would do just the opposite, or subtract. A federal wilderness area in Montana might have 14° east declination, in which case Forrest would have to subtract 14° from a map bearing to obtain a field bearing.

◇◇◇◇◇◇◇◇◇◇◇◇

BOTTOM-LINE TIP: Adjusting for Declination
First, find the declination on your map in degrees. It should say a number of degrees from 0 to about 24. If you are east of 0° declination, you add the number when converting a map bearing to a field bearing. If you are west of 0° declination, you subtract the number when converting a map bearing to a field bearing.

◇◇◇◇◇◇◇◇◇◇◇◇

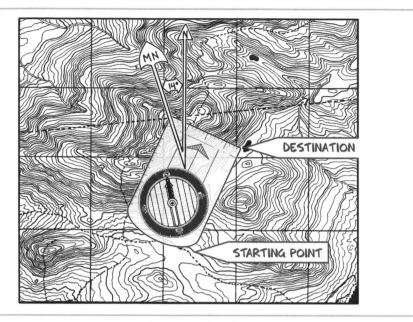

Figure 6.19
Step 3: Add or subtract declination to your map bearing.
(In this example, add 14°.) The result is called a field bearing.

Route Planning and Guideposts

After the Stumps had taken declination into account, they were ready to head out and find Bartlett Pond. We recommend that you do what the Stumps did before they left: they stopped and thought about the terrain on their route. They took a look at the map and tried to predict what the trip would be like. They asked a number of questions: Were there any obstacles to look out for, such as cliffs or large rivers? Did alternate routes need to be considered to avoid swamps or mountainous terrain? How much altitude would be gained? Was water available along the way? Did they anticipate how thick the terrain was going to be? Was the terrain wet or insect-ridden? How long did they think it would take?

These were all questions that the Stumps considered before they headed out. For experts and novices alike, however, the most important question is "What guideposts are there to help find the way?"

Guideposts are clearly identifiable, natural or human-made landforms that can be used to help you keep from getting lost. In case you do get lost, guideposts help you find your way. There are three general types of guideposts: handrails, backstops, and checkpoints (Figure 6.20). They each help make your hike safer and more enjoyable.

Handrails are features that parallel the line of travel to the left or right. A river or a highway might serve as a handrail. The handrail serves as an indicator to tell you whether you have drifted off to the left or right of your chosen route.

Backstops serve as a "gone too far" warning or a "dead end." A mountain, river, highway, or lake might be that indicator that tells you, "Whoops, we missed it. We better turn around and try again."

Certain selected landmarks called *checkpoints* or "way" points can be used to confirm your exact location. These features should be used frequently to evaluate your progress and help determine on the map whether you are traveling as planned. A river, pond, hunting camp, trail, or campsite could all serve as checkpoints.

The Stumps checked their route, found some handrails, determined backstops, and even found one or two checkpoints. The family headed out, and although the terrain didn't fit their image of the map as exactly as they thought it would, they found their way to Bartlett Pond with little difficulty. Forrest was ecstatic and the rest of the family was impressed, because not

Figure 6.20
Some topographical features can serve as checkpoints, handrails, and backstops, depending on your route.

only did they find the pond, but it was a beautiful spot. Besides, because they remembered the insect repellent, the bugs were tolerable and they should be able to enjoy their picnic lunch with little bother from the blood-sucking monsters. Wait a minute, they did bring the lunch, didn't they?

As they sat on the edge of the pond soaking up the rays and the panoramic view of the mountains, Woody said, "Hey Dad, what mountain is that one over there with the rock slide that looks like Bugs Bunny?" Forrest did have to admit it did look like Bugs Bunny, but he had no idea what mountain it was. How did he find out? He pulled out the map and compass. He had read up on map and compass before leaving home and so was eager to put his newfound knowledge to work.

First, he oriented the map. *Orienting the map* means to line up the map so it faces the same way as the observer so that north on the map is lined up with north on the earth. The map can be oriented one of two ways. If the terrain is obvious, just rotate the map until the features on the map line up with the features observed. This takes a little practice with map interpretation. The second way, using a compass, is easy and accurate. Set the compass housing for the declination indicated on the map. Place one of the long sides of the compass base plate along either of the north/south margins of the map, making sure the "direction of travel" arrow is heading in a northerly direction. Turn the map, with the compass on it, until the magnetic needle is "boxed" by the orienting arrow. Once the needle is boxed, the map is now oriented.

SAFETY TIP: Expert Advice
Don't expect to get good map advice from local "expert" outdoor people. Most of them are excellent in the outdoors and can find their way through their local backwoods. However, their knowledge is often based on first-hand exploration, and they may never have looked at a map of the area. We once asked a local to point out on the map where we were. The gentleman pondered the map for a while then pronounced that it was terribly inaccurate but that we were here, and pointed at a location on the map. The spot turned out to be 4 miles from our actual location.

In Woody's case, if the features were distinct enough, he would be able to look out and compare them with the map. He might have been able to identify a number of them in this way, but if he ran into trouble, he knew another approach. He could take a field or sight bearing with his compass and plot that bearing on the map. Remember, the Stumps took a sight bearing to hike up Little Burn Mountain. In this case he pointed the "direction of travel" arrow at "Bugs Bunny Peak" and "boxed" the needle; that is, he turned the housing until the orienting arrow boxed the magnetic needle.

Next came the tricky part. The first time he took a map bearing and converted it to a field bearing, he added declination. Now he was converting a field bearing to a map bearing and had to do the opposite. Subtracting the 14° declination (Figure 6.21) left Woody with a bearing of 242°.

To plot that on the map, he had to line up one side-edge of the compass base plate with his location on Bartlett Pond. While keeping that edge on his location, he had to rotate the base plate (not the compass housing) until the orienting arrow and orienting lines lined up with north on the map.

If he drew a line along the edge of the base plate from his location on Bartlett Pond, it would intersect with "Bugs Bunny Peak." He may have to extend the line if the peak is farther away than his compass is long on the map, but "Bugs Bunny Peak" had to be somewhere on that line. By interpreting the contour lines he was able to determine which mountain it was. Fortunately, Woody wasn't too disappointed that it was called Haystack Mountain rather than Bugs Bunny Peak.

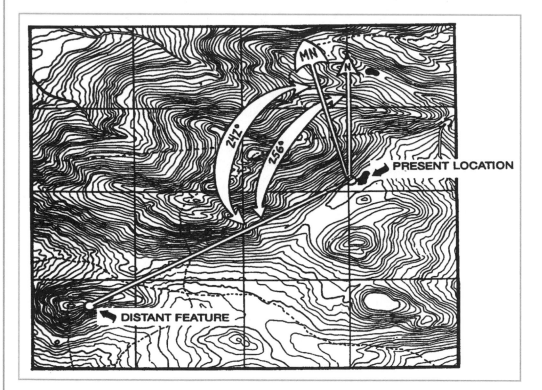

Figure 6.21
Convert a field bearing taken from a visible feature
into a map bearing by adding or subtracting declination
(in this example, subtract 14°).

TECHWEENIE TIP: Altimeters

Altimeters can be useful by providing additional information to help determine one's location. Altimeters calculate your elevation and, if regularly calibrated, can help pinpoint your exact location. With the advent of wrist-worn instruments like Avocet's Vertech II Alpin and Casio's Pathfinder for under $200, you can't miss. Nike's ACG Ascent is even less expensive, running well under $200. These instruments (the term "watch" hardly describes what they are) provide for an extremely compact and accurate altimeter/barometer. Which is the one for you? If you're looking for the most high-tech, accurate, and sophisticated watch, the Avocet Alpin is the instrument of choice. It will keep track of the altitude and barometric readings in either conventional feet and inches of mercury respectively or in their metric equivalents. In addition, it will track your daily total ascent and rate of ascent and will even keep track of your total feet ascended over a period of time. The weather function shows the barometric trend and is easily adjustable to compensate for elevation change. Of course the Avocet Alpin also keeps regular time and has a date and alarm function and a split/lap timer. We liked the split/lap timer on hikes as it allowed us to easily track hiking, resting, and total time throughout the day.

If you are not the type of person who reads the directions, you will be frustrated using the Avocet Alpin. We have had students who owned them over a year and still did not know how to use most of the functions. It is not intuitive and will take time and practice to learn. Once you have mastered the use of this fine instrument, however, you will wonder how you hiked without it.

Jack has had great success with his trusty Nike ACG Ascent Compass watch, which adds a digital compass feature to the mix. This watch provides him with compass readings and altitude at the touch of a button, and even generates a weather forecast based on saved barometric readings. Nike's "Zero Drift" technology supposedly compensates or adjusts for weather-related pressure changes, which ordinarily would change altimeter readings. For example, most barometric altimeters determine your elevation by measuring the pressure of the air on the instrument. This changes constantly, leaving the hiker with the puzzling situation of having gone to bed having been told by his or her watch that the elevation was, say, 2,500 feet only to wake up to have their watch read 2,000 feet. Of course this really means that the weather has changed, not the altitude. In any event, wrist mounted altimeter/barometers can be a helpful addition to the backcountry techweenie's widget wardrobe.

Triangulation

A variation of the above technique can also be used to figure out where one is when three known points can be recognized. Suppose the Stumps were really gluttons for punishment and were willing to go on another off-trail adventure. This time, they planned to hike up Scarface Mountain.

The Stumps' previous adventures gave them the confidence to take an alternative route rather than the heavily used trail. They had done all their homework, but despite their best efforts, when they reached the top of a small mountain and looked to the right, they saw the namesake scar of Scarface Mountain about a half a mile away. The Stumps were surrounded by small hills, and as Forrest looked at his map he realized that he was not sure which one they were on. They saw the scar on Scarface. They saw what appeared to be McKenzie Mountain.

Heck, they clearly saw the 1980 Winter Olympic Village (since turned into a federal prison), but Forrest still wasn't sure exactly where they were. By plotting these three points on his map, he used *triangulation*, the process of locating an unknown point by using intersecting bearings taken on three known points. In this case, the Stumps first had to take a field bearing of the scar on Scarface Mountain. They converted this field bearing to a map bearing taking into account declination (since they are east of 0° declination, they subtracted 14° degrees). They then placed the edge of the compass base plate on the scar with the "direction of travel" arrow facing the scar.

Keeping the front tip of the base plate on the scar, they rotated the compass base plate around the landmark until the orienting arrow and the orienting lines pointed to true north on the map. Forrest then drew a pencil line on the map along the compass base plate edge that touched the scar. He then repeated this procedure for each of the other landmarks.

Once all three landmarks have been plotted, the lines should intersect at one point (the lines may have to be extended). The spot where the lines intersect is your approximate location. Don't be disappointed if the lines don't meet precisely at some given point. Given the level of sophistication of normal compasses and one's skill level, an approximate location should determine which mountain you are on and satisfy the need to know "where you are."

TRICKS OF THE TRADE: Drawing Declination Lines

Drawing pencil lines parallel to magnetic north/south across the map will eliminate the need to add or subtract when taking map bearings. However, this method is discouraged until participants have a thorough understanding of why and when to add or subtract when taking bearings. Don't be confused by the Universal Transverse Mercator (UTM) grid lines marked on metric maps such as in Figure 6.19. They do not correspond exactly to true north.

Advancing with the Map and Compass

Like any skill, improvement with map and compass takes practice and requires a natural progression. Start off slowly, use the map on your trail hikes, and let it help you figure out where you are. Use the map with the compass on mountaintops to figure out what the features around you are. Don't despair if you take the wrong trail intersection and don't realize it until an hour later. Learn from your mistakes. Plan your first off-trail hikes carefully so that your family and friends want to go again. Remember your lunch. Before you know it you'll be venturing off the trail and finding a whole new world that was inaccessible to you before.

TRAIL TECHNIQUES

"Trail techniques" is a term coined by wilderness education pioneer Paul Petzoldt. In his classic book, *The Wilderness Handbook*, he defines trail techniques as "the means by which one prevents fatigue and avoids mistakes which might lead to survival situations. These skills involve efficient use of backpacks, group organization along the trail, conservation of energy, and safe maneuvering over varied terrain."[1] We look at trail techniques as the practices that allow a group to hike efficiently, comfortably, and safely while minimizing the chances of getting lost.

PHILOSOPHY TIP: The Journey

Some people think hiking down the trail is the price you have to pay to get to your destination. We think that hiking should be thought of as a metaphor for life. Life is appreciating the journey, not just rushing to the destination. Just as life has ups and downs, good times and bad, so does hiking. In life we may try to make our journey smoother, but few people want to eliminate life's adventures. We feel the same way about hiking.

Have you ever been on a trip where you or a companion feel like you have been run over by a railroad train? Have you ever arrived in camp with your tongue dragging on the ground and large blisters on your heels, feeling dehydrated and ready to bite off your partner's head if she reminds you one more time that she thought it was only 3 miles to the campsite? After 7 hours of trail torture she lets you know that she's never going camping with you ever again. That may be some people's idea of fun, but we believe these events can be prevented with a little foresight and effort. Not only do we find these types of experiences extremely unnecessary, but we think they are unsafe as well. Once an individual's energy reserves are depleted, they are helpless in dealing with the minor or major emergencies that develop in the backcountry.

There is a classic Adirondack story of a young man in 1974 who did nearly everything wrong in his hike to Lake Colden in the central High Peaks Wilderness Area. He and his partner were dressed poorly, had little to drink and eat, and had not slept well the previous night. The young man eventually collapsed of hypothermia a short distance from a popular camping area. When the young man's companion reached other campers, none of them were able to help because they were all too exhausted or borderline hypothermic themselves. The young man died by the time his companion could round up enough help. It is sad enough that through their own ignorance these two young men got into this tragic situation, but it is even more distressing that most of the nearly two dozen people the companion encountered could not help them because the potential rescuers themselves were exhausted.

Conservation of Energy

It is for this reason that we believe that energy conservation is one of the most fundamental trail technique concepts. *Energy conservation* entails using as little energy as possible to accomplish a given task efficiently and comfortably. It involves coordinating the heartbeat and breathing to regulate one's pace rather than the reverse. This idea is sort of like the tortoise and the hare. Some would argue that hiking is a time to stretch oneself to one's limits and energy conservation is contrary to this philosophy. We don't disagree, but we feel that challenging oneself physically is great as long as energy is conserved so that the hiker can deal with emergency situations and can enjoy his or her companions' company and the natural beauty of the surroundings.

How do you conserve your energy while hiking? There are five things you can do to keep energized all day: regulate your pace, use rhythmic breathing techniques, use the rest step, take regular rest stops, and drink and eat frequently.

Pace

Regulating pace to conserve energy is a simple concept, but it is difficult to master. By slowing down the rate at which we hike, we save energy. It is that simple; don't let others tell you otherwise. What is a good pace? A good pace is one at which a conversation can be carried on at all times and group members can hike all day with occasional short rests and not be exhausted at the end of the day. Although this sounds simple, it becomes complicated because of personal differences. What is an easygoing pace for some is torment for others. How do you deal with this? It only makes sense for the faster hikers to slow down rather than make the slower hikers speed up. We tell our students who are training to be outdoor leaders that they can only hike as fast as the slowest person.

Rhythmic Breathing

The idea of *rhythmic breathing* is to synchronize your walking steps with your breathing. Think of yourself as a big 18-wheel tractor trailer trying to maintain a constant RPM. On the flats you keep a regular rhythm, which allows you to breathe regularly and have a moderate heartbeat. When you come to a hill, like the truck, you downshift and slow your pace without increasing your heart or breathing rate. You don't maintain your regular pace and just start breathing harder and have your pulse start racing. The idea is to have your breathing and heart rate maintain a steady pace whether hiking uphill, downhill, or on level terrain.

Rhythmic breathing is developed by coordinating the number of steps with the number of breaths. On level terrain with a moderate load, you may take three large steps for every breath. As the terrain gets steeper, the load heavier, or the oxygen thinner, shorten the step length and the number of breaths between steps.

The goal is to maintain a comfortable pace and still make forward progress. This skill does not come naturally to many people, but with practice it eventually becomes second nature.

The Rest Step

The *rest step* uses the skeletal structure to provide support and give the hiker's muscles a rest while climbing steep inclines. Lock the knee with each step, putting weight on the skeletal system instead of depending on the muscles for support. The steeper the terrain, the shorter the distance between steps and the longer the period of rest between steps. Dipping the shoulder on the side of the front foot takes the weight of the pack off that shoulder, allowing it to rest. Like rhythmic breathing, the rest step doesn't always come naturally. With practice, the rest step becomes a natural part of your gait.

When possible, walk as flatfooted as possible, preventing the tiring of calf and foot muscles. As you walk, swing the foot up to the next step, lifting it no more than necessary. This saves on muscle exertion.

Rest Breaks

Although some people like to see how far they can hike without a rest and others honestly don't feel the need to rest, we believe that breaks are an important part of a camper's trail techniques. Just as it is counterproductive to wait until you are dehydrated to drink water, the idea of taking a rest is to *prevent* exhaustion. You don't want to take a break because you are exhausted.

If people in your group are finding it difficult to make it from one rest break to the next, either the pace is too fast or the time between breaks is too long. When backpacking with moderate-weight packs, we recommend starting easily and establishing set hiking and resting times. You might set a pace of hiking 30 minutes and resting 5 minutes for the first hour or two. If the group is strong you might move it up to 40 or 50 minutes of hiking with a 5-minute break. Remember, the idea is to rest before getting tired, not when the group is already tired.

It is important for all group members to know when break times will be. For physically weaker group members, knowing how much longer they have to hike before a rest gives them a goal to shoot for; they know that a break is at the end of the tunnel. We advocate short breaks of 5 minutes to minimize lactic acid (a waste product of muscle activity) buildup. We acknowledge that although this may be a worthy goal, it is difficult to achieve. Whatever length of time is decided on, try to stick to it unless judgment dictates otherwise.

When taking a break, try to anticipate other people hiking by. Move to the side of the trail, or preferably off it, to be out of the way of others who may pass by. We remember one trip in a remote section of the Adirondacks where, even though the chances were low of encountering anyone (it was during the middle of the week, in late fall on one of the least-used Adirondack horse trails), the student leader of the day had the discipline to make sure the group was well to the side of the trail. Suddenly, six horseback riders traipsed through. They were very grateful for our group's courtesy, and the student took great pride in knowing he had done the correct thing.

Trail Nutrition

Taking in plenty of food and liquids helps maintain good morale and provides strength and energy. We encourage grazing, or the art of eating and drinking regularly and frequently, to maximize energy levels. Regular handfuls of gorp, candy, cheese, or pepperoni and a few gulps of water, powdered fruit drink, or iced tea go a long way in keeping up spirits and energy levels. See Chapter 4 for additional information on nutrition.

Knowing Where You Are

As advocates of campers taking responsibility for their own actions, we can't overemphasize the importance of knowing where you and your companions are at all times. Ask yourself if the trail is going where you expect it should. How does the terrain compare to the map? Where was the last trail marker, blaze (paint or hatchet mark), or cairn (pile of rocks marking a route)?

Trail Courtesy

As a courtesy to other people you encounter, use judgment in stepping to one side of the trail to let groups pass. When hiking on horse trails, come to a complete stop and stand on the downhill side when encountering horses. Horses are very easily spooked by humans wearing backpacks and can be injured more easily running downhill than up. Speak softly to the horseback riders and make the horses aware of your presence.

Hiking

When hiking uphill, try to maintain an upright posture and avoid leaning into the hill. Although leaning into the hill gives a sense of security, standing upright improves balance and chance of a quick recovery if footing is lost. Standing upright also improves your traction by putting all of your weight directly on your feet. Hiking downhill takes more effort than many people realize. When hiking downhill, if you feel the gravity and momentum urging you to break into a run, fight it by bending the knees slightly and using small steps to stay in control. If your boots give you problems on the downhill trek, don't be afraid to try some different lacing approaches to minimize discomfort. If you usually keep the lower eyelets loose and upper ones tight, try reversing it. Keep experimenting until maximum comfort is found.

Figure 6.22
The practice of contouring saves precious energy.

When hiking off-trail, the art of contouring can conserve energy and be easier and safer. *Contouring* is hiking along the same elevation rather than hiking up and down the terrain. Use your judgment to determine whether contouring around a hill rather than going up and over it will save energy or time.

Change clothes along the trail as necessary. Don't get too hot or cold just because you don't want to ask your companions to take a short break. We encourage our students to take clothing breaks whenever necessary to maintain a comfortable body temperature.

When hiking in thick growth where branches may slap you in the face, it is generally easier for you to be responsible for keeping a safe distance from the person in front of you than for that person to hold branches for you.

Low-Impact Trail Thoughts

There are a number of little commonsense tips that help minimize our impact on the outdoors. The most obvious of all is taking care to make sure you and your companions leave no litter along the trail. We go to great lengths to avoid leaving anything that wasn't in the wilderness before we entered it, other than human waste. Human waste is a special case in which catholes should be used for solid waste and judgment should be used for liquid waste disposal. We won't disgust you with the story of the camper one of us encountered squatting in the middle of the trail! Check Chapter 5 for a more thorough review of this topic.

Try to keep the noise down as you trek down the trail and also try to stay in the trail treadway even when it's muddy. Walking on the sides of the trail just makes the trail wider and harder to maintain. Stay on existing trails—don't start new paths or walk on evolving human "herd paths." Also, never cut across switchbacks. Switchbacks are designed to protect steep areas by minimizing erosion. Cutting switchbacks creates direct paths for water runoff, which greatly accelerates erosion.

Always try to walk on durable surfaces, such as open rocks, sand, and gravel, in order to minimize trail erosion. Most of us have seen deeply eroded trails in remote places that truly mar the landscape. Let's try not to create more of these scars. Hike in single file on trails in order to keep treadways narrow. Conversely, spread out your group when hiking cross-country, in order to avoid creating pathways. Hiking cross-country often requires specialized knowledge of indigenous ecosystems. Consult land management agencies to be aware of the impact of cross-country travel on fragile life-forms.

Make sure that you never crowd or harass wildlife. Although most people greatly appreciate wild creatures, they should curb the instinct to get close and touch animals. We can easily adversely affect wild animals' feeding and migrating patterns by crowding them. In fact, being too close sometimes invites animals to feed on you! Keep your distance.

Trail Organization

Most of us don't travel in large hiking groups, but regardless of your group's size there are certain things that should be considered. First, don't allow your group to split up except in the rarest of circumstances. In a number of parts of the country, groups splitting up is the number one cause for organized searches. The old line, "Don't worry, I'll catch up," is inappropriate and inconsiderate. Wait for your companions, because they may not know the right way, may not have the same level of experience that you have, or may not have the same understanding of where you are heading or meeting.

If your group consists of more than two people (and they always should) there are two group roles that we feel are essential for safe travel. The *scout* sets the pace and determines the route. In small groups this task can be shared, but one person should have the clear responsibility. We are advocates of President Harry S. Truman's famous quote, "The buck stops here." Someone needs to be ultimately responsible for a given job. The role of *sweep*, the last person in the group, is to make sure no one falls behind or drops anything and that the pace is appropriate. With larger groups, the sweep makes sure the group does not get too spread out.

Blister Prevention and Care

Preventing and taking care of blisters is important for ensuring enjoyment and maintaining safety. We have seen people evacuated from the wilderness because of poor blister care. Think of a foot blister as a second-degree burn created from the heat generated from the sock and boot rubbing against your skin.

Blister Prevention

Good blister prevention starts with good socks. Don't try to save money on socks. We have hiked thousands of miles and our feet have been grateful for the high-quality socks we wear. We recommend wearing two pairs of socks. Two socks will rub against each other and the boot, minimizing friction against the foot. We prefer one light polypropylene sock and one heavier wool/synthetic blend sock. Adjusting your socks and boot laces can help prevent blisters or minimize their discomfort.

Good walking technique can go a long way in preventing blisters. In particular, walking flatfooted helps because the foot does less bending and so generates less friction.

Probably the most important thing to do to minimize blisters is to promptly treat hot spots. A *hot spot* is an irritation felt on the foot well before a blister forms. It may feel "hot" or just irritated. If this happens, stop immediately. Don't worry about holding up the rest of your companions. If you don't stop, you will eventually get a blister and have to treat it as well as deal with the discomfort.

Get out the moleskin from your first aid kit. If you have never used moleskin, you are missing out on one of western civilization's greatest inventions. Contrary to rumor, moleskin does not come from large mole farms located in Hope, Arkansas. Moleskin is a sturdy synthetic felt-like fabric with an adhesive backing that reduces friction on the skin. For hot spots, cut out a round or oval piece larger than the hot spot (square edges tend to curl off more readily), peel off the adhesive backing, and place it over the hot spot. Leave it on until your camping trip ends or it falls off.

We have friends who put petroleum jelly on their feet at the start of a trip, stick strips of duct tape on their heels, or place moleskin on the most likely places they get blisters. This is all good medicine for preventing blisters and may head off further troubles down the trail.

Blister Treatment

Once the blister has formed, we recommend catching it early and using the same procedure as listed above, with one exception. The one exception is to cut a small hole the size of the blister out of the center of the piece of moleskin. This "donut" is then placed over the blister. Sometimes you may want to use two pieces of moleskin on top of each other to raise the level of the moleskin above the blister. Some people prefer molefoam over moleskin. Molefoam is thicker and we don't like it for that reason. From our experience it takes up more room in the boot and can cause additional friction.

A more recent technology works extremely well for blisters. Second Skin™ is a thin layer of gel that has a cooling effect on hot spots and blisters and relieves soreness. In fact, it practically eliminates friction. However, it is a more expensive alternative and additional tape is necessary to apply it because it has no adhesive.

Physical Fitness

Physical fitness is an important consideration when traveling in the backcountry. Being physically fit allows for more enjoyment because fatigue doesn't occur as quickly. It also helps to minimize frustration and interpersonal conflict as well as helps the hiker avoid injury and illness. Strength and stamina also provide an extra margin of safety in emergency situations. We work hard to stay in shape for our monthlong wilderness ventures, yet no matter how hard we work, the mountains seem to get steeper and the trails longer while our students seem to get stronger and faster. Without prior physical conditioning, our trips wouldn't be much fun at all.

CONCLUSION

It is while traveling during our outdoor adventures that our most serious emergencies can occur. Getting lost, exhausted, dehydrated, and injured are mostly preventable phenomena. Practicing the skills introduced in this chapter will go a long way in preventing injury and mishap.

Notes

[1]Petzoldt, P. (1984). *The new wilderness handbook (2nd ed)*. New York: W.W. Norton.

References

Braasch, G. (1973, Fall). Reading a map at a glance. *Backpacker*, p. 34.

Drury, J., Ed. (2005). *The backcountry classroom: Lessons, tools and activities for teaching outdoor leaders*. Guilford, CT: Falcon Guide.

Hart, J. (1977). *Walking softly in the wilderness*. San Francisco: Sierra Club Books.

Jacobson, C. (1988). *The basic essentials of map & compass*. Merrilville, IN: ICS Books, Inc.

Kjellstrom, B. (1976). *Be expert with map and compass: The orienteering handbook*. New York: Charles Scribner's Sons.

Mehaffey, J., Yeazel, J., DePriest, D. (2004). *Important features for a hiking G.P.S*. Retrieved Dec. 14, 2005, from: http://www.gpsinformation.net/

Petzoldt, P. (1984). *The new wilderness handbook* (2nd ed.). New York: W.W. Norton (Original work published in 1974).

Simer, P., & Sullivan, J. (1983). *The National Outdoor Leadership School's wilderness guide*. New York: Simon and Schuster.

Vivian, E. (1973). *Sourcebook for environmental education*. St. Louis: C.V. Mosby.

Warren, J.W. (1986, May). Map and compass fundamentals. *Adirondak, (4)*, 12–16.

Wilderness Education Association. *Instructor's Manual* [Manual]. Unpublished.

CHAPTER 7
Safety and Emergency Procedures for the Backcountry

"Thou shalt not forget that the first-aid kit that saves lives rarely comes stuffed in a bag but in the human brain that stores skills."

—*Buck Tilton*

Topics:
- Judgment
- The Importance of Medical Training
- Pre-Trip Physical Conditioning
- Backcountry Skill Levels
- Pre-Trip Checklist
- Emergency Procedures for the Backcountry
- Evacuation Routes and Emergency Contacts
- Hypothermia
- Altitude-Related Illnesses

People often think of safety in the backcountry in terms of response. We think that the rugged outdoor woman or mountain man should be able to provide traction for a fractured femur with fishing line and a spatula. We picture movie characters suturing open wounds in the field with an awl and thread. We marvel at the resourcefulness of any of the MacGyver-style outdoor survival manuals that trumpet improvised water stills, tourniquets, and litters. How do we gain such skills? The more important question is, why do we need them? Instead of the paradigm of response-oriented emergency procedures, we suggest a proactive safety program for backcountry traveling groups that begins weeks before the first step beyond the trailhead. Thorough preparation wedded with good judgment should be sufficient to deal with almost all wilderness medical emergencies. Unfortunately, no matter how we prepare for emergencies, fate, lack of luck, or probability sometimes throw the backcountry traveler situations they are vastly unprepared for. Some people say this risk is the reason for wilderness travel.

JUDGMENT

Judgment and self-confidence are very important elements in your backcountry emergency response program. Students of emergency medicine discover that almost every procedure has a very specific algorithm, or pattern for use. They also discover that these specific approved methods change almost continually and that their administration is governed by judgment. In other words, although medical providers need to know their systems and techniques, how and when to use these techniques remains largely dependent on situational variables.

What is judgment and how do you gain it? Judgment is the ever-increasing sphere of information and wisdom that is available to help a person make sound decisions under a variety of circumstances. This pool of information is gained by constantly increasing one's experiences in widely different situations and then consciously evaluating and drawing sound conclusions from each experience.

 BOTTOM-LINE TIP: Judgment
Judgment is knowledge gained from conscious and thoughtful experience.

We urge you to apply judgment to everything you read in this chapter. Indeed, look at all the information in this book with judgment. We do not attempt to write gospel truths about outdoor experiences in these pages. We understand, and hope that you will understand, that the information in these pages cannot conduct a safe backcountry trip. You conduct a safe backcountry trip and should apply this and other sources of information in the specific contexts of the hundreds of different situations you will encounter.

BEING PROACTIVE FOR SAFETY: PRE-TRIP CONSIDERATIONS

The Importance of Medical Training

What this chapter will not do is to provide a thorough discussion of methods for emergency medical treatment. We have neither the space nor the official capacity to do so. We urge any backcountry user to acquire some level of emergency medical training from any of the several community and private organizations currently offering them. There is no substitute or excuse for not having medical training appropriate for the backcountry activity and setting of one's trip.

Outdoorspeople also need to recognize that all medical courses are not created equal. Unless the course includes material designed specifically for the backcountry traveler, the course will be oriented to the care provider who can count on help from the ambulance squad in short order. These "community" oriented courses do not cover what you need to know: namely, how to stabilize and care for your patient for several hours or days in situations miles from professional help.

Standard First Aid provides a minimum of information and techniques for dealing with emergency situations. It describes methods for stabilizing simple fractures, open wounds, and heat-related illnesses. Coupled with cardiopulmonary resuscitation (CPR), Standard First Aid is the bare minimum of training recreational backcountry users should have for short outings.

First Responder, Wilderness First Responder (WFR), and *Emergency Responder* courses provide more detailed training that covers environmental hazards and backcountry medical protocols as well as evacuation techniques. These courses are considered the state-of-the-art for outdoor leaders and are offered in 7-to-10-day intensive sessions by several different training companies, including SOLO and Wilderness Medical Associates. We believe that at least one member of any group planning a serious wilderness adventure should have WFR training.

A higher level of training, *Emergency Medical Technician* and *Wilderness Emergency Medical Technician*, offers a very comprehensive training of all body systems and advanced techniques such as intubation and oxygen administration. These courses run for entire semesters at colleges or are available in intensive one-month marathon sessions by some of the commercial training companies. This level is generally more than enough training for most trips under one month in length in continental U.S. wildernesses.

For extended international expeditions or extremely hazardous wilderness activities, backcountry travelers should consider paramedic-level training or enlist the help of a physician's assistant, nurse practitioner, or medical doctor. See your local medical school.

Obviously, obtaining appropriate medical training takes some degree of prior planning, time, and money. Training is the type of focused, thoughtful experience that contributes most rapidly to the formation of outdoor judgment and should be considered an essential step before venturing into the backcountry.

Pre-Trip Physical Conditioning

Another step that should be considered to contribute to a safe, enjoyable backcountry experience is assessing and developing an appropriate level of physical conditioning. We've seen too many wilderness experiences ruined for individuals and the group around them by travelers possessing inadequate strength and stamina for the wilderness setting.

Pre-trip physical conditioning contributes to expedition safety because a fit backcountry traveler is less prone to exhaustion and exhaustion-related injuries, such as fractures, strains, concussions, and wounds related to heavy lifting and fatigue-related falling. Increased energy and immunity levels, a happy by-product of fitness, help to reduce the occurrence and spread of illness that can run rampant in groups.

Fitness also contributes to morale and positive interactions between group members. Generally speaking, fit backcountry travelers can enjoy themselves more than exhausted travelers and will be more likely to continue their relationships with the wilderness.

We suggest that backcountry travelers assess their fitness level several months before the planned trip and work to either maintain a good level of fitness or improve a low level. Consult books or people about your workout, but generally, try to work out with the same activities you will be using in the backcountry. That is, if you plan to backpack on your trip, go out on hikes while carrying a loaded pack and hike distances as closely resembling your upcoming trip as possible. This way, you will be gaining strength and stamina as well as activity-specific skills.

Building Backcountry Skill Levels for Safety

Possessing an appropriate level of activity and outdoor living skills is just as important as physical fitness for backcountry safety. While there is plenty of room in backcountry activities for novice skill levels, it is very important that some members of the party possess significant skill levels and time logged in the field. The trip should not be "over the head" of at least two members of the party, hopefully the party leaders. In other words, the place for pushing the leaders' limits is with parties of highly experienced peers; novices should be accompanied by competent and comfortable outdoor people capable of supplying information and leadership in safety situations.

Take opportunities to build each person's overall skill level in anticipation of your trip. Growing skill levels contribute to enjoyment, increasingly challenging trips, empowerment, leadership, and trust between group members. Most importantly, improving skill levels increases the human resources available to deal with backcountry medical emergencies.

PRE-TRIP CHECKLIST

Several tasks require either the direct or indirect participation of all group members. The group can divide these tasks between members, but someone must ensure that all are accomplished with appropriate quality. It is not good enough to have a vague idea of whom to call in the case of emergency, for example. Safety and emergency procedures need to be clearly researched and spelled out for everyone's thorough understanding.

Sharing Medical Histories

We have been taught by our society that our medical concerns are our own private business. In the case of backcountry activities where a small group of people face physical hardships and an absence of immediate emergency medical support, it becomes essential that the leaders, or in some cases all members, know everybody's relevant medical conditions and history.

Your group may want to sit down and share each person's relevant medical histories, paying attention to allergies, orthopedic injuries and fractures, medical conditions such as diabetes or hypertension, current medications, and illnesses. If a prospective group member is unsure of his or her health or if other group members voice sufficient concern, a physical examination by a doctor could help clarify the picture.

Most people will gladly share their particular physical concerns. You may find that some people need to be asked to stop talking about all their old football injuries or childhood illnesses!

Maintaining Equipment

Designate someone to check out and repair all tents, stoves, packs, ropes, vehicles, and any equipment that the group will rely upon during the upcoming trip. We hope you never have to experience the distinct frustration of trying to set up a tent on the first night, during a rainstorm, only to find out that you've left one tent pole in the attic. Oh, yes—it happens! Hopefully, all equipment was put away cleaned and repaired in anticipation of the next trip. Try to set this proactive precedent to reduce headaches as your next trip approaches.

Considering the Trip Environment

Take a look at the trip's geographic location and the terrain and do some research to give your group some idea of what to expect from the environment. Find out the weather history for your trip's time period for the years preceding the trip. Look at the effects of local insects, plants, and animals on your plans. Check to see that trails go where you want them to and that bridges do in fact exist where you plan to cross a river.

Historically, can you expect a 10-foot snowpack at higher elevations? Can daytime temperatures reach the low 80s while nighttime temperatures dip into the 20s? Is flooding a consideration with spring rains? Do black flies swarm in clouds of bloodsucking insanity? Does poison ivy wind its way throughout the forest floor? Do grizzly bears routinely invade camps, scaring the daylights out of campers?

Find out the answers to all your questions and plan for potential hazards and emergencies accordingly. Federal, state, and local land managers are generally more than happy to share information with you, since a well-prepared group is generally responsible and safe.

Obtaining the First Aid Kit

Outdoor experts and their preferred first aid kits are as numerous and varied as opinions about politics. Everyone will tell you something different. Some minimalists will bring only a roll of adhesive tape, gauze, and moleskin, while eager would-be sawbones bring $300 field surgery cases for dealing immediately with almost any problem. In general, it is important that the kit match your ability and training; you should know how to use each item (Figure 7.1). Consult Dr. Forgey's book on the subject, *Wilderness Medicine*, for a thorough discussion of first aid and first aid kits.

You may want to purchase one of the many excellent prepackaged first aid kits for sale by several companies. These companies have spent years researching and testing their first aid kits, so that you don't have to worry about what to bring. In most cases (unless you work in a hospital), the commercial kits are actually cheaper than if you were to buy each item separately. Be sure that you know how to use each item, however. It makes little sense to bring items that require training and knowledge beyond your level.

Make sure that your first aid kit is up-to-date. Don't bring Uncle Wally's Vietnam War emergency kit. Check that medications, if any, are not expired and that quantities of consumable items (pain pills, bandages) have been renewed.

Also, make sure that everyone in the group knows who is carrying the first aid kit, where it is, and who is capable of using it.

SAMPLE WILDERNESS FIRST AID KIT
(Adaptable for multiweek North American trekking.)

EMERGENCY KIT
- 1 pair trauma scissors
- Blob mask
- 6 pairs latex gloves
- Povidone/Iodine solution or ointment (Betadine)
- 2 Epi-pens/Ana-kit
- 1 pencil
- Memo pads
- 2 quarters
- 6 incident report kits
- 1 risk management form with emergency information (filled out)
- SOAP notes (forms for recording medical observations)
- 2 cravats (large triangular cloths for slings and lashing splints, etc.)
- 4 large safety pins
- 15 4 x 4-in. sterile gauze pads
- 2 gauze rolls (4-in. Kerlix)
- 2 trauma dressings or blood stoppers

PERSONAL CARE KIT
- Nail clippers
- Splinter tweezers
- OB tampons
- 1 tube antifungal cream (Micatin, Tolfonate 1%)

WOUND CARE
- 1 ace bandage
- 18–24 Band-Aids (fabric)
- Tegaderm, or tube gauze
- 1 package of moleskin
- 1 roll of adhesive fabric athletic tape
- Antibacterial ointment (Triple antibiotic ointment, Neosporin, Polysporin, Polymixin, Bacitracin, etc.) in foil packets
- 1 tube of Hydrocortisone ointment 1%
- 3 x 4-in. Spenco Second Skin

MEDS
- 24 aspirin
- 24 Acetaminophen (Aceta-Gesic, Tylenol)
- 24 Ibuprofen (200 mg) (Mobegesic, Motrin, Advil, Datril, Nuprin, etc.)
- 12 antihistamines (Benadryl)
- 12 decongestant tablets (Sudafed)
- 12 antacid tablets (Dimacid, Gaviscon, Mylanta, Teralac, or Maalox)
- 12 anti-diarrhea tablets (Loperamide, Diasorb, Imodium A-D, etc.)

Figure 7.1
Adapt the sample first aid kit list to fit your trip.

EMERGENCY PROCEDURES FOR THE BACKCOUNTRY

Before you head into the field, make sure that at least the trip leaders, and preferably the entire group, are familiar with a standard procedure for action in the event of a medical emergency. This will reduce anxiety and confusion in the event of an emergency, increase confidence and sense of group safety overall, and may save lives due to increased efficiency of group response. While we encourage backcountry travelers to obtain high-quality medical training, this section should be thought of as a framework for administering medical care.

These emergency procedures are organized roughly in the order in which they would occur in the actual emergency situation.

Immediate Considerations in an Emergency Situation

- **Stop and think**. Look around the scene of the accident and/or consider the context for the illness or injury. Decisions should not be rushed but should be carefully thought out within the time limits of the situation. Make sure the setting is safe for you to enter.
- **Delegate emergency roles**. The leader should clearly emerge in an emergency situation and should enlist group members with suitable skills to take different roles. It is important to give everybody in the group something to do. Accidents and illnesses can be very upsetting to group members; helpful activity is the surest way to keep everybody calm. Consider all these roles:

  1. *Emergency medical caregiver*. Designate the person with the highest level of training and confidence.
  2. *Recorder*. This person should take accurate notes, including the time of the incident, mechanism of injury, patient vital signs, treatment given, patient name and relevant history, etc. Use a standard incident report form (Figure 7.2) when possible. It helps keep you organized in a time of crisis.
  3. *Messengers*. If necessary, form a messenger party of three to four individuals to run for help.
  4. *Assistants*. These people can help by setting up tents, bringing warm clothing and food, or otherwise helping with the physical well-being of the group as a whole.

- *Care for the patient and the group*. Make sure that not all attention is focused on the current patient. In dangerous or poor weather conditions, neglected group members soon become patients themselves. Try to create a calm, caring atmosphere with lots of tender loving care for the patient.
- *Decide on a course of action*. After administering initial care, the leader and the medical person should decide if outside help is necessary. Does the patient need to be evacuated? Can the patient walk out or is outside assistance necessary?

Wilderness Education Association

Wilderness Risk Managers Committee Incident Report Form

If you have any questions regarding how to complete this form properly, please consult the accompanying instruction sheet.

Affiliate: _____

Program Type: NSP   PSC   WSP   WEW   (circle one)

Course Name: _____

Name: _____

Age: _____ ❑ Male ❑ Female ❑ Staff ❑ Student/Client

Incident Date: _____/_____/_____   Time _____:_____ a.m./p.m.

Total Days of Course: _____   Day Incident Occurred: _____

Type of Environment. Check all that apply:
❑ River ❑ Lake ❑ Ocean ❑ Forest ❑ Mountain ❑ Cliff ❑ Glacier ❑ Snow/Ice ❑ Desert ❑ Cold Environment

Surface Condition. Check the two most significant:
❑ Wet   ❑ Dry   ❑ Snow   ❑ Ice   ❑ Trail   ❑ Rock   ❑ Uneven   ❑ Flat   ❑ Sloped

Type of Incident. Check most significant:
❑ Injury   ❑ Illness   ❑ Motivation/Behavioral   ❑ Near Miss   ❑ Fatality

Is this a Lost-Day case? ❑ NO   ❑ YES, Number of days lost _____

Did the patient leave the field? ❑ NO   ❑YES, Date: _____/_____/_____

Evacuation Method: ❑ Unassisted ❑ Walking Assisted ❑ Litter Carry   ❑ Vehicle ❑ Helicopter ❑ Other _____

Did the patient visit a medical facility? ❑ NO ❑ YES If yes,   ❑ Outpatient?   ❑ Admitted?

Victim returned to the course? ❑ NO   ❑ YES, Date _____/_____/_____

Property Damage ❑ NO   ❑ YES. If yes, ❑ Vehicle   ❑ Equipment ❑ Other: _____

(continued)

Figure 7.2
Sample incident report form.

Wilderness Risk Managers Committee Incident Report Form (continued)

Type of Injury. Choose the most significant:

- ❏ Blister(s)
- ❏ Burn
- ❏ Dental
- ❏ Dislocation
- ❏ Eye injury
- ❏ Fracture
- ❏ Frostbite
- ❏ Head injury (change in LOC)
- ❏ Head injury (no change in LOC)
- ❏ Ligament sprain
- ❏ Muscle strain
- ❏ Immersion foot
- ❏ Near drowning or immersion
- ❏ Soft tissue (bruise, wound, abrasion)
- ❏ Sunburn
- ❏ Tendonitis
- ❏ Other (explain)

Anatomical Location of Injury. Choose most appropriate:

- ❏ Abdomen
- ❏ Ankle
- ❏ Chest
- ❏ Elbow
- ❏ Eye
- ❏ Face
- ❏ Foot
- ❏ Forearm
- ❏ Hand/Fingers
- ❏ Head
- ❏ Hip
- ❏ Knee
- ❏ Lower back
- ❏ Lower Leg
- ❏ Neck
- ❏ Pelvis
- ❏ Shoulder
- ❏ Thigh
- ❏ Toe
- ❏ Upper Arm
- ❏ Upper Back
- ❏ Wrist

Type of Illness. Choose most significant:

- ❏ Abdominal pain
- ❏ Allergic reaction
- ❏ Altitude illness
- ❏ Apparent food-related illness
- ❏ Chest pain or cardiac condition
- ❏ Dehydration
- ❏ Diarrhea
- ❏ Eye or ear infection
- ❏ Flu symptoms/"cold"
- ❏ Heat illness
- ❏ Hypothermia
- ❏ Nausea or vomiting
- ❏ Nonspecific fever illness
- ❏ Skin infection
- ❏ Upper respiratory illness
- ❏ Urinary tract infection
- ❏ Other (explain)

Type of Activity. Check the activity at the time of the incident

- ❏ Backpacking
- ❏ Camping
- ❏ Canoeing
- ❏ Caving
- ❏ Cooking
- ❏ Cycling
- ❏ Dog sledding
- ❏ Glacier travel
- ❏ Hiking (no pack)
- ❏ Horseback riding
- ❏ Independent travel
- ❏ Initiative game
- ❏ Mountaineering
- ❏ Portage
- ❏ Rafting
- ❏ Rappelling
- ❏ River crossing
- ❏ River kayaking
- ❏ Rock climbing
- ❏ Ropes course
- ❏ Running
- ❏ Sailing
- ❏ Sea kayaking
- ❏ Service project
- ❏ Ski (telemark/downhill)
- ❏ Ski touring
- ❏ Snowboarding
- ❏ Snow/Ice climbing
- ❏ Snowshoeing
- ❏ Solo
- ❏ Swim/Dip
- ❏ Transportation
- ❏ Other (explain)

(continued)

Wilderness Risk Managers Committee Incident Report Form

Contributing Factors. Rank in order of priority the major categories ①, ②, ③, etc.

_____ Altitude	_____ Loose rock (not rockfall)
_____ Avalanche	_____ Misbehavior
_____ Animal encounter	_____ Missing/Lost
_____ Carelessness	_____ Not following instructions
_____ Cold Exposure	_____ Overuse injury
_____ Dehydration	_____ Plant poisoning/toxicity/contact
_____ Equipment	_____ Technique
_____ Exceeded ability	_____ Preexisting medical condition
_____ Exhaustion	_____ Psychological issue
_____ Fall on rock	_____ Rock fall
_____ Fall on snow	_____ Screening
_____ Fall/Slip on trail	_____ Sunburn
_____ Falling tree/branch	_____ Supervision
_____ Fitness/ability	_____ Technical systems failure
_____ Hygiene	_____ Unknown
_____ Immersion/submersion	_____ Visibility
_____ Instruction	_____ Weather
_____ Inattention	_____ Other (explain)

Narrative: Describe the incident and provide details: distances, times, sizes, sequence of events, and so forth, to present a clear picture of the incident.

_____

_____

_____

_____

_____

Analysis: Include any suggestions, observations or recommendations regarding the incident. Why did it happen? Follow up care and any diagnosis or other outcome.

_____

_____

_____

_____

Prepared by: _____ Position: _____

Signature: _____ Date: ____/____/_____

Reviewed by: _____ Position: _____

Signature: _____ Date: ____/____/_____

Considerations for Getting Outside Assistance

- **Send at least three capable and physically strong messengers to walk out and find help.** Four is the ideal number, because if one of the messengers is injured on the way out, another may stay with the injured person while the last two continue out. Nobody should travel alone if it can be avoided. Make sure an adult or one of the people with the most experience goes with the messenger party and another similarly qualified person stays with the patient.
- **Send an accident report form** or a detailed written description of the patient's symptoms, vital signs, medical history, and treatment given with the messenger party.
- **Send a map with the accident location marked on it.** Do not rely on the messenger party's memory for the exact location of the patient.
- **Put all requests and information in writing** so that tired and nervous messengers don't forget crucial items. Ideally, make two copies of all requests and information; one stays with the patient while the other goes with the messenger party. This way, the patient's caregivers keep a record of what they asked for!
- **Give the messengers vital telephone numbers,** both for emergency medical services and for the patient's family or for the trip's sponsoring agency.
- **Make contingency plans for all reasonable eventualities.** What if help arrives in half a day? One day? Three days? What if nobody from the messenger party returns? What if the patient's condition worsens? What if it rapidly improves? What if somebody else gets sick?

SAFETY TIP/PHILOSOPHY TIP: Cell Phones

Should you bring a cell phone on your wilderness trip? This is a somewhat controversial question. Some wilderness areas have considered banning them while others encourage their use. Many feel that the use of cell phones are not appropriate in wilderness areas as wilderness is a place to be self-reliant and get away from technology. While we share some of these philosophical concerns and would just as soon see them outlawed from wilderness areas, we recognize that they can be a vital tool in helping acquire outside assistance after an incident has occurred. There are two things to keep in mind if you decide to take a cell phone into the backcountry:

1. It may not work! Cell coverage is notoriously spotty in remote areas. It may work in some areas and may not in others.
2. Don't let it take the place of a good emergency plan! Make an emergency plan as if you don't have a cell phone. If you have one and it works, great; it may speed your emergency care. If it doesn't work, your plan still will.

TECHWEENIE TIP: Emergency Beacons

Should you bring an emergency beacon? EPIRBs (Emergency Position Indicating Radio Beacons) or PLBs (Personal Locator Beacons) as they are called for personal use, are completely self-contained radio transmitters designed for emergency use. When activated, they transmit an internationally recognized distress signal. They can be found for as little as $150, but beware how you use them.

continued

Cleveland, Ohio, canoeist Carl Skalak Jr. became the first—and second—person in the contiguous United States to be rescued with a Personal Locator Beacon (PLB), got arrested and thrown in jail for the honor, and lost his $1,800 Kevlar canoe in the process.

It started when Skalak, an avid outdoorsman taking his 12th trip into the Adirondack Park of Northern New York, set out November 10, 2003, for a peaceful trip in the western part of the park. Though forecasts gave no hint of bad weather, trouble started on the second day of the trip when a storm came in. Within 24 hours temperatures dropped and portions of the river froze, blocking his way out. After waiting out the 3-day blizzard, still unable to get out due to the frozen river and heavy snowfall, he activated his PLB, which transmitted his location via satellite to the National Oceanic and Atmospheric Administration (NOAA), Virginia's Air Force Rescue Coordination Center (AFRCC), and finally emergency services in New York. Seven hours later, an Army helicopter picked him up.

All would have been fine, as search and rescue people said he did exactly what he was supposed to do, were it not for rescue number two. When Skalak returned to retrieve his gear, as luck would have it he ran into still more rain and snow. After several days of strenuous hiking, he finally made it back to where he had stashed his canoe. Arriving cold and wet, he found that someone had stolen his canoe. With no canoe to paddle out, limited rations, wet boots and clothes, and temperatures in the teens, he spent the next few days trying to dry out and stay warm before activating the beacon again just 18 days after making history for its earlier activation.

He was arrested the day after the second rescue and thrown in jail, facing charges from the state of New York's Department of Environmental Conservation (DEC) for both rescues for "inappropriate use" of the technology.

Beacon manufacturer ACR Electronics is happy both rescues worked flawlessly but advises users to activate them only when absolutely necessary. They claim that they should "only be activated in situations of grave and imminent danger when conventional communications are unavailable and all other means of self-rescue have been exhausted." Our guess is that Skalak won't be flipping the switch again anytime soon on his PLB.[1]

Evacuation Procedures

If the patient's condition is serious and the distance from medical attention is such that medical care is days away, evacuation may be considered. Consider these factors:

- **Time.** How long will it take for your group to physically evacuate the patient? Is the patient stable? Will his or her condition improve or worsen with time?
- **Distance to help**. Can your group reasonably and safely evacuate the patient over the terrain between your present location and the road?
- **Terrain.** Is the surrounding terrain dangerous, extremely challenging, swampy, confusing? Will you get the patient and the group into more trouble than they are in now by attempting an evacuation?
- **Weather.** Is a storm blowing? Should you wait for fair weather? Is the weather good now but likely to worsen?
- **Patient's condition.** Will an evacuation endanger the patient? Is the patient's condition so critical that you have to move immediately?

- **Cost.** Depending on local regulations, evacuations may be directly charged to the patient or indirectly to taxpayers. Helicopter evacuations can cost in the tens of thousands of dollars. Is such assistance absolutely necessary?
- **Mental and physical condition of the group.** Perhaps most importantly, can your group effectively meet the intense strain of a physical evacuation? Will the rigors of the evacuation cause extreme physical and mental damage to individuals?

If you determine that the patient must be evacuated by the group, consider the transportation options. The most preferable is that the patient can walk out his or her their own power. The patient may need to be carried out by group members via litter or other carrying system. The patient may need to be carried out by rescue squad or forest rangers. Lastly, the patient may need to be evacuated by helicopter or vehicle.

Evacuation Routes and Emergency Contacts

Long before you arrive at your trip location, your group should take a close look at good maps of the trip area to determine the routes the group will take in the event of an emergency evacuation. It is important to choose the quickest and easiest path to the location most likely to provide a helpful contact with the public.

Bear in mind that this path may not be the shortest in terms of distance, nor does it have to be to the closest human habitation. What if the shortest route is over a mountain or involves crossing a dangerous river? What if the nearest people are living in a militant doomsday-cult commune the next valley over? In these instances, choose a safe, longer path to more potentially reliable human contacts, such as a ranger station.

Also, make sure that you choose appropriate evacuation routes for each stage of your trip. The route may change if your path leads over a high mountain pass or crosses a difficult river; you may evacuate to the far side after the midpoint.

Choose an evacuation route that enables you to reach a telephone or 2-way radio. Find out where the nearest telephone is by contacting local officials. Also get a complete list of local emergency telephone numbers, including search and rescue squads, ambulance, helicopter, rangers, sheriff's department, local hospitals, and state police. In addition to emergency telephone numbers, compile a list of each trip member's family telephone numbers.

Once you have your routes and numbers, photocopy your map, mark your itinerary and evacuation routes, and send them to the local rangers, members of your family who are staying home, and any other people who should know where you are going. Make a packet of information including a copy of your route, emergency numbers, planned return time, and instructions for what should be done if you don't return on time. Leave a copy of this packet at your home, tacked in some conspicuous place, like your refrigerator. This enables relatives or officials to know your whereabouts in case they need to locate you. Of course, this also allows burglars to know when you are expected home, so exercise your judgment!

HYPOTHERMIA

One time Eric had a situation develop on a spring college backpacking trip in New Mexico's Rocky Mountains. On their first day of backpacking from the trailhead, one student became very tired. She had trouble hefting her backpack but refused help. She was wearing sunglasses even though the day was not bright and soon complained of a headache. Even though she was urged by other people to drink water, she did so only sporadically. After about 2 hours, she sat down in the spring snow on the side of the trail, vomited a small amount, and began shivering.

The student leader called for a complete halt and dealt with the situation with expedience and good decision making. He had two people set up a bivouac shelter and had the sick student crawl in her sleeping bag inside. He had two others light a stove to heat up soup and sent three others ahead on the trail to look for a suitable campsite. Eventually, the group camped near where the student had fallen ill, and the student regained her strength and health after a good night's sleep and a hot meal.

The student had rapidly fallen prey to *hypothermia*, or the lowering of the body's core temperature below 98° F. The situation was compounded by incomplete acclimatization to the altitude (9,000 feet), dehydration, exhaustion, and a light wind. She hadn't helped matters with her refusal to accept aid or to drink water copiously. This erosion of sound judgment is itself a classic symptom of hypothermia: Stricken people often deny the onset of the condition, making diagnosis and prompt treatment more difficult.

Prevention

What had somehow failed in this anecdote was the communication to the student of the importance of prevention for avoiding hypothermia. Wilderness medical expert Dr. William Forgey cites five factors that are crucial in preventing hypothermia in backcountry situations.[2]

1 **Pre-trip physical conditioning.** Being in good shape prevents exhaustion, which dramatically reduces the body's ability to produce heat. Poorly conditioned travelers do not have the stamina to keep their bodies moving to stay warm in hypothermia conditions.
2 **Adequate nutrition.** Hungry travelers are cold travelers. High-calorie and high-fat food items keep travelers warm and active for long periods and build reserves of energy (aka fat) in the body for emergency situations.
3 **Avoiding exhaustion.** As stated above, exhaustion soon leads to hypothermia. In fact, exhaustion is the single biggest warning factor of developing hypothermia. Plan trip routes according to the strength and stamina of the group and stop to camp before travelers become exhausted.
4 **Preventing dehydration.** Dehydration leads to decreased blood volume levels in the body. Low blood volume restricts blood and heat flow to extremities, precipitating hypothermia. Keep hydrated by drinking approximately 1 pint of water an hour when exercising vigorously.
5 **Adequate clothing.** Always bring appropriate layers of clothing in anticipation of poor weather. Bring a wind and a rain layer to keep inner clothing layers dry and warm. Avoid cotton. See Chapter 2 for more details about clothing.

Symptoms

If you can't count on the hypothermic patient to tell you that he or she is feeling cold due to impaired judgment, how can you promptly diagnose this potential killer and take steps to help? While the classic symptom of hypothermia is shivering, many people in this stage are already very cold, and treatment will have to be more dramatic than if the condition were addressed at an earlier stage.

Hypothermia is directly linked to exhaustion. While an exhausted person is not necessarily hypothermic, he or she will soon become so without heat, rest, and nutrition. Social withdrawal, or noticeable silence, often attends the onset of hypothermia. People become less talkative as they become colder.

Hypothermic people become increasingly uncoordinated as the condition worsens. Many people will have trouble operating buttons or zippers, touching their pinkies with their thumbs, or walking a straight line. Eventually, deeply hypothermic patients have blue and puffy skin, memory lapses, and difficulty speaking.

What this all means is that, essentially, you must anticipate the conditions under which you and your fellow travelers will develop hypothermia and make sure that your group has provided food and shelter to deal with these situations before they develop.

Treatment

There are two distinct types of hypothermia, each caused by different conditions. The form you will most likely encounter is *chronic hypothermia*, which is the cooling of the body's core temperature over a period of several hours due to cold weather, wetness, exhaustion, or other compounding causes. *Acute hypothermia*, sometimes called immersion hypothermia, occurs with the sudden exposure of the body to extreme cold, such as when the victim falls through ice and is immersed in freezing water. The core temperature falls rapidly and the victim can quickly fall into shock. Victims of acute hypothermia need immediate care and should be evacuated as soon as possible. See Forgey's excellent book on all types of exposure-related emergencies, *Hypothermia: Death by Exposure,* for more acute hypothermia treatment details.

The treatment of chronic hypothermia involves restoring core temperature through several methods. The first step for all degrees of hypothermia is to replace wet clothing with dry layers, especially against the skin. For cases of mild hypothermia, encourage the victim to generate his or her own heat through moderate exercise. Also, make sure the victim is hydrated by providing warm, non-caffeinated liquids. Provide calories for internal heat generation by offering high-calorie, "quick-burning" foods (carbohydrates, such as simple sugars, etc.).

For more advanced hypothermia, have the victim change into dry clothing and get into a dry sleeping bag. Provide warm, high-calorie liquids and simple foods. Consider heating water and pouring it into *tightly sealed* water bottles, which are placed inside the sleeping bag with the victim. As a last resort, zip two sleeping bags together and have one or two *warm and healthy* group members get into the sleeping bags with the victim. Through cuddling, all three people in the sleeping bags should warm up fairly quickly. Be sure that the would-be rescuers don't get chilled by the cool victim. Also, make sure that the rescuers don't get too warm and begin to sweat on the victim.

ALTITUDE-RELATED ILLNESSES

An infrequent but not insignificant effect of ascending to altitudes above 6,500 feet is altitude-related illnesses that may interrupt or alter trip plans and, in the worst case, cause severe sicknesses. As elevation increases, the thickness and oxygen content of the atmosphere decreases, which causes a host of physiological changes in the mountaineer's body. While some people climb mountains to "get high," others find that getting high makes them very ill.

Prevention

Altitude-related illnesses may be treated by ensuring slow ascents at altitudes above 9,000 feet (1,000 feet per day) and light physical activity for the first 2 to 4 days at high elevation. This adjustment period allows the body to change and adapt to the new alpine environment.

Symptoms

The oxygen-poor alpine environment starves the body for the oxygen it needs for its normal function. Stricken travelers may complain of fatigue, headaches, nausea, and breathlessness. Acute mountain sickness (AMS), high-altitude pulmonary edema (HAPE), and high-altitude cerebral edema (HACE) may develop. You may consult mountain medicine books for thorough discussions of each. At this point, you should be concerned with the prevention and immediate treatment of altitude-related illnesses.

Treatment

With any of the three altitude-related sicknesses, the most expedient treatment method is rapid descent to lower elevations. Usually, a descent of 1,000–3,000 feet brings quick relief to the stricken patient.[3] If you have reason to suspect HAPE or HACE or if the victim is more than moderately ill, take the victim to a hospital for a complete examination.

CONCLUSION: PROACTIVITY

Before your group dreams up a wilderness odyssey and parachutes into the heart of a trackless backcountry jungle, make sure you bring along a Florence Nightingale or Hawkeye Pierce to patch yourselves back together. Better yet, make yourself into one of these figures! Wilderness medical training is easily obtained and, in the big picture, is an inexpensive step you can take to increase your backcountry judgment.

Proactive, well prepared approaches to backcountry medical situations, together with clear and thorough communication of trip-related information to critical agencies and individuals, is our goal. Ask yourself how much advance time you think is necessary to devise and activate a thorough emergency plan, and we think it's likely that you'll begin 1 to 2 months before the trip date. Good luck, and remember that situations anticipated and planned for seem less likely to happen than if not planned for. When you think about this saying, you can begin to see why it is true: As your mind analyzes and prepares for a situation, you learn how to prevent the situation from happening through timely action and basic awareness.

Notes

[1]Cockrell, D., Ed. (1991). *The wilderness educator*. Merrilville, IN: ICS Books, Inc.

[2] Canoe rescue: Stranded canoeist becomes first person in lower 48 to be rescued with Personal Locator Beacon. Retrieved Dec. 14, 2005, from http://www.paddlermagazine.com/issues/2004_2/article_243.shtml

[3]Cockrell.

References

Drury, J., Ed. (2005). *The backcountry classroom: Lessons, tools and activities for teaching outdoor leaders*. Guilford, CT: Falcon Guide.

Johanson, K.M. (Ed.). (1984). *Accepted peer practices in adventure programming*. Boulder, CO: Association for Experimental Education.

van der Smissen, B.J. (1980). *Legal liability: Adventure activities*. Las Cruces, NM: Educational Resources Information Center.

"Leadership consists not in degrees of technique but in traits of character; it requires moral rather than athletic or intellectual effort, and it imposes on both leader and follower alike the burdens of self-restraint."

—Lewis H. Lapham

"Good leaders know what they know and know what they don't know."

—Paul K. Petzoldt

Topics:
- Planning
- Leadership in Action
- Expedition Behavior and Group Development

THE THREE SUCCESS FACTORS

When we think about practical leadership for the outdoors, a host of factors, concerns, strategies, and tips come to mind. Entire libraries have been written about the controversial, challenging, and ever-changing aspects of people leading people in goal-oriented settings. Where do we start and how do we boil down all the leadership information into a usable package?

We find that there are three basic (and universal) factors to successful outdoor leadership. They apply to all situations and groups, from the casual and relaxing family outing to the rigorous demands of the mountaineering expedition. (Or should we say the rigorous demands of the casual family outing?) These critical success factors, *planning, leadership*, and *expedition behavior*, affect all aspects of your trip. You'll realize that leadership starts months (or years) before the trip through planning, goal setting, and clarifying how people treat each other. It continues on the trip when the group needs to make critical or recreational decisions. It ends months after the trip when everyone reflects on the experience and applies what they learned to the next outing. We'll see how our family, the Stumps, use the three factors in their big summer vacation.

PLANNING THE STUMPS' VACATION

The "Round-Table" Discussion

The post-Christmas blues hit the Stump household, and to boost spirits and distract the kids from thinking about all the presents they didn't get, Forrest and Holly asked them for suggestions for the summer's family vacation. Ideas ranged from the boring (stay home and take Driver Education) to the extravagant (stay at the Tahiti Hilton and take sea kayaking trips around the islands). Forrest and Holly encouraged this brainstorming session. After much discussion of what they wanted to get out of a summer vacation and what kinds of things they wanted to do, everyone agreed on a trip up the Alaska-Canada Highway with the potential for side adventures along the way.

Papa Stump asked, "Where in Alaska do we want to go, and what do we want to do?" Willow suggested, "Why don't we go to the library and get some books on Alaska so we have an idea of the possibilities?" Woody agreed with the idea and offered to pick some up on his way back from school the next day. Moss retorted, "Aw, I'll just hop on the web and I'll have the score way before you do." He turned on his wireless laptop, opened up his internet browser and was soon heard saying "No way!" and "We gotta check this out" to himself as he discovered Alaska's treasures on the web.

The next day, after dinner was finished and the dining room table was cleared, Woody spread out the half-dozen books he had found. Holly had also picked up a couple of books and a few maps from the AAA office. As they perused the materials, ideas started to pour out. Woody suggested an overnight hiking trek over the historical Chilkoot Pass. Holly wanted to see native artwork and grizzly bears. Willow wanted to see eagles and glaciers. Moss wanted to fish for salmon. Forrest wrote down all the ideas and added his own: to camp in Denali National Park. He said, "I've wanted to see Denali ever since my college roommate climbed it in the early 1970s."

Holly suggested that Forrest read the list aloud to see if they could combine some of the ideas. She started by suggesting that she would probably see grizzly bears in Denali National Park and so would be willing to go there. "Besides, I bet they have hundreds of different wildflowers to see!"

Willow suggested, "I don't want to carry a heavy pack up over the Chilkoot Pass, but Woody, what would you think if we took this rafting trip through the Chilkoot Eagle Preserve? It's only a day trip, but then we could go camping at Denali National Park."

Moss stuck to his guns and emphasized his desire to go salmon fishing, "I found a charter boat that takes you out and you also get to see the glaciers calving into the bay!"

"I'd go for that!" said Willow, enthusiastically.

Papa Stump endorsed both trips and said, "I'll make a deal. You three get all the information on the fishing and rafting trips, and as long as the cost stays within our budget, we can do it. It's your responsibility, however, to make all the arrangements. All your mother and I want to do is pay the bills and get us all there. Okay?"

The family agreed, and as the months flew by, they made many phone calls, sent faxes, banged out emails, and wrote letters to finalize the vacation plans. The 4-week tour of Canada and Alaska started to take shape. It was highlighted by a day of salmon fishing by charter boat, a rafting trip through the Chilkoot Eagle Preserve, and a 4-night stay at the Wonder Lake campground in Denali National Park, under the shadow of Denali, North America's highest mountain.

A Contract for Fun

Before it was time to climb into the family van and take on the challenge of this adventure, Holly called for a final family meeting. "A couple of months ago at work we had a staff development day where team-building consultants came and conducted a whole day of team-building exercises. They introduced a concept called the *Full Value Contract* that I thought might be helpful during our trip."

"It sounds exciting," said Woody, with a pained expression.

"Well, let me explain it, and if you want, we can try it," Holly said. "The basic Full Value Contract has three components: Play Fair, Play Hard, and Play Safe. To play fair means that whatever rules the family determines by consensus will be abided by. To play hard means that we give activities and discussions our best effort. In other words, we bring quality to whatever we do. To play safe is the one I think is most valuable. It means that we won't hurt anyone physically or emotionally. That's something that is hard to do because we all like to use sarcasm in our family, and I'm convinced it's not healthy. I know I've been hurt by it, and I know I've hurt others. What do you think?"

"It sucks," blurted Moss. "It sounds so goody-two-shoes, and I think people ought to just chill and not take things so seriously."

"That's easy for you to say. You're usually the one who never lives up to these rules," Willow stated firmly.

After a lively discussion, clarification, and Papa Stump's tale of his distant relative Leo Stump Buscaglia, the famous family counselor, they wrote down what a Full Value Contract might look like during the trip. They eventually found something they all could live with. They even came up with a recognition system for the person who best modeled the Full Value Contract on a given day.

The Stump Family Contract:

We, the undersigned, do hereby agree to the principles described below, in order to ensure family harmony, individual enjoyment, smiling faces and to avoid unnecessary nastiness on our monthlong family trip in the majestic Great Northern Wilderness.

1. We will always do our best to share work equally, share fun equally, and give things a fair chance. (We will stretch ourselves to do new things, like eat salmon, raft wild rivers, and go shopping in outlet malls.)
2. We will try to treat each other well, with love and respect, and minimize our mean jokes, realizing that each of us can be the object of mean humor and that it hurts.
3. We will always try to tell each other both when things are great (compliments are welcome!) and when things are not going well (constructive complaints). We will do so in a kind way and focus on the problem, not the person. We all make mistakes—that's part of being human!

Signed, Moss, Willow, Woody, Holly, and Forrest

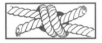

BOTTOM LINE TIP: Full Value Contract

"The Full Value Contract is the process by which a group agrees to find positive value in the efforts of its members. . .(It) is expressed in encouragement, goal setting, group discussion, a spirit of forgiveness, and confrontation."[1] It has become a standard component of "adventure-based counseling" programs and was made an industry standard by *Project Adventure* of Hamilton, Massachusetts.

The day of departure finally arrived, and with tension and expectations high, the Stumps loaded up the van and headed out. Their first challenge as they pulled out of their suburban driveway in northwest Washington was to make their way across the U.S.-Canada border and find a nice campsite before dark.

LEADERSHIP IN ACTION

Stranded on the Al-Can!

As the Stumps drove toward Alaska, the implications of their planning and the family's ability to work and have fun together (i.e., their ability to function), began to affect the tone of their vacation. Late one afternoon nearly a week into the trip, the van's engine computer went haywire. The van stopped dead in its tracks 23 miles from the nearest gas station and nearly 40 miles from the nearest major service station. The importance of leadership became extremely apparent.

While Moss and Woody, oblivious to the van's situation, poked fun at Willow's adolescent complexion, Holly said, "Thank goodness for AAA membership!" Forrest gulped and reluctantly confessed that he forgot to renew their membership. "The renewal notice came just before Christmas and I forgot to renew it in the holiday rush," he said sheepishly. The kids continued their bickering—Moss suggested to Willow that she invest her life savings in the Stridex medication company.

Holly couldn't believe Forrest's forgetfulness and started complaining about how the situation was typical of his schemes. "We haven't had a real vacation in 17 years of marriage and now we're going to spend a month stuck between Upper Liard Village and Teslin in the middle of nowhere in British Columbia!" The Full Value Contract seemed to have flown out of the window, and things appeared to be falling apart.

Finally, between hearing Holly go on about how he'd ruined her life, hearing Moss and Woody calling Willow "zitface," and realizing the seriousness of their situation, Forrest snapped. "Quiet, everyone! Quiet! Let me think! Moss, I want you and Willow to look around outside and see if there is anywhere we can camp. I think I saw some level areas along the way. Find a decent place, get out the tents, and prepare to spend the night. Woody, I want you to go down to the river and get water for cooking. Holly, would you make sure warmer clothes are available for everyone? It's going to get cold soon. Then after Moss and Woody find a decent camping spot, would you get some dinner started?

Figure 8.1
Does the Full Value Contract have to fly out the window?

"I'm going to try to flag down a car to send a message about our predicament to the nearest service station. It looks like we'll be here for the night, and then we'll stay at the nearest village for as long as it takes to get the van fixed. Let's make the best of it, gang— we're all in this together. Just consider it part of the adventure."

The kids calmed down and got started on their tasks. As they stood outside of the van, Forrest had a few quiet words with Holly.

"I'm sorry I yelled, honey," said Forrest. "It just seemed like I had to get things moving."

"That's all right, Forrest," said Holly. "I don't know if you had to raise your voice like that, but let's make sure we have a little check-in with the kids before we go to sleep tonight to make sure they understand the situation and have a chance to talk with us. We should take another look at the Stump Family Contract, dear."

Critical Success Factors for Outdoor Travel

When the van broke down, all three of the critical success factors, planning, expedition behavior, and leadership came into play (see Chapter 9 for more on trip planning). Had the Stumps anticipated breakdowns and devised a contingency plan? When the auto repair went into the third day and it looked as if they might miss the salmon fishing trip, was there an understanding among the family members of acceptable and unacceptable behavior in terms of the family getting along? Or did the arguments start fast and furious, culminating in fisticuffs?

The third and biggest challenge is leadership. How were all these incidents handled? Who made the decisions and how were they made, communicated, executed, and evaluated? This is the art of leadership, and we feel it is as important in ensuring a fun and safe family vacation as it was for General Dwight Eisenhower in defeating Hitler's Third Reich.

The Argument for Leadership: Anarchy, Dictatorship, or Something in Between?

Human nature is funny about leadership, especially in the case of vacations. Nobody usually wants to be leader, or even wants to have a leader, but if nobody takes charge and makes sure things get done, they don't get done. Also, people reflexively seek someone to blame when something doesn't go as planned. Furthermore, nobody wants to take orders on his or her vacation. Isn't that what leaders do—give orders? We'll see that the answer is both yes and no.

We strongly believe in the need for a formal leadership role in backcountry travel. Someone needs to take the ultimate responsibility when major decisions need to be made. That doesn't mean that many decisions can't be decided by the group, but that when the cowchip hits the fan, and you and your companions are approaching the summit of the mountain, the wind picks up and the weather is obviously deteriorating, someone has the authority to say, "We're turning back," and not be challenged. In these sorts of crises, there should be no vote and no attempt at consensus, because someone we trust is telling us that based on their judgment we should turn back. As Forrest's great ancestor George Washington Stump once said, "Leadership is complex stuff!"

There are those who argue that the idea of having leadership on peer or family camping trips rings of dictatorship and prevents spontaneity and freedom. But who is more free, the group who anticipates the need for planning, expedition behavior and leadership, or the group that doesn't? People who plan for leadership take a larger role in their own destiny (or more pragmatically, in the enjoyment of their adventure). Given good leadership and planning, the group will have the time and energy to take part in free and spontaneous activities. For instance, how much enjoyment is the group going to have if it spontaneously decides to go camping, but, due to the lack of planning, forget, the rain gear and matches? Will the wilderness suffer from the group who spontaneously heads into the woods without a means of burying its human waste or doesn't bother to repack food from glass and canned containers?

"LEADERSHIP IS COMPLEX STUFF!"

Figure 8.2
George Washington Stump

 BOTTOM-LINE TIP: Outdoor Leadership
In some way, every outdoor adventure needs a leader to turn to for information, planning, ultimate decision making, and effective action, especially in emergency situations.

We feel strongly that Howard Zahnizer, author of the 1964 Wilderness Act's definition of wilderness, came up with the right word when he described wilderness as "an area where the earth and its community of life are *untrammeled* by man." *Untrammeled* is defined as "not limited or restricted; unrestrained." We think that definition applies not only to wilderness but to wilderness travelers as well. We argue, however, that the sense of freedom will be strongest when good leadership, expedition behavior and planning are part of the wilderness travel equation.

PHILOSOPHY TIP: Leadership

"To act is easy; to think is hard."[2]

—*Goethe*

Defining Leadership

What is leadership, and what does it look like in outdoor travel? There are almost as many definitions of leadership as there are leaders. William H. Spoor, former CEO of Pillsbury, found over 350 definitions of leadership.[3] The definition we have found that conveys the essence of a leader's responsibility is that leadership is "the process of influencing an organized group toward accomplishing its goals."[4] In the Stumps' case, leadership was provided by anyone who helped contribute positively to the planning and participation of the family vacation. In outdoor travel, it takes on many "looks." One aspect is the planning that goes into finding where to go, how to get there, what the rules and regulations are, getting permits, buying food, and so forth. All these tasks take coordination, and the individual taking that role is usually considered to be the leader.

Once outdoors, leadership may look considerably different. Outdoor leadership is usually centered around decision making, taking responsibility, and facilitating daily goals, such as getting to camp before dark, climbing a mountain, getting dinner, and having fun. Leadership occurs whether it is planned for or not. Whether one leaves these things to chance or anticipates and plans for them illustrates one's leadership style.

What's Your Style?

What leadership style do you favor? Do you like to get things done efficiently regardless of the implications? Are you a detail person who wants all the details attended to precisely? Do you worry about how the group members feel and want to make sure everyone is happy, or do you like to come up with the ideas and then jump into doing things without worrying about the details or all the implications? Early leadership theory suggested that individuals had a dominant leadership style and should be encouraged to use that style. Current leadership theory centers around the situational aspects of leadership and suggests that different situations require different styles of leadership. Depending on the situation, we may use any one of a range of leadership styles.

What Leadership Styles Did the Stumps Use?

Leadership situations have three fundamental components: the leader, the followers, and the situation.[5] Looking back on the Stumps' predicament, the situation was their van breaking down in a remote section of the Al-Can highway during the family vacation. The leader in this case appeared to be Forrest Stump, although there didn't seem to be a formal designation to that effect. He certainly appeared to assume the leadership role in this instance. The followers were the rest of the family.

The kids were doing what kids do (in violation of the Full Value Contract, we might add), and Holly played a co-leadership role. Married couples play different leadership roles. In this case, it was apparent that Forrest played a traditional "head of household" role. As the major decision maker, he had a range of leadership styles he could utilize.

Hersey and Blanchard's Situational Leadership Theory[6] calls for using a specific leadership style based on the maturity of the group. Although defining the maturity of the group is a challenge—maturity includes experience, knowledge, responsibility, problem-solving ability, and the ability to meet deadlines—the theory is very useful for its commonsense approach. Although we don't subscribe to all aspects of Hersey and Blanchard's Situational Leadership Theory, we think their descriptions of leadership are very useful in clarifying the leader's roles.

The four situational leadership styles include *telling*, in which followers are told what will happen or what to do; *selling*, in which the leader presents an idea and tries to "sell" it to the followers; *participating*, in which followers are encouraged to come up with ideas and play a role in their implementation; and *delegating*, in which responsibility and power is delegated to the followers. The style a leader should use depends on the group's maturity.

In Forrest Stump's case, early on during the planning phase of the trip he used a *participating* style. The family's maturity was fairly high in terms of deciding where they wanted to go. They could and wanted to make important decisions. Thus, the whole family participated in making the decision of where to go for vacation. During a portion of the planning, he also used a *delegating* style. He left it entirely up to the children to organize and plan the rafting and salmon fishing trips. In this case, the kids' maturity level is unclear. What is clear, however, was that their motivational level was extremely high. If they wanted to go on these adventures, they would learn whatever skills were necessary to accomplish their goal.

When the car broke down, Forrest used a *telling* style with the children and a *selling* style with Holly. In this case, given the time of day and stress of the situation, it seemed to be the most appropriate style to accomplish the task at hand. After his telling-style outburst, Forrest turned to a participating style with his check-in with Holly and the kids later that evening. He sensed that the family would need to review the events of the crisis and share their impressions and concerns.

BOTTOM-LINE TIP: Choosing a Leadership Style

The situation and the group's maturity and needs determine which style a leader will use. Leadership styles can evolve or can be consciously determined. Try to make your choice a conscious one, rather than a reflex or reaction to stressful situations. Inevitably, we occasionally use the wrong style for a particular situation. Take the opportunity at a later time to discuss the situation with the people around you. An honest feedback session can really clear the air and accelerate the progress of the group!

Leadership Application: From Textbook to the Trail

How does this translate to the everyday camper? The obvious answer is that it's situational—in other words, it depends. If you're with a group of peers, the first thing you should do is to determine who the leader is going to be. Is it going to be the most experienced person, the one people respect most, the best communicator, or the most rational personel in settling arguments? Any number of criteria could be used to help decide.

With a peer group of roughly the same experience, the style which would probably be least useful would be that of *telling*. In our culture, peers don't like to be told what to do, so probably a *selling* or *participating* style would be most appropriate.

Let's take another look at the Muskrat Pack's late spring canoe trip to the Drifting Paddle National Canoe Area (DPNCA). Remember, Anne is your best paddler, since she's worked part-time for a rafting company for the last two years and is a certified American Canoe Association whitewater canoe instructor. If you recall, Juan is the only person who has been to the area. He canoed on several of the lakes a few years ago. Stella has great camping skills, since she took a National Outdoor Leadership School (NOLS) course last summer. You're the novice. (Remember? That's why you're reading this book!) You do, however, have the most experience working with groups of people and in facilitating complex decision making. You've worked your way up from substance abuse counselor to assistant director of the whole program.

Let's look at how the leadership roles and styles might evolve with a peer group. It was important to have the decision of where to go be at the very least a *selling* decision and ideally a *participating* one. If you have no say with your peers about where you're going, you may not want to go. Perhaps Juan *sold* the group on the Drifting Paddle or they brainstormed ideas and the DPNCA came up. What we're almost certain is that the group wasn't told where they were going to go.

On the other hand, if you were going on an Outward Bound course at the Hurricane Island Center in Maine and you had never been to Maine, you would expect the Outward Bound staff to use a *telling* style. In this case, the leadership's knowledge is high and yours is low.

Once on the trip, you may turn to Anne for canoeing tips and she may well use a *telling* style. She's probably not going to try to sell you on the idea of using a draw stroke in a given situation. She's going to tell you that it's the best stroke to use and that you *should* use it. Similarly, in any dangerous situation she's going to use a *telling* style, not a *participatory* one. Her knowledge level is high, and the rest of the group's is considerably lower.

As you can see, each individual in this peer group brings his or her own expertise. How that compares with the needs, knowledge, and maturity of the rest of the group will determine what type of leadership style you will use.

Juan is the resident expert on the area, and he may want to use a leadership style that enables him to share that expertise without using a *telling* style. As previously mentioned, people often don't take kindly to a telling style, and besides, he has only been through a portion of the DPNCA once, so his expertise is probably limited. If he uses a telling style and doesn't know as much as he would like us to believe, then he will suffer from a credibility problem. He will probably want to share his information in a qualified way. "As I remember it . . . As the ranger explained it to me . . ." This type of comment helps clarify that he is not an expert but might have information to contribute.

Stella, the resident wilderness expert, probably wants to use a *selling* style. She has a fair amount of wilderness experience, although in a different environment, and will hopefully find a style that allows her an opportunity to share her knowledge without sounding like an over-bearing authority. On the other hand, there may be times when she sees something unsafe going on where she should use a *telling* style to make sure no one gets hurt.

Your expertise in working with groups provides you with the challenge of helping the group to maximize its enjoyment of the trip within a framework of group understanding. You would probably be able to help the group clarify goals and understand group development stages and typical group roles. You may want to facilitate the group as these stages and roles evolve and assist in difficult decisions that arise. To do that in a supportive way as a peer probably will require a *selling* or *participatory* style.

With peer groups there can be a leadership role for everyone, although we believe there ultimately has to be one person the group can turn to who will either facilitate or take responsibility for the final decision.

◈◈◈◈◈◈◈◈◈

TRICKS OF THE TRADE: Getting a Response from Your Followers

It is often frustrating trying to get a response from your fellow campers when asking questions such as, "Does anybody want to take a break? Do you want to set up camp? Do you want to stop for lunch?" it is common to get no response at all. We suggest two things.

1. Try asking questions in a reverse form. Instead of asking, "Does anybody want to take a break?" ask, "Is there anybody who *doesn't* want to take a break?" It is important in terms of safety that if one person needs a break, then a break should be taken to help people avoid ex-

continued

haustion. If the question is asked in this way, it would require a unanimous vote to *not* take a break.

2. Keep in mind that if you have to ask these questions, it probably means you think someone in the group needs a break, wants to set up camp, or is hungry for lunch. If that is the case, then you probably don't even have to ask the question. Just do it. We sometimes tell students, "If you have to ask the question, you already know the answer."

BOTTOM-LINE TIP: Situational Leadership Styles

Situational leadership reinforces the fact that there is no "best" style of leadership and provides four styles:

1. *Telling*: leader-centered. The leader tells the group what to do.
2. *Selling*: problem-oriented versus people-oriented leadership. The leader proposes solutions to problems.
3. *Participating*: shared decision making. The leader has the group actively involved in identifying and solving problems.
4. *Delegating*: the leader delegates decision making and assumes a supportive role.

EXPEDITION BEHAVIOR AND GROUP DEVELOPMENT

What Is Expedition Behavior?

Paul Petzoldt, wilderness education pioneer, defines good expedition behavior as "an awareness of the relationships" that exist in the out-of-doors, plus "the motivation and character to be as concerned for others as one is for oneself." He further states that poor expedition behavior is characterized by "a breakdown in human relations caused by selfishness, rationalization, ignorance of personal faults, dodging blame or responsibility, physical weakness, and in extreme cases, not being able to risk one's own survival to insure that of a companion."[7]

The consequences of good and bad expedition behavior are obvious. The expedition members who practice it are more likely to enjoy the trip, meet objectives, make friends, and have a safe experience, while those who don't, won't. What can you do to promote good expedition behavior? Let's look back at the Stump vacation and see what they did. They clarified their goals by asking, "What are we looking for in a vacation?" Expectations were discussed and the entire family was empowered to have some say in where they were going and what they were going to do. They discussed and adopted a Full Value Contract. They conducted periodic check-ins, especially after difficult days, to keep communication open and address concerns as a group.

PHILOSOPHY TIP: The Facets of Expedition Behavior

Petzoldt outlined several different relationships that make up expedition behavior. These need attention either before or during outdoor trips. Timely and positive communication in each facet generally leads to healthy expedition behavior.

Individual to Individual: This relationship is the heart of good expedition behavior. One-on-one interactions are critical and spread to affect the whole group. The classic example of individual-to-individual expedition behavior is between tent partners. For instance, one person always leaves the tent unzipped, allowing black flies to enter. This drives the

continued

other tent partner berserk. This issue can be resolved either through calm discussion or an emotional explosion.

Individual to Group: This relationship addresses how our actions as individuals affect the rest of the party. Remnants of lunch in beards, perpetual lateness, and off-color humor are ways that one person may adversely affect the group. On the other hand, cheerfulness and a willingness to help others on the part of one individual can really bring a group up.

Group to Individual: This is where a group can affect an individual both positively and negatively through peer pressure, support (physical and emotional), and other ways.

Group to Group: Two separate recreational groups may come into contact in the outdoors. How each group conducts itself has an enormous positive or negative impact on the experience of the other group. Radios, loud voices, and litter have negative group-to-group impact; sharing information and providing plenty of privacy between groups have positive group-to-group impact.

Individual and Group to Multiple Users: Sometimes, outdoor recreators using different travel modes come into contact. Hikers may run into horsepackers or all-terrain vehicles. While each group may be tempted to frown at the choice of the other group, respect and consideration enhance the experiences of all concerned.

Individual and Group to Administrative Agencies: Rangers and park officials have a job to do in maintaining a safe and environmentally sound outdoor experience for us, as well as protecting the landscape. Please respect regulations and policies.

Individual and Group to Local Populace: As the outdoors become more and more used, recreators have an increasing impact on the people who live in and around these beautiful areas. Be careful to respect property lines, regulations, and local cultures. The growth of exotic eco-tourism vacations brings an even greater need for cultural and environmental sensitivity.[7]

Group Development Stages

Groups appear to go through similar stages of development (Figure 8.2). Space shuttle crews, professional athletic teams, corporate project teams, and even family and peer groups go through these same developmental stages. The first stage, *forming*, is characterized by polite conversation, the sharing of perfunctory information about each other, and generally low trust. At this stage, the group can be described as a collection of individuals. Some call this the honeymoon stage, and even though friends and families already know each other, they go through a somewhat similar stage when embarking on a new adventure by being exceptionally polite and feeling the new situation out.

The second stage, storming, usually is demonstrated by conflict within the group as members try to organize themselves into roles and sometimes show impatience with each other's differences. Members may interrupt or disagree over plans or ideas as they vie for attention and leadership within the group in the storming stage.

As group cohesiveness develops with members listening, accepting differences, compromising, and working together to reach consensus, the group enters into the *norming* stage.

Finally, in an ideal setting, groups become interdependent and efficient in focusing on accomplishing group tasks in the *performing* stage. These stages are not static or linear, as a particular group may hop from stage to stage and move both forward and backward. The impor-

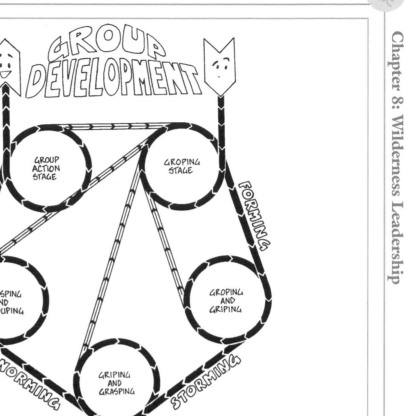

Figure 8.2
The four stages of group development.
Note that these stages are not linear.

tant thing to realize is that the group development stages are normal and most group experts would argue that a group can't reach the performing stage without going through the other stages.

What does this mean to most campers? Be prepared, and don't be surprised as the group you are camping with goes through these stages. By letting them occur and facilitating them without fighting them you will have a better chance of reaching the performing stage.

PHILOSOPHY TIP: Teamwork
"Snowflakes are one of nature's most fragile things, but just look at what they can do when they stick together."
—Vesta M. Kelly[9]

If understanding expedition behavior and group development are the first steps in ensuring that our group has a good time, what other things can we do to help us get along? As individuals we can come into a group with a relaxed and tolerant attitude. By keeping things in perspective, not taking offense, maintaining a positive attitude, and managing conflict effectively, one can contribute positively to the success of a wilderness outing.

Different Strokes for Different Folks

We all know that people are different, are motivated by different things and react differently to different situations. We believe that understanding these differences makes it easier to practice good expedition behavior. When we understand our differences we can appreciate that even in homogeneous groups there is a tremendous diversity in thinking.

Contrasting with this diversity within a group, most individuals have a distinct and dominant approach to working in groups, and that in turn impacts their decision making, leadership, and interaction with others. For example, you might be a person who needs to "get to the point" quickly and gets frustrated with your friend who wants to "talk about their feelings." You can see the potential for conflict!

The best way we can think of to describe how we approach teamwork as individuals is to think about whether you are left- or right-handed. If you are predominantly right-handed, it doesn't mean you can't do anything with your left hand. It just means you are more comfortable doing things with your right hand. In addition, anybody who has broken their dominant hand knows they can learn to do many things with the other hand. In fact, many athletes learn to be ambidextrous because it enhances their athletic performance. We would argue that people need to become "ambidextrous" in their approach to teamwork to become better learners and more productive members of wilderness camping groups.

There are many psychological profiles and other personality inventories that help give understanding about individual differences. We prefer to look at how one approaches teamwork as a way of understanding why people do certain things. In particular, we like Bonney and Drury's IP3, which describes four collaborative tendencies. The IP3 recognizes that we don't use just one teamwork approach, but a blend of the four. One style usually emerges as our dominant approach to teamwork.

IP3: Your Key to Understanding Yourself and Your Group

The IP3 (Ideas, People, Product, Process) concept, adapted from the work of Ichak Adizes by Bruce Bonney and Jack Drury in 1995, describes the characteristics and behavioral tendencies of four categories of people: Ideas, People, Product, and Process. This useful format helps you take advantage of the strengths of each personality/learning type while acknowledging the areas of potential weakness as well. The following IP3 material is adapted from Bonney and Drury's book, *The Backcountry Classroom*, Second Edition.

As you read this section, ask yourself, "What kind of person am I?" It's likely that you tend to be like one or two of the following four personality/learning types. You are probably not "just" one type, but are a blend of the four. The IP3 format allows you to see how the preferences and tendencies that you and your camping partners embody affect your group for good or ill. Knowledge of your tendencies also might encourage you to try to develop strengths in your weak areas.

Ideas **People**—"Ideas" group members see the big picture and are frequently visionary and creative. Ideas group members want to know what the possibilities are, and their favorite question is, "What if . . . ?" They need flexibility and dislike rigidity.

In a group setting, this is how ideas people might contribute to reaching goals:

- They are visionary.
- They are risk takers.
- They are flexible and comfortable with chaos.
- They operate intuitively.
- In the extreme, their greatest strength is their ability to come up with visionary and creative ideas.

By contrast, this is how ideas people sometimes hinder collaborative work:

- They sometimes don't follow the rules.
- They frequently struggle to focus on just one idea and follow through on it. As a result, they may look unorganized or inconsistent.

- They are not too concerned with details and frequently struggle to work with people who are.
- They need their ideas validated by others.
- They can be perceived as impulsive and unrealistic.
- They tend to be dramatic.
- In the extreme, their greatest weakness is their tendency to be "arsonists" —they go around planting ideas (starting fires) but not following through and frequently not allowing others to follow through, thus preventing problem solving or task accomplishment. ("Forget what I told you to do yesterday; I've got a better idea today!")

Ideas people have a pattern in their communication. When they say yes, they actually mean maybe. The reason is that they will most likely come up with a new idea, one they think is better, shortly after they have okayed the existing idea or project. By contrast, when they say no, they mean no because they already have a better idea in mind.

People **People**—"People" group members value people and focus on relationships. They want to know who is involved in the decision and whom the decision will affect. People group members crave harmony and dislike divisiveness and conflict.

How people people contribute to collaborative work:

- They are sensitive to people's feelings.
- They like to build community.
- They value cooperative efforts and enjoy being part of a team.
- They bring a sense of inclusiveness to a group.
- In the extreme, their greatest strength is caring about people.

How people people sometimes hinder collaborative work:

- They sometimes appear wishy-washy because others don't know where they stand.
- They don't want to offend people and as a result don't always share their true feelings.
- They don't like hard-and-fast rules that can divide people.
- They tend to be slow to react until they have checked everyone else's opinion.
- They avoid risk taking and tend to avoid pressure situations.
- In the extreme, their greatest weakness is their tendency to be a "soaped fish" —no one can get a handle on them and see where they stand.

When people group members say yes, they usually mean maybe. They don't want to commit to something until they have checked with others. When people group members say no, they also mean maybe for the same reason. They don't want to commit to a decision until they have checked with others.

Product **People**—"Product" group members value achievement, focus, and quality. Product group members want to know what needs to be done. They need results and dislike drift or indecisiveness.

How product people contribute to collaborative work:

- They value performance and producing a quality product.
- They are committed to getting the job done.
- They take pride in being task-oriented and getting many things accomplished.
- They value expert knowledge.
- In the extreme, their greatest strength is getting high-quality results.

How product people sometimes hinder collaborative work:

- They are often stubborn and tend to work alone and do things their way.
- They tend to hate meetings and would rather just get on with the job.
- They tend to be authoritative.
- They tend to see one "right" answer and don't like to "waste" time exploring creative alternatives.
- They are considered insensitive because they worry more about getting the job done correctly than people's feelings.
- They can be too rigid and defeated by their own perfectionism.
- In the extreme, their greatest weakness is their tendency to be a lone ranger workaholic. Since they believe they have the best solution and can do the best job, they tend to want to do it all.

When product people say yes, they mean yes. They are very literal and have difficulty understanding why others aren't. When product people say no, they mean no for the same reason—they mean what they say!

Process **People**—"Process" group members value procedure. They want to know how something is going to be done. They need structure and dislike chaos.
How process people contribute to collaborative work:

- They usually are well organized and self-disciplined.
- They attend to details and get things running smoothly.
- They are practical and direct.
- In the extreme, their greatest strength is bringing order out of chaos.
  How process people sometimes hinder collaborative work:

- They don't like surprises or changes to plans.
- They generally are not tolerant of "rule breakers."
- They tend to be insensitive to people and allow rules to be more important than people.
- They sometimes appear inflexible.
- They are reality-oriented and can be impatient with those who are considered to have their "heads in the clouds."
- In the extreme, their greatest weakness is the tendency to become a "bean counter," where details become more important than the overall goal.

When process people say yes, they mean yes. They are satisfied that rules have been followed and criteria met and that individuals have worked within the system. When process people say no, they mean maybe. If the rules are followed and if the criteria are met and if you work within the system, you can change a no to a yes.

Hopefully you see yourself somewhere among the teamwork approaches. We encourage wilderness leaders to try to become more "ambidextrous" so they can exhibit qualities of all types of people. Leaders should learn to stretch and see the value of all teamwork approaches. Leaders shouldn't get in the rut of feeling what he or she thinks is the only way. We all win if we can appreciate what people with other teamwork approaches bring to our group. Don't forget that people virtually never have just one teamwork approach but have a blend of them, with one dominant tendency.

Decision Making in Outdoor Pursuits

When the Going Gets Tough: Dealing with "Group Think"

Peer groups are subject to a phenomenon known as "group think," where groups make poor decisions due to a sort of mindlessness or single-mindedness. This process keeps out everything but what the group thinks and wants to be true. It provides an illusion of invulnerability and collective rationalization that may frequently be the cause of wilderness disasters.

"The weather isn't that bad . . . the snow won't be as deep on the other side of the mountain . . . we won't need our flashlights . . ." are all comments characteristic of group think. In order to minimize its impact we suggest using two "flags." These flags can be used to provide a warning to the group that someone is concerned for the group's safety or for the protection of the environment.

If you or a companion sees anything unsafe that makes someone uncomfortable, your group should have an understanding that anyone can call a halt to a given activity by raising the safety flag. All too often, people feel uncomfortable sharing their concerns until it is too late. Before your group goes out, the safety flag concept should be discussed and adopted. The safety flag can be invoked by any group member at any time and the group agrees to immediately address the issue. The activity won't be continued until all group members are satisfied that the issue has been addressed.

Suppose you are with your friends Juan, Anne, and Stella in the DPNCA and you come to a section of a river that looks too scary to you. You raise the safety flag and tell them you think the level of whitewater is over your head. If your group has adopted and lived by the Full Value Contract, you can make that statement without fear of ridicule. As the group discusses your safety flag, any number of resolutions might come about. They could convince you that it isn't that bad by paddling down first and demonstrating that it looks worse than it is. You may suggest one canoe carry around or line through the rapids while the other runs them. The group may decide to carry the gear around and paddle canoes with no gear in them. The possible solutions are endless, but the bottom line is that the solution somehow demonstrates that the safety concern can be handled.

Along with the safety flag we advocate the adoption of the eco-flag. The eco-flag is similar except that instead of personal safety, we substitute environmental safety. If anyone feels that the environment is going to suffer from a specific activity, they raise the eco-flag and the group stops and addresses the environmental concern.

Using the DPNCA river scenario, perhaps as you break camp you toss the leftover burnable garbage into the fire ring with the idea that the next camper can use it to start their campfire. Stella raises the eco-flag and tells you that she doesn't feel that is appropriate. You discuss it and come to the resolution that if it is good fire starter then you'll pack it and use it yourself at the next campsite. Stella is satisfied that the campsite is left cleaner for the next camper, and you have some dry fire starter for the next campsite. Having an understanding of the flags before the trip allows Stella to feel comfortable addressing the issue.

Mindful Decision Making: Slow Down, Think Clearly, and Get Better Results!

The eco-flag and the safety flag are examples of techniques for mindful decision making. What we want to avoid are situations where we either rush to a quick decision or where we do things that are in effect critical decisions without even being aware that we've just made a decision. You might think of paddling a canoe down a whitewater river for the first time. You and your partner are making decisions constantly. You can imagine a situation in which you are in the bow and see what looks like an easy rapid. As you are approaching, you are making many quick decisions: Which side of the river do we paddle to? How fast should we go? Should we back paddle, drift, or forward paddle? How big is the obstacle? Is there a good line to follow? Is there clear water beyond? Should we actually shoot this rapid or get to shore to scout it out? By the time you've read these statements, it's probably too late to do anything but go through the rapid! You've made a decision by hesitating—the decision to go through the rapid without scouting it, which could be a very poor decision.

In the majority of situations in the backcountry, you have more time at your disposal. You can take a few minutes to clearly and calmly consider all the information. Actually, many outdoor leaders will tell you that you never will have "all" the information on which to base a decision. They're right. But don't use this philosophical point to excuse you from doing any thinking before just plunging in!

We like to think of effective decision making as "mindful" decision making, as opposed to instinctual or subconscious decision making. Most decisions will be better, or at least better informed, if you take a few minutes to gather information, come up with two or more options, and weigh the options before choosing a course of action. In our canoeing example, you would be better served to pull the canoe over, walk along shoreline, open the guidebook, consult the map, ready the rescue equipment, and talk with your canoe partner before shooting a questionable or difficult rapid. It will take you 5 or 10 minutes, but is probably worth it, considering a potentially deadly (or at least uncomfortably wet) possible outcome.

QUALITY CAMPER TIP: The Decision-Making Process

Everyone uses some sort of decision-making process, whether consciously or unconsciously. We advocate conscious decision making and provide this generic model for consideration:[10]

1. Identify the problem.
2. Clarification and analysis—Gather facts, examine assumptions, recognize constraints, understand values, and consider group dynamics.
3. Brainstorm options—Consider the positive and negative consequences and contingencies.
4. Make the decision.
5. Implement the decision.
6. Evaluate the decision.

We recommend both individuals and groups develop their own decision-making or problem-solving strategy and then ritualize it; that is, make it part of the natural sequence of dealing with problems.

Figure 8.3
Raise your flags if you think the group should
stop to consider a safety or ecological issue.

CONCLUSION

Use of the flags and mindful decision making demonstrates the finesse aspect of leadership and decision making. Without a supportive atmosphere, in this case set up by the use of the Full Value Contract, the flag concept won't work. Keep in mind that leadership styles are situational and no two situations are exactly the same. Although every leadership style has its place, our experience tells us that in most instances with peers and family a *selling* or *participating* style is preferred. Experience tells us that when we are told what to do rather than asked (*telling* vs. *selling*) it discourages commitment and a sense of empowerment, but if we have a role in decision-making processes, we feel a sense of ownership and commitment. The disadvantages of the *selling* and *participatory* approaches is that they generally are slower, and if consensus is not part of the process, there are winners and losers.

 **PHILOSOPHY TIP: Knowing One's Strengths and Limitations**

"It's not what we don't know that hurts, it's what we know that ain't so."

—*Will Rogers*[11]

Finally, remember that "immutable rules are the tools of fools." The crucial aspect of leadership is that of judgment. Use your previous experience and intuition and not some cookbook-like recipe to guide you through decision-making processes. This, along with an honest appraisal of your strengths and weaknesses, will get you through more tough situations than all the leadership theory found in the Library of Congress.

Notes

[1]Schoel, J., Prouty, R., & Radcliffe, P. (1988). *Islands of healing: A guide to adventure-based counseling*. Hamilton, MA: Project Adventure. p. 33.

[2]Hughes, R.L., Ginnett, R.C., & Curphy, G.J. (1993). *Leadership: Enhancing the lessons of experience*. Burr Ridge, IL: IRWIN.

[3]Spoor, W. *William H. Spoor dialogues on leadership: The leadership riddle*. The Nelson A. Rockefeller Center for the Social Sciences, Dartmouth College.

[4]Roach, C.F., & Nehling, O. (1984). Functionalism: Basis for an alternative approach to the study of leadership. In J.G. Hunt, D.M. Hosking, C.A. Schriesheim, & R. Stewart, *(Eds.),Leaders and managers: International perspectives on managerial behavior and leadership*, Ed. Elmsford, NY: Pergamon.

[5]Hughes et al.

[6]Hersey, P., and Blanchard, K.H. (1982). *Management of organizational behavior: Utilizing human resources* (4th ed). Englewood Cliffs, NJ: Prentice Hall.

[7]Petzoldt, P. (1984). *The new wilderness handbook* (2nd ed.). New York: W.W. Norton & Company. (Original work published in 1974).

[8]Drury, J., Ed. (2005). *The backcountry classroom: Lessons, tools and activities for teaching outdoor leaders*. Guilford, CT: Falcon Guide.

[9]Hughes et al.

[10]Drury & Bonney.

[11]Hughes et al.

References

Buell, L. (1983). *Outdoor leadership competency: A manual for self-assessment and staff evaluation*. Greenfield, MA: Environmental Awareness Publications.

Capel, K.E., & Clark, M.B. (1990). *Measures of leadership*. West Orange, NJ: Leadership Library of America.

Johnson, D.W., & Johnson, F. (1987). *Joining together: Group theory and group skills* (3rd Ed.). Englewood Cliffs, NJ: Prentice-Hall, Inc.

Jones, J.E. (1973). A model of group development. In J.E. Jones, & J.W. Pfeiffer, (Eds.), *The annual handbook for group facilitators*. LaJolla, CA: University Associates, 129.

Kalisch, K. (1979). *The role of the instructor in the Outward Bound process*. Three Lakes, WI: Wheaton College.

Petzoldt, P. (1984). *The new wilderness handbook* (2nd ed.). New York: W.W. Norton & Company. (Original work published in 1974).

Rosenbach, W.E., & Taylor, R.L. (Eds.). (1984). *Contemporary issues in leadership*. Boulder, CO: Westview Press.

Schoel, J., Prouty, D., & Radcliffe, P. (1988). *Islands of healing: A guide to adventure based counseling*. Hamilton, MA: Project Adventure, Inc.

Shaw, M. (1981). *Group dynamics: The psychology of small group behavior* (3rd ed.). New York: Simon & Schuster.

CHAPTER 9
Begin with a Happy Ending: Trip Planning

"I have always found that plans are useless, but planning is indispensable."
—*Dwight D. Eisenhower*

Topics:
- Guidelines for Trip Planning
- Trip Vision
- Itinerary and Safety
- Food, Materials, and Finances
- Interpersonal Relations
- Introductory Cooking
- Weather, Logistics, and Miscellaneous

By now you've absorbed all the necessary book knowledge and are thought of as the neighborhood expert on backcountry travel and camping. You can walk down the street and hold your head high, confident that you can tackle any suburban experience with your knowledge of fabrics, wind pants, maps, stove-top ovens, and catholes. Now you need to strap on the boots and hit the trail.

In your mind you picture it clearly: you're on the west buttress of Mount Tremendous, contemplating a suction-cup traverse of a mile-high wall of granite on a faint ledge the width of a pencil line. The wind blows the first snowflakes from an approaching storm. Suddenly, the Japanese crew shuffles by on its way to greener elevations, having been defeated and battered by the cruel summit. A team of Sherpa climbers limps off the summit next, muttering something about it being Miller Time. A small herd of mountain goats walks by next, hungry, wet, and discouraged, all bleating plaintively. You begin to have second thoughts about the climb.

Well, maybe next summer. What's that? The phone's ringing . . .

Ah, life! Juan, your best friend from college, calls and suggests that you organize a reunion trip for your paddling group, the Muskrat Pack, on the Green River in Utah.

"Why me?" you ask.

"Because you just read the book," Juan says. "You must have a lot of time on your hands."

How do you go about planning a major trip and using all your backcountry knowledge? Wilderness outings involving several people require a significant amount of forethought, preparatory work, and information gathering.

PHILOSOPHY TIP: Trip Planning
Forrest Stump's ancestor, the Mongolian warrior chief Vanilla the Bun, had a saying about outdoor leadership in general and trip planning in particular. "The art of leadership is not as much about knowing the right answers as knowing the right questions to ask."

"THE ART OF LEADERSHIP IS NOT AS MUCH ABOUT KNOWING THE RIGHT ANSWERS AS KNOWING THE RIGHT QUESTIONS TO ASK... AND CRUSHING ALL WHO DARE TO OPPOSE YOUR WILL!"

Figure 9.1
Vanilla the Bun was known for his keen insight.

You don't need to know everything about camping, backcountry travel logistics, and wilderness trivia to plan a safe expedition. You do need to know which questions you should ask and answer. You want to avoid dangerous, frustrating, or embarrassing surprises when preparing for the trip, driving to it, or traveling in the backcountry. Reducing surprises and maintaining a capable, can-do attitude when they inevitably arise are hallmarks of a good planner and leader. This chapter provides a guide and shortcut to organizing and devising questions in planning wilderness adventures.

GUIDELINES FOR TRIP PLANNING

Wilderness trip planners should approach backcountry adventures of any length seriously and not underestimate the complexity and potential hazards of a challenging new environment. Too many trips are planned the morning of the first day of vacation, when the trip members converge at the local Piggly Wiggly to buy provisions. At this point, it is not uncommon for frustrations to arise as members quibble over bringing fresh versus dry food, cases of soda and beer versus drink mixes, and just how much work each person thinks lies ahead as the group moves from campsite to campsite. Who calls the shots?

Proper Prior Planning

This vision of chaos illustrates several of our guidelines for trip planning. The first and most important is to start the planning process early. Give yourself much more time than you think you need for the group to plan all aspects of the adventure. You will find that time slips by all too quickly and that the date creeps closer with alarming rapidity. You will need time to meet with your trip partners, order maps, obtain food and equipment, and plan your travel route.

Next, organization is critical for minimizing glitches, oversights, and snafus. (We borrowed these terms from the government.) Make list after list of tasks to do, things to buy, and so forth. In fact, make lists of lists, and delegate tasks to responsible group members. Play on each person's strengths. If someone works at a sporting goods store, put them in charge of ordering gear. Put someone with knowledge of nutrition and camping provisions in charge of food. Do everyone a favor, though, and instill a system of checks and balances for each job. That is, double-check what everyone is doing to avoid surprises. For instance, maybe not everyone is willing to try powdered carrot juice at every meal for 2 weeks.

Lastly, anticipate problems. Use this chapter to ask the right questions. Think about what could go wrong at each phase of the trip, and ask yourself how the group would deal with it. Do you have what you need?

TRIP PLANNING CONSIDERATIONS

We offer 13 broad considerations that thorough trip planners should address when organizing a complex outing for several people. Some of the considerations apply to educational or institutional trips and can be altered or dropped to suit private recreational ventures. We organized the 13 considerations into five topic areas, which are roughly sequential in the planning process. The five topic areas are *Trip Vision; Itinerary and Safety; Food, Materials, and Finances; Interpersonal Relations;* and *Weather, Logistics, and Miscellaneous.*

TRIP VISION

This trip planning topic addresses "big picture" questions such as "Why are we going on this trip?" and "Who's in charge, and how should they act?"

Goals and Objectives

Before you can move out and make route plans, food plans, or activity plans, your group needs to agree on why it's going on the trip. People often have vastly different ideas about why they want to go into the backcountry. One friend might want to summit as many mountain peaks as possible; someone else might want to set up a base camp and fish for 4 days. One person might want to haul a full backpack over long days and steep climbs. Another might want to curl up with his or her laptop computer and catch up on work projects. If these people don't understand each other's goals, then subtle or overt conflicts may arise. Head them off before they occur by talking.

You get the point. The group should take the time at the earliest opportunity to state, clarify, and come to agreement on personal goals for the trip. Also pay attention to group goals. Here are some typical examples of each:

- Individual goals: to fish, to relax, to have fun, to eat good food, to push oneself physically, to summit three peaks, to have some time alone, to sleep late, to rise early, to get some time with one's husband or wife, to connect with everyone on the trip.
- Group goals: no one gets hurt, to protect the environment, to remain friends with everyone, to meet everyone's needs and desires, to involve everyone in decisions, to not put people down verbally, to be supportive of everyone emotionally, to get down the river, to climb the mountain, to see the wildlife.

Leadership

Although leadership doesn't always have to be as formal as on a commercially guided trip, we recommend the recognition of the roles a leader needs to take and the formal delegation of those duties among the group members. Make sure the buck stops somewhere. Chapter 8 contains a more detailed discussion of leadership in a variety of settings.

ITINERARY AND SAFETY

Now that you have a clear idea of your group's goals and values for its wilderness adventure, you are prepared to take a look at the particulars of where to go and what to see. It is logical to devise a simple emergency plan as you go.

Itinerary

When planning your day-to-day route, make sure to consider what your group members desire to see and experience. Try to meet as many individual goals as possible while staying within group-agreed limitations. A popular and practical compromise often involves traveling to a central location and establishing a base camp, from which small groups can travel to meet individual goals. Keep in mind:

- **Group physical abilities and limitations.** How far should you move each day? Start small on beginning trips in terms of distance traveled and elevation gained.
- **Planning for rest days.**

- **Planning so that each campsite has a relatively convenient water source** (spring, stream, lake).

Consult Resources

Make sure you do some research to take advantage of current information. There are few things as frustrating as driving hundreds of miles only to find your prime campsite has been closed for the season or paved over as a parking lot for a fried chicken shack.

Consult these resources:
- **Human**—has a friend visited the region recently? Ask rangers about trail conditions, campsite availability, and the like. Hire a guide.
- **Written**—Buy or borrow guidebooks, magazine articles, and books that pertain to your trip area. Consult brochures and backcountry management agencies to learn about local regulations concerning camping and travel.
- **Photographic**—Are there photos of your area? Can you find snapshots of the mountain you want to climb or the river you want to negotiate?
- **Maps**—Find both old and new maps of your trip area.

Emergency Planning

For a more thorough discussion of emergency procedures, see Chapter 7. In short, be sure to have a written plan that addresses:

- **Preventative measures.** How will you avoid health and safety hazards? Bring a first aid kit, have the proper training, treat health concerns promptly (e.g., blisters, hypothermia, illness).
- **Emergency procedures** in the event of emergency situations. Who will treat an injury? Who will organize the rest of the group? How will you proceed if someone breaks a leg?
- **Evacuation options.** What is the easiest path out of the wilderness in case of an emergency? Plan different evacuation routes for each stage of the trip as necessary. Leave a written copy of your evacuation plan with the management agency and at home. Don't forget to take one with you!
- **Post-emergency plans.** Counseling care for group members, contacting relatives, working with the media (public relations).
- **Medical history and insurance.** Depending on the length, remoteness, and type of activities of your trip, you may want to have a complete medical history of group members or a more informal review of major medical concerns. In addition, medical insurance may be a requirement for participation or you may agree to go without. The entire group should be made aware and be part of the decision-making process. For ambitious trips, we recommend complete medical history forms, physical examinations, consent for treatment, and proof of insurance. If working with friends who have no health insurance, trip accident insurance is available through a local insurance agency.
- **Liability.** This applies primarily to professionally guided trips or program trips. If you are the leader, be sure that your program has an overall risk management plan with adequate liability insurance. Make sure every participant signs an assumption of risk form complete with a waiver of claims and liability releases.

FOOD, MATERIALS, AND FINANCES

Food Planning

Refer to Chapter 4 for a thorough discussion of methods for provisioning. In terms of overall trip planning, how will the group select food items? How will amounts and nutritional balance be determined? Who will purchase and pack food? How will any necessary resupplies be coordinated and arranged?

Food presents one of the most challenging and detailed areas of trip planning and must be tackled with plenty of advance time and good attention to group needs and desires.

Equipment and Clothing

This is another area that needs plenty of lead time for the best results. The trip leader should determine a list of equipment needed for the particular environment and activities to be engaged in. Next, inventory and check existing gear to see what needs repair or replacement. Distribute a list of required personal gear to all trip participants well in advance, so that they may acquire missing items. Order and shop for missing gear items with plenty of time to spare, so that, if necessary, returns or exchanges can be made.

After equipment has been purchased, make a plan for how it will be distributed. Many people wait until the roadhead to divide up camping gear such as stoves, tents, and food, and would be better served to plan ahead and take care of such shuffling earlier to facilitate a swift departure.

Finances

To avoid financial scandal, make sure the person handling trip finances prepares a written budget and keeps accurate accounting of money spent. Money has a knack for generating controversy, misunderstanding, and distrust very quickly, and an organized approach to record keeping goes a long way to support friendships on the expedition and afterward.

In the same vein, make sure that people pay their share of the expenses before the trip begins. Often, people who "front" money for other trip members begin to resent the people who wait to honor their financial responsibilities. You don't want this cloud hanging over your backcountry vacation.

INTERPERSONAL RELATIONS

Skills and Knowledge Training

Especially for more ambitious outdoor activities and routes, the group should assess and take appropriate steps to advance trip members' skill and knowledge levels. If the group is motivated primarily by reaching an itinerary goal, for example a summit, few things cause as much contention as a group member or members who can't function at the skill, knowledge, or endurance level as the other members. While sometimes this results in "accidents," like rocks inside packs or cannibalism, ability-level tension often divides the group emotionally or physically into small and resentful cliques.

Take steps to bring everyone to similar knowledge and skill levels by enrolling in short skill classes, going on preparatory trips, and reading up on skills and trip locations. No matter how you work to prevent it, however, ability level tension will always exist and can be dealt with in a positive manner through perceptive leadership.

Expedition Behavior

How does the group ensure that everyone will get along for the duration of the trip? Is this possible? Are we nuts? Actually, you don't need to hire an expedition psychiatrist to keep people from dumping cayenne pepper in each other's sleeping bags. If you stick to a few basic expedition behavior techniques, most interpersonal friction can be expressed and soothed in its infancy.

Firstly, and perhaps most importantly, make sure the group comes together in the planning stages of the expedition to unify trip goals. See the *Goals and Objectives* section above for more information. Next, while in the backcountry, have regular or semi-regular group meetings to discuss progress, revise plans, and bring up interpersonal issues. Depending on the group members, group meetings can be therapeutic or explosive, but they should occur in order to deal with real issues in a healthy and timely manner. Things will only get worse if they are brushed aside. Good communication usually brings groups to a higher level of cooperation, function, and friendliness. Also refer to Chapter 8 for more information about group development.

WEATHER, LOGISTICS, AND MISCELLANEOUS

Weather

We cannot expect people on trips to come up with accurate weather forecasts for the 6 and 11 o'clock news. We do recommend that trip members do some research into the historical weather patterns of the area to be visited. Do 8 in. of rain usually fall during the month you plan to visit Winking Squirrel State Forest? Does the daytime temperature historically soar to 130°F in the week of your trip to Blistered Heel National Desert?

Just before you pile into the station wagon, obtain a long-range and short-range weather forecast from the National Weather Service for the trip area. You may want to bring in a weather radio for updates. Be advised, however, that weather patterns in mountainous or remote regions often vary significantly from the weather in populated regions covered by most forecasts. You've probably heard that mountains make their own weather. It's true, so do sea coasts.

You can also learn to "read" local weather conditions to obtain fairly accurate 24-hour predictions while in the backcountry. Using wind speed, wind direction, cloud patterns, and barometer, you can usually do as well as your evening meteorologist at predicting weather trends.

Transportation

Just as important as what you do when you get there is how you're going to get there. For most informal trips, transportation is fairly simple. You drive to the trailhead, do your trip, and return to the trailhead. You only need to research safe parking at the trailhead. A variation involves leaving a car at each end of a route, so that you minimize retraced paths.

If the group is large, however, or is staying in the woods for several weeks at a location far from home, transportation needs become complex. We recommend writing all the transportation needs on a calendar or single document and then filling in vehicles and drivers to meet each need. On longer trips, we often have resupply days where a friend meets us at a trailhead and replenishes our food, fuel, medical supplies, and other equipment. This resupply agent can also carry messages out, bring mail in, or help with evacuating sick or injured group members.

Make sure you rely on well-functioning vehicles that won't break down and leave you stranded. Just as importantly, rely on well-functioning individuals who won't forget you, dismiss you, or otherwise leave you stranded. Divide costs for gas, oil, and repairs among group members, if appropriate. THIS IS IMPORTANT: MAKE SURE ALL DRIVERS HAVE ACCURATE MAPS AND DIRECTIONS TO TRAILHEADS, complete with the exact time of each rendezvous written down. Once you've had a lost or late resupply agent, you'll appreciate the importance of extremely explicit directions.

Post-trip Considerations

Plan ahead for logistics and events that will take place when you emerge from the backcountry. You might be tired, rested, drained, or energized. Or maybe all of these things. Regardless, you probably don't want to scramble to plan for some basic amenities as soon as you hit the pavement. Plan ahead for shower facilities for the group. You might also want to stop at a laundromat, use telephones, buy junk food, and have a celebration dinner at a local restaurant.

Also, how will the group end its time together? Is there a provision for people to evaluate the trip and each other? Can people make recommendations for next time? How will gear be cleaned, inventoried, and returned?

 **BOTTOM-LINE TIP: Trip Planning Checklist**

Trip Vision
- Goals and Objectives
- Leadership

Itinerary and Safety
- Itinerary
- Consult Resources
- Emergency Planning

Food, Materials, and Finances
- Food Planning
- Equipment and Clothing
- Finances

Interpersonal Relations
- Skills and Knowledge Training
- Expedition Behavior

Weather, Logistics, and Miscellaneous
- Weather
- Transportation
- Post-trip Considerations

CONCLUSION

A well-run trip is capped by a smooth and thoughtful post-trip period. People will remember the last image of the trip left in their minds: either a warm, cheerful celebration, or an exhausting and frustrating struggle with logistics. Good luck and we'll see you in the woods!

References

Drury, J., Ed. (2005). *The backcountry classroom: Lessons, tools and activities for teaching outdoor leaders.* Guilford, CT: Falcon Guide.

Wilderness Recreation Leadership Program. (1984). *Winter practicum manual.* [Manual]. Saranac Lake, NY: North Country Community College.

Wilderness Recreation Leadership Program. (1985). *Winter practicum manual.* [Manual]. Saranac Lake, NY: North Country Community College.

Wilderness Recreation Leadership Program. (1986). *Winter practicum manual.* [Manual]. Saranac Lake, NY: North Country Community College.

EPILOGUE:
The Stumps Meet the Muskrat Pack

WOODY GOES TO COLLEGE

The September after the infamous Stump family adventure to Alaska, Woody Stump packed up and went off for his first year of college. After copious research using college guides, guidance counselors, and ratings from *Outdoor Maniac* magazine's Top Ten Camping Colleges, Woody selected a small private college in St. Louis, Missouri. Woody's choice, Wynotgota College, offered him the widest selection of programs, since he had no idea what he wanted to major in, and had an active outing club, which would help him enjoy his time away from studying.

"Besides," Woody told his parents, "it has been proven that healthy recreation improves kids' studies in college."

As the weeks went by, Woody adopted study habits (i.e., procrastination and sleeping through lectures) that freed up large chunks of his time and allowed him to engage in his passion, outdoor activities. He was elected to the events board of the Wynotgota Healthy Outdoor Activities! club (WHOA!) and immersed himself in planning the national conference for the Champions of the Wilderness (COW), which was to be held in January at the college.

In his preparations for the conference, Woody contacted Wynotgota College alumni who were active in the WHOA! and who were still involved in outdoor recreation and wilderness-related issues. His goal was to convince active alumni to come to the conference and serve on panel discussions or present workshops based on their wilderness work. One evening in October, he made his first phone call.

SYNCHRONICITY, OR YOU KNEW THIS WAS COMING!

Woody's first phone call on his WHOA! alumni list was Stella Storm, from Mystic, Connecticut.

"Ms. Storm?" said Woody.

"Yes, who is this?" said Stella.

"I'm Woody Stump, from WHOA! at Wynotgota College, and I'm calling to . . ."

Well, you get the picture. Stella had many fond and fuzzy memories of Wynotgota from the late '70s and was honored to attend the conference with the members of the Muskrat Pack. The club suited the conference theme well as an example of a private peer recreational club that uses public wilderness. After a few quick calls, Stella made sure that everyone in the Muskrat Pack would be able to attend the combination conference and mini-reunion at their beloved alma mater.

Of course, as soon as Woody learned of the Muskrat Pack, his imagination ran wild. He was captivated by visions of their exploits and thought it was cool that a group of "older people" still got together to enjoy the outdoors. He was so excited that he invited his parents to attend the conference and meet the Muskrat Pack.

"Dad, we can even do a PowerPoint slide show on our Alaska trip!" said Woody during a semimonthly phone call.

"That's great, Woody! I've been rehearsing a script for the presentation. I've got it down to under 4 hours!" said Forrest.

"Come on, now, dear!" said Holly, also on the Stumps' speaker phone. "You don't want to bore them yet. We haven't even met them!"

"They'll warm up quick!" said Forrest. "How can they resist the Greatest Adventure of All Time?"

"Well, I'm going to ask them to bring slides of their own greatest adventures, so you'd better cut out about two thirds of our adventures, Dad," said Woody. "And, Mom? Do you think you could advance me a little money for some textbooks?"

THE COW CONFERENCE AT WYNOTGOTA COLLEGE

The weeks marched by and Woody's finals came and went. He managed to hang on and pass all of his classes and still be active in planning the Champions of the Wilderness conference. After winter break, Woody returned to campus early for the last preparations for the big conference. Soon, the big weekend arrived and Woody's honored guests took their place at the head table in the campus gymnasium.

"And lastly," said the president of the outing club from the podium, "I am pleased to introduce members from the Muskrat Pack, which is an active outing club that formed right here at Wynotgota College in 1978! I'll bet you were using dugout canoes back then, heh-heh! From the right is Juan Marquez, Anne Angelo, Stella Storm, and . . . the writing is smudged on this card . . . well, one other distinguished graduate! Welcome to the COW National Conference!"

BACK AT THE GOLDEN ARCH MOTEL

After the festivities, workshops, events, and speakers were finished that night, Holly and Forrest invited the Muskrat Pack over to their motel room to look at slides and socialize. Juan, Anne, and Stella drove over from their motel and left the other Muskrat Pack member, who was fighting a cold and feeling poorly, back at the room. Woody was excited to finally talk with his idols and ask them all about their adventures. Everyone chatted over refreshments and onion dip before the slide show.

"Well, Anne," said Forrest, "tell me about yourself. When did you start canoeing? What was your favorite canoe trip? What type of boat would you recommend we should purchase? Did Woody tell you we traveled to Alaska this summer?"

"Forrest, give her a little space," chuckled Holly.

Anne laughed. "Well, Forrest, I first canoed as a baby; I loved the Green River; it depends on the type of paddling you do; and yes."

THE POWERPOINT PRESENTATIONS

After a few minutes of introductory socializing, Forrest made an announcement.

"Okay, everybody. How about looking at our PowerPoint?"

Since nobody protested, Forrest set up the screen, powered up his laptop and the LCD projector, and dimmed the lights.

"Alright everybody, here goes," said Forrest. He projected the first slide. "Here we are on the first day starting on the Fraser Canyon Highway in British Columbia. Notice everybody's smiling?"

"That didn't last long," said Woody. "We had a big blowup later when our van broke down on the Al-Can."

Over the next hour, Forrest flashed through slides of their trip through spectacular scenery in Canada and Alaska. They saw images of raw and stunning wilderness as pristine as it was when the first people saw it. They also saw slides of RV-lined roads around Portage Glacier, highly impacted camping areas, and the streets of downtown Anchorage. They saw shots of eagles, salmon, and bears along with all-terrain vehicles, motorboats, and trailers.

Forrest recounts "The Stumps' greatest adventure of all time" with the Muskrat Pack.

After a short break, Stella inserted her iPod Shuffle into Forrest's laptop computer and uploaded her PowerPoint presentation incorporating pictures from several of the Muskrat Pack's paddling trips. The Stumps were treated to pictures of many of North America's wild and scenic rivers and lakes. They saw the Allagash, the Everglades, the Adirondacks, the Ozarks, rivers in the Pacific Northwest, the Southwest, and Canada. Woody couldn't believe his eyes and was full of questions. He dreamed of his next adventure and made mental plans. He also started thinking about all the natural areas he had seen.

THE BIG DISCUSSION

"You know," said Woody, "after our big family trip, some camping trips I've been on at college, and after seeing your PowerPoint, Anne, I have a completely different idea of what wilderness really is."

"What do you mean?" said Juan.

"Well, I used to think going to the wilderness meant going to almost anyplace that had big trees, bushes, and trails. You know, like anyplace that didn't have a lawn," said Woody. "We started out camping at state parks and KOA campgrounds and I thought they were really wild. Sleeping in a tent or trailer at a campground was rugged for me! Now that I've seen places like the Yukon and Alaska and have camped 10 miles from the nearest road, I have a different idea of what wilderness means. Now those state campgrounds and KOAs seem only one step wilder than a mall parking lot!"

"I know what you're saying, Woody," said Juan. "But those campgrounds are still a valuable and important place for a lot of people to go. Many people get feelings of peace, contentment, beauty, and contact with nature when they're car camping. I, for one, really enjoy having restrooms, fireplaces, and signs at the places I camp. But there are times when I choose a more remote type of trip."

"Yeah, I know," said Woody. "But it really isn't the same. They shouldn't call using camp-grounds a wilderness experience."

"You know what problem you're getting at, Woody?" said Stella. "The *definition* of wilderness. You have one definition of your wilderness experience. Juan and most car campers might have a different idea of what makes for a wilderness camping trip. But aside from the million shades of gray that exist in each outdoor camper's mind, the governmental agencies have a specific definition for wilderness. They also have designated certain regions as wilderness and apply a whole list of specific rules for what can go on within wilderness boundaries. So in this way, people may have ideas of what is *wilderness-like* to them, but they often have no idea of what *wilderness* is, according to regulations."

"Sounds complicated," said Forrest.

"It isn't, really," said Stella. "Soon after my first canoe trip in college, I learned about the differences between what is allowed on a wilderness river and a non-wilderness river."

"Yeah, namely motorboats," said Anne. "I'm sure you know what it's like to expect quiet and solitude and then encounter powerboats and radios."

"But remember, sometimes you want a trip with powerboats and radios," said Juan. "They can be a lot of fun!"

"You're right, Juan. In fact, you're both right," said Stella. "We have large tracts of land that still have great natural beauty. Some of these areas are near cities and highways, while others are very hard to get to. What the agencies and the wilderness advocacy groups need to do is to get the word out that there are some places suited for motorized and high-intensity use and others for very primitive and low-intensity use. Our big problem is that everybody wants to use the same places! Everybody wants to go to Yosemite and the Grand Canyon, and each person, from the car camper to the pure wilderness minimalist, wants to have their type of experience, unmolested by the other types of users."

"What I'm learning is that there is a place for everyone to get what they want if they would only learn about the different rules and regulations for each area," said Juan. "People just don't know that they can't run their snowmobiles in a designated wilderness area, and that areas that are just as beautiful but are not called wilderness are just down the road."

"What really bugs me," said Woody, "is that I can't go to the really awesome places like Yosemite Valley and have the experience that I want—which is, namely, no people. Why can't I have my true wilderness experience at any of the most amazing places? It really bugs me!"

"I know what you mean," said Anne. "We all do, don't we? I remember when the Drifting Paddle National Canoe Area was so unused that you could drink from the lakes. It was rare that you had two groups camped on the same lake. You often had a wilderness lake all to yourself!"

"Now the Drifting Paddle is overrun with groups: outing clubs, Scouts, school groups, college groups," said Juan. "I don't mind it so much, but the rest of our group really dislikes the noise, litter, and impact. We've had to shift canoe trips to a more remote system of lakes up in Canada."

"Unfortunately, Woody," said Stella, "there really is no immediate answer to your problem. As areas become popular, the agencies do their best to protect the resources, but aside from limiting access, it is very hard to maintain the type of wilderness experience you want at these well-known places. It's almost like we have to sacrifice the most spectacular or easily accessible places to higher-intensity use. But there is some consolation, still. If you want a really remote wilderness experience, try using less popular National Forests or lands managed by other agencies like the Bureau of Land Management. There are millions of acres of remote and little-used areas that might not have the spectacular beauty of the National Parks, but offer solitude and few signs of other people."

"You mean I have to settle for Brand X," grumbled Woody.

"Often, Brand X is much better than the leading brands," laughed Anne. "Go generic!"

THINKING LIKE THE MOUNTAINS

"You know," said Holly, "we've been having a great discussion about what wilderness means to people, but what about what wilderness means to the planet?"

"What do you mean?" said Forrest.

"Well, although we love wilderness and natural areas for their beauty and the great times we have when we travel in them, some people think that wilderness is much more important for the role it plays in keeping the world as healthy as it can be," said Holly.

"Mom's right," said Woody. "I've read that most of us naturally look at the wilderness from a people-centered viewpoint, which means how much we value the wilderness for the great things it does for us. Other people think that wilderness is important just because it's a place we haven't completely messed up yet, and the forests, bugs, and everything else that's there can keep the Earth's ecosystems functioning in a somewhat healthy way."

"Can you imagine if every last bit of the world were paved, farmed, mined, grazed, or developed?" said Juan. "Many scientists think that the Earth needs wilderness and other natural areas in order to keep all life in balance. Some people even think that humans need natural areas in order to keep the world healthy enough for us to survive."

"And that's another example of what Woody calls a people-centered viewpoint," said Holly. "In other words, we need to keep these areas healthy in order to keep us healthy. I'm so glad you're learning something in your studies, Woody!"

"I read that in a book outside of class, Mom," said Woody. "It was called *A Sand County Almanac*, by Aldo Leopold."

"Great book!" said Anne. "He said something about learning to think like mountains in addition to our perspective as humans. I think I know what he meant, but I'm not sure I can put it into words."

"I think it was something like, think about how each living and nonliving thing affects one another before, during, and after the influence of people," said Woody. "Think of each choice you make from the perspective of the ancient mountain, which hosts a whole world of life on its shoulders, and sees everything: every birth, every death."

"Well said, Woody!" said Forrest. "I'm really proud of you! You're really turning into quite a thinker."

FORREST IN A REFLECTIVE MOOD

"You know," said Forrest, after the computer and LCD projector were put away and the Muskrat Pack members were standing in the doorway with their coats on. I have a whole different feeling about our natural areas and the things we do as campers now. I've learned so much in the past year. I used to think nature was an immense playground and that nothing we did as campers could really hurt anything in the big picture. Now I realize that the big picture is really billions and billions of smaller pictures when seen close up. And if we trash too many of these little pictures, the effects add up quickly.

"We just can't use the same camping methods that we had when I was a kid. Heck, what I did as a kid was a lot different than what my folks did—and for that matter, what my grandad did when he used to go fishing on the Missilappagoola. . ."

"There you go again, Dad," said Woody. "What are you trying to say?"

"Sorry, Woody," said Forrest, "but I was saying that we've got to start looking at what we do in terms of the effects we have on the ecosystems, firstly, and then the experiences of other campers."

"You said a mouthful, Forrest," said Stella. "It's like when I'm teaching my biology students, I tell them that the first step is to be aware of the issues and problems. Make sure you have accurate information. Then, do something about it! Get involved some way, if only through the example you set with your own actions."

"But don't forget to have fun," said Juan. "Let's keep the enjoyment in the outdoors. Too much of this heavy talk can make you want to stay on the couch. We've got to keep getting outdoors and keep encouraging more people to use the outdoors in ways that keep ecosystems healthy."

"But now," said Anne, "we've got to go. Thanks for having us, and we hope to see you sometime in the wilderness!"

"We should plan a trip together," said Juan. "How about it, Woody?"

"You bet, Juan!" said Woody. "I'm really glad I got to meet you folks!"

"Goodbye!" said Holly and Forrest.

"Well, family, all this talk about the value of wilderness and natural areas aside from people values has got me thinking," Forrest said as he rubbed his chin. "It reminds me of my great-aunt Sabrina Boone. You've heard of Daniel Boone? Well, Sabrina was. . ."

Appendix

Apples (dried): Add to hot cereal, eat raw, or rehydrate for baking.

Apricots (dried): Add to hot cereal, eat raw or rehydrate for baking.

Baking Powder

Beef Base: Start with less than a teaspoon as it is very salty. Add base to water. Bouillon cubes may also be used.

Brownie Mix: Mix: water = 8:1.

Bulgar: Prepare the same way as rice. Can be used with or instead of rice, or combined with veggies to make a tabouli salad.

Candy

Cashews

Cheese Cake Mix: Add to already-mixed milk, stir, and let set.

Cheese: Cheddar, Mozzarella, Muenster, Colby.

Chicken Base: Start with less than a teaspoon as it is very salty. Add base to water.

Chili base: Mix with water to taste.

Cocoa: Mix with water to taste.

Coconut: Add to granola or use for baking.

Cream of Wheat: Water: Cream of wheat = 4:1.

Egg Noodle: Bring water to a boil, then add noodles and about a tablespoon of oil (to keep noodles from sticking together).

Fruit Drink: Orange, Lemon, Fruit. Add to purified water. When using iodine, let the water sit for 30 minutes (or per instructions) Before adding drink mix.

Flour (unbleached and whole wheat): Whole wheat can be mixed with unbleached flour. Use between a 2:1 and 1:1 ratio (unbleached: whole wheat).

Gingerbread Mix: Add enough water to form a thick, runny consistency.

Honey: Use in addition to or instead of other sweeteners.

Jello: Use as a high energy hot drink. (It is difficult to make Jello gel in the field.)

Macaroni: Bring water to a boil, then add noodles and about a tablespoon of oil (to keep pasta from sticking together).

Margarine: Add a little to every dinner for a good source of energy.

Milk (powdered): Mixes best when cold. Water: milk = 2:1.

Mushroom Soup Base: Add water to base, to taste.

Nuts (mixed)

Oatmeal (rolled, not instant): Cooks in 10-12 minutes.

Onions (dried): Rehydrate 12-15 minutes in hot water.

Pancake Mix: Add cold water.

Peanut Butter

Peanuts

Pepperoni: Can be cut up in dinners, or used for lunch.

Popcorn

Potatoes (powdered): Good as a thickener, in potato pancakes, or just as potatoes.

Prunes: Add to hot cereal, eat raw, or rehydrate for baking.

Pudding (instant chocolate or vanilla): Add milk, stir, and let set. Milk: pudding = 4:1

Raisins (regular and golden): Add to hot cereal, eat raw, or rehydrate for baking.

Rice: Add to water, then boil for 15-20 minutes. Water: rice = 2:1.

Salt

Soy Sauce

Spagetti: Bring water to a boil, then add pasta and about a tablespoon of oil (to keep pasta from sticking together).

Sugar (white and brown): Use in addition to or instead of other sweetener.

Sunflower seeds
Tea (regular and spiced)
Tomato base: Add water to base.
Trail mix
Texturized Vegetable Protein (TVP): An inexpensive meat substitute. It has meat texture but very little taste and no fat. Best if rehydrated in hot water for 15-20 minutes.
Vanilla
Vegetables (dried, mixed): Rehydrate 12-15 minutes in hot water.
Vegetable oil: Add to dinners, use for popcorn, pancakes, etc.
Vinegar
Walnuts
Wheatena: Water: Wheatena = 4:1.
Yeast

Index

About the Authors

Eric Holmlund

Eric Holmlund currently serves as an Associate Professor in the Forestry, Natural Resources and Recreation Division of Paul Smith's College and coordinator of the Recreation, Adventure Travel and Ecotourism Program (B.S.). He is also the Director of the Watershed Stewardship Program, which conducts recreation resource research on the St. Regis Lakes chain, Upper Saranac Lake and St. Regis Mountain, and provides public education on controlling exotic aquatic invasive species and minimizing recreational impact to the St. Regis Mountain trail and summit. Holmlund brings students from Paul Smith's College to Costa Rica to study ecotourism and adventure travel. He also teaches courses in environmental literature and nature writing at Paul Smith's College. Holmlund has served as the Director of the Outdoor Education Program at St. Lawrence University and as a senior instructor for the Wilderness Education Association (WEA). He has taught WEA outdoor leadership expeditions for North Country Community College, Southern Illinois University, Slippery Rock University, University of Alaska-Anchorage, University of Colorado-Ft. Collins, and Wesleyan University. These expeditions were set in the Adirondack Park, Missouri, Arkansas, Illinois, New Mexico, Utah, and Alaska. Holmlund has served as course director and instructor for the New York City Outward Bound Center. He has designed and facilitated leadership and team building programs for a wide range of corporate and educational clients.

Jack K. Drury

Jack has been working with learners of all ages and walks of life ranging from youth at risk to corporate executives for 30 years. Jack is co-owner of Leading EDGE, a professional development organization of experienced educators who design and facilitate learning experiences for educators, businesses, nonprofit organizations, and government agencies. Jack was the founding Director of the Wilderness Recreation Leadership Program and an Associate Professor at North Country Community College in Saranac Lake, New York. He has taught Wilderness Education Association (WEA) courses since 1979 and has been an Education By Design Institute Coordinator affiliated with the Antioch New England Graduate School since 1992. He is past-president of the WEA, a veteran of numerous National Outdoor Leadership School (NOLS) courses and has been fortunate enough to lead and participate in ventures throughout North America, Central America, Europe, and Siberia during all the seasons.